Jan 1971.

A HISTORY OF THE CHRISTIAN CHURCH

THE CATHOLIC CHURCH
FROM 1648 TO 1870

A HISTORY OF THE CHRISTIAN CHURCH

———

APOSTOLIC AND POST-APOSTOLIC TIMES
Leonhard Goppelt

A HISTORY OF THE REFORMATION
IN GERMANY TO 1555
Franz Lau and Ernst Bizer

THE CATHOLIC CHURCH
FROM 1648 TO 1870
Friedrich Heyer

THE CATHOLIC CHURCH
FROM 1648 TO 1870

BY

FRIEDRICH HEYER

PROFESSOR OF ECCLESIASTICAL HISTORY
UNIVERSITY OF HEIDELBERG

TRANSLATED BY D. W. D. SHAW

ADAM & CHARLES BLACK
LONDON

THIS EDITION PUBLISHED 1969

A. AND C. BLACK LTD
4, 5 AND 6 SOHO SQUARE, LONDON, W.1

© 1963 VANDENHOECK AND RUPRECHT
ENGLISH TRANSLATION © 1969 A. AND C. BLACK, LTD
SBN 7136 0906 0

Translated from the German, *Die Katholische
Kirche vom Westfälischen Frieden bis zum Ersten
Vatikanischen Konzil*, being Section N, Part I,
of Die Kirche in ihrer Geschichte: ein Hand-
buch, edited by Kurt Dietrich Schmidt and
Ernst Wolf (Vandenhoeck and Ruprecht,
Göttingen and Zurich)

PRINTED IN GREAT BRITAIN
BY W & J MACKAY & CO LTD, CHATHAM

CONTENTS

TRANSLATOR'S NOTE

While this translation covers the complete text of the original German edition of *Die Katholische Kirche vom Westfälischen Frieden bis zum Ersten Vatikanischen Konzil*, the footnotes are restricted to those in the German edition which refer either to standard works readily available in English-speaking countries or to works translated into English. Any reader who wishes details of sources or bibliographical data should consult the very full notes and bibliography in the German edition. Because comparatively few of the German works referred to in the sections of this book dealing with the history of the Catholic Church in Germany have as yet been translated into English, a short bibliography of English works dealing with this area has, at the author's request, been included at the end of the translation.

D.W.D.S.

ABBREVIATIONS

American Ecc. Rev.	American Ecclesiastical Review
Diss.	Dissertation
E.T.	English Translation
Fliche/Martin	Ed. A. Fliche and V. Martin, *Histoire de l'Eglise depuis les Origines jusqu'à nos jours*, (21 vols.), Paris, 1948–52.
IER	Irish Ecclesiastical Record
NZMW	Neue Zeitschrift für Missionswissenschaft
Préclin/Jarry	E. Préclin and E. Jarry, *Histoire de l'Eglise*, Vol. XIX, I and II, *Les Luttes politiques et doctrinales aux XVII et XVIII siècles*, Paris, 1956 ff.
RHE	Revue d'Histoire Ecclésiastique
Th.Q	Theologische Quartalschrift

CHAPTER I

THE PAPACY AND NATIONAL ABSOLUTISM

In the tribune of St Peter's Cathedral stands Bernini's Cathedra Petri, descending from the clouds of heaven, chosen by the dove to be the bearer of the Spirit. It had been commissioned by Alexander VII to house the sacred relics and forcefully expresses the consciousness of the divine institution of the papacy, which the success of the Counter-Reformation seemed to have ratified anew.[1] This position had been made possible by Rome's alliance with the national princes in their struggle for absolute powers.

Just how dangerous it was for the papacy to achieve success by this policy cannot be overlooked. The absolutist Catholic Powers themselves tended to envelop the papacy more and more. In setting up their own kind of national churches over against Rome, they imperilled the universal unity of the Church. Moreoever, when it suited their own purposes, they showed no hesitation at times in backing current movements for Catholic reform.

In the "De ecclesiastica potestate" controversy, which was revived again between 1643 and 1664, the absolutism of the princes was given theological justification: the infallibility the Pope asserted, his superiority over the Council and the political outreach of his authority were all questioned. The new feature was that concern was now not with Occam's arguments or Aristotle's "Politics", as it had been before, but with arguments from history. Père Combéfis's researches led to the revelation, in his *Historia haeresis Monothelitarum*, that one pope, Honorius, had been condemned as a heretic by a General Council. The error with which he was charged had been committed in the exercises of the magisterium. In fact, the Centuriators of Magdeburg had already brought this fact to light, but Pighi, Baronius and Bellarmine had put minds to rest by declaring that the Acts of the Sixth Ecumenical Council had been forged, and that Honorius's name

[1] The relics of the See of Peter, which had been a symbol of the apostolic succession as early as the third century, were deposited by the chapter in Bernini's construction (begun in 1657) at the Festival of the Cathedra Petri, in 1666 (R. Wittkower. G.L.B. London, 1955). The esteem in which Rome was held is evidenced by the number of pilgrims, 700,000 in all, who visited it in the Jubilee year 1650. Cp. É. Préclin and E. Jarry, "Les luttes politiques et doctrinales aux xviie et xviiie siècles": *Histoire de l'Eglise*, xix, Paris 1955, I 15f. L. V. Pastor, *Geschichte der Päpste seit dem Ausgang des Mittelalters*, Vol. xiv, 515-19 (E.T. *History of the Popes*, London 1923, Vol. xxxi, 322-7).

had been inserted at a place where originally the name of an oriental patriarch had stood. Now Combéfis proved the authenticity of the sources,[1] and even though the Curia placed his book on the Index, in France this merely confirmed the view that the Romans lacked the integrity of true "érudits".

Some idea of the tension that characterized this period can be grasped by setting Bernini's creation of the Cathedra Petri over against Combéfis's historical proof of a heretical pope.

I. THE GREAT POWERS ENVELOP THE CURIA

The first place where the conflicts came to a head was the Conclave in Rome. The aim of the Catholic powers was to make political use of the Curia, and in the College of Cardinals and through it, in the Conclave, they found the ideal medium for exercising their influence. In 1605, for the first time, Spain commissioned a cardinal to use its veto against an unacceptable candidate for pope, i.e. it exercised its right of exclusion (*Jus exclusive*), and by the middle of the seventeenth century the Emperor, Spain and France had all established their title to the *Jus exclusive*.[2] In the College of Cardinals, parties were formed and with these the powers had to deal every time there was a papal election: the "Zelanti", who followed their own party line in the Curia, and the "squadrone volante".[3] If they sided with the crown cardinals, the election of a pope who suited the Emperor and Spain, or, on the other hand, France, could be carried through. The Peace of the Pyrenees of 1659 had marked the demise of Spain as a world power, but for a long time thereafter the feeling nevertheless persisted in France that Rome was backing Spain against France. Antoine Arnauld, for instance, was convinced that there were so many Spanish cardinals that the Curia would always be under Spanish control.[4]

Mazarin's protest against the election of Innocent X in 1644 reached Rome too late. In the Conclave of 1665 the cardinals Innocent had appointed—although not guilty of nepotism, they were united in their rejection of outside state influences—were moving in a neutralist direction *vis-à-vis* the national powers. Cardinal Sacchetti was the most promising candidate, but his election was blocked by the Spanish and Imperial party

---

[1] A. G. Martimort, *Le Gallicanisme de Bossuet*, Paris 1953, 172f.

[2] As late as the Conclave of 1903 the right of exclusion was claimed by Austria, but this was followed by the threat of excommunication in the Constitution, "Commissum nobis", of 20th January 1904.

[3] A term coined by the Spanish ambassador at the time of the 1655 Conclave.

[4] In 1676 Astorgas could still boast that he would elect the Pope despite France. The French ambassador had great difficulty in preventing this. Spanish influence in the Curia was strengthened by the fact that Naples was ruled by a Spanish Vice-Regent.

with their rights of exclusion. Mazarin's opposition to Fabio Chigi (Alexander VIII), whose attitude at the Peace Congress of Münster had given rise to dissatisfaction among the French, had first to be silenced by a note from Sacchetti. Even so, Mazarin considered the outcome of the election a setback to French policies, and reacted by making unreasonable demands of the Pope in the affair of Cardinal Retz, whom Mazarin feared as a potential rival, and who, after his arrest, escaped to Rome. Mazarin, indeed, went the length of recalling the French chargé d'affaires in Rome.[1]

When Louis XIV resumed diplomatic relations through the Duke of Créqui, the ambassador arrogantly demanded an extension of his "fredom of quarter" (the area in which he was entitled to have diplomatic immunity) so as to include the area surrounding his residence, the Palazzo Farnese. This led to a clash between Créqui's men and Corsican troops in the papal service, in the course of which a page was killed at the Duchess's side. The Pope was ready to give immediate satisfaction, but Louis XIV could not let slip this opportunity of humiliating the Curia. The papal nuncio was expelled from France, Avignon was occupied, and an expedition was organized against the Papal States. Alexander VII was shown no mercy and in the Peace of Pisa (12th February 1664) was forced to accept the most extravagant French demands. Despite the fact that the Corsicans involved in the outrage had been tried, and two of them executed, it was stipulated that the Corsicans be for ever disqualified from papal service and a monument commemorating the disgrace erected in front of the Corsican barracks.[2]

In 1667, in an amazingly short Conclave, the cardinals agreed upon Rospigliosi, the former Secretary of State (Clement IX), and the French ambassador in Rome, the Duke of Chaulnes, reported to his king that the result was a foregone conclusion: he would not have named the president of a Paris merchants' guild with greater confidence than that with which he had named the Pope on this occasion. For the first time, the decisive influence in the Conclave was French.

The Conclave of 1669 dragged on for four months, because there was no party among the electors strong enough to carry their candidate through. The French ambassador exercised France's right of exclusion against Cardinal d'Elce; the Spanish ambassador exercised Spain's against Cardinal Broncaccio. They could only reach agreement by switching to a wholly insignificant figure, the 80-year-old Roman nobleman, Emilio Altieri (Clement X), who was to achieve nothing of importance as pope.

[1] Pastor, op. cit., E. T., xxx, 48–9.
[2] Castro had to be withdrawn to Parma and compensation had to be paid to Este or the further occupation of Comacchio.

France and Spain now concentrated on having men they approved of appointed as cardinals so as to build up their influence in Rome.

The Conclave of 1676, however, could not overlook the fact there was one outstanding "papabilis", Benedetto Odescalchi. This was an exceptional situation. Even so, it was only when they were assured of Louis XIV's concurrence that they proceeded to elevate Odescalchi. As Innocent XI, Odescalchi turned out to be the only papal figure of importance in the age of absolutism.[1] Untainted by nepotism, stabilizing the finances of the Papal States, refusing to emulate Maecenas in the way he developed baroque Rome, Innocent XI was independent enough really to tackle the spiritual problems of the time and, by his papal decisions, to pave the way for their solution. His pontificate was marked by the condemnation of four "heresies". The sudden change of policy which caused Innocent XI to condemn "Quietism" and to anathematize "Jansenism", may well have been due to pressure from the French ambassador. Yet in the question of "Gallicanism", the Pope did not shrink from a dangerous conflict with the French throne. Rigorous in matters of morals—in his personal behaviour and in his enactments, he set himself against the lavish extravagance in Rome—in his decree of 2nd March 1679, Innocent XI condemned the sixty-five theses of "Probabilism" proposed by the University of Louvain and broke the dominance of probabilist "Laxism" within the Jesuit Order by having the Probabiliorist, Thyrsus Gonzalez, of the University of Salamanca, elected as General of the Order.

After 1699, with the last of the Hapsburgs on the Spanish throne and without an heir, the problem of the Spanish succession arose and on the solution of this problem the future shape of Europe was to depend. The Emperor Leopold I, like Louis XIV, was married to a sister of the Spanish King, who was without issue. The Spanish Primate, Cardinal Portocarrero, who was backing the French claim to succession and who had got the unanimous approval of the Council of State, obtained an authoritative statement from the Pope in favour of the French claimant. In view of all that was at stake, it was inevitable that the Conclave of 1700 should serve as a prelude to the War of the Spanish Succession. The Imperial and French parties stood in flagrant opposition to each other, but neither was strong enough to stop the Zelanti electing Cardinal Gian Francesco Albani (Clement XI). Afraid that Italy would fall under Hapsburg domination,

---

[1] Despite French counter-measures, Innocent XI carried through a Christian political programme with regard to the Turks, shocked as he was by the Turkish occupation of Crete in 1669 and the siege of Vienna in 1683. The Pope endorsed the alliance between Leopold I and John Sobieski and supported the campaign which put an end to Turkish control of Hungary. A Capuchin, Mark of Aviano, went with the army, preaching repentance, as Apostolic Delegate. The historical picture of Innocent XI has to be freed from Jesuit misrepresentation.

which he, as an Italian prince, wished to avoid as far as the Papal States were concerned, Clement XI was also inclined to support the French, and his attitude led to the occupation of part of the Papal States by the Emperor Joseph I's troops. This forced him to enter into secret articles recognizing the Emperor's brother as King of Spain. By so doing, the Pope provided Philip VI (of Anjou), the French pretender to the throne, who had all along possessed *de facto* power, with the opportunity of breaking off relations between Spain and the Curia and of blocking papal revenues from Spain.[1]

At this point any respect that the powers had retained for the papacy vanished. The pontificates of the Age of Enlightenment—of Innocent XIII, Benedict XIII, Clement XII, Benedict XIV, Clement XIII and XIV, Pius VI—shed no great light on the European scene. In 1729, when Benedict XIII canonized Pope Gregory VII, the Parlement in Paris refused to allow the service prescribed for the new saint to be celebrated, on the ground that to honour a pope who had forced an emperor to Canossa would be an affront to royal authority. Joseph II, too, reacted by directing the priests to strike out the relevant prayers in their office-books with printer's ink. Of the eighteenth-century popes, Benedict XIV was the most impressive, "a priest without presumption" (as Walpole of England described him in his eulogy); "the greatest of all the canonists" (according to the Protestant, E. L. Richter). Benedict introduced the historical method into the study of canon law long before the same development took place in secular jurisprudence. His concordats reflect his anxiety to reach a settlement with the absolutist powers and made far-reaching concessions in the matter of the right of presentation to benefices. (In Seppelt's view, this was a shrewd judgment as to the actual state of power.[2] Where princes were engaged in introducing their subjects to new methods of work so as to commercialize the economy and make a start with industrialization, the papacy was able to help by sanctioning a reduction in the number of public holidays.

With Pius VI (from 1775), the Pope himself adopted the role of absolute ruler, and in the manner of a sovereign developing his realm, set about draining the Pontine marshes and building up his Vatican Museum.

When the papacy was forced by the distribution of power to hand over ecclesiastical functions to the states, the question still debated was whether this was done as a matter of papal privilege or in pursuance of the sovereign rights of the princes.

[1] The Pope was opposed to the Court of Vienna because when Prussia became a monarchy (1700) the Curia's concurrence had not been obtained.

[2] F. X. Murphy, "Pope Benedict XIV", in *The American Eccles. Review*, 138, 1958, pp. 303–15.

The complete lack of respect for the See of Rome is well illustrated by the way the Parma question was settled. Parma was really a papal fee, but without any deference to papal suzerainty the Emperor ceded it to Don Carlos, Elizabeth of Farnese's son, and it later fell to the Emperor himself.

In 1787, the King of the Two Sicilies for his part discontinued the practice of sending "the White Palfrey" and 7,000 gold pieces as tribute to Rome. Up till then, the handing over of these tokens of recognition of papal suzerainty had been the occasion of a popular festival ("omaggio della chinea") and had served to bolster Rome's sense of its own importance.[1]

"I cannot deny", wrote Alvise Mocenigo, the Venetian ambassador, from Rome in 1737, "that there is something unnatural in the spectacle of all the Catholic governments in such utter dissension with the Roman Court that no reconciliation can be envisaged which would not strike a severe blow at the very heart of the Court. Whether it be the effect of greater enlightenment or a spirit of violent exploitation of the weaker party, it is certain that the princes are proceeding with quickened pace to deprive the Roman See of all its secular privileges."

2. GALLICANISM

France had advanced further than other countries and took the lead in the disputes which inevitably took place as state churches, congenial to the absolutist outlook, developed. Not that advocates of Ultramontanism were lacking to continue the tradition of Bellarmine and his treatise "On the Temporal Power of the Pope".[2] But over against them a form of Gallicanism had been striving to gain the ascendancy. Its theory had been propounded since 1606 by Edmond Richer, Syndic of the Faculty of Paris, and was based on the teaching of Gerson, d'Ailly and John Major.[3] Its constant concern was with the principle: maximum exclusion of the Pope to achieve solidarity within the state church. It is, however, necessary to distinguish between different "Gallicanisms".

[1] H. Daniel-Rops, *L'ère des grands craquements*, Paris 1958, 300 (E.T. *The Church in the Eighteenth Century*, London, 1964, p. 239).

[2] parlement forbade printing and sale of Bellarmine's Tractate.

[3] In 1606 Richer edited the works of Gallican theologians of the age of the Councils. In 1611 he launched his "Libellus de ecclesiastica et politica potestate". To A. Duval's "Elenchus libelli de ecclesiastica et politica potestate" (Paris, 1612), he replied with "Demonstratio libri de ecclesiastica et politica potestate" (Paris, 1622). Published posthumously, in connection with the development of Gallicanism, were "Apologia pro Johanne Gersonio" (Leyden 1677), "De Potestate ecclesiae in rebus temporalibus" (Cologne 1692), "Traité des appellations comme d'abus" (Cologne 1701). In 1663 the Court, through its officials, contrived to forbid the presenting of pro-Bellarmine theses in doctoral disputations in the Faculty. The fact that the Faculty at once gave way has been seen by Catholics as an error which endangered doctrine and opened the way for Jansenist possibilities.

The doctors of the Sorbonne in their doctoral disputations and in pursuit of their 400-year-old practice of "Censures" contended for "their Maxims". Richer's followers claimed that spiritual authority lay with the episcopate, but presbyterian tendencies, too, were active among them and after Dr Arnauld was expelled from the Faculty in 1656, they tended to drift towards Jansenism and the recalcitrant "four bishops" who sympathized with it. Parlement treated the Gallican privileges not as exceptional concessions granted to the kingdom but as the assertion of a basic freedom. For it, the "old law" was valid, Gratian being the last recognized authority, and so it refused to take account of subsequent developments in papal law.[1] The Gallicanism of the "assemblée du clergé de France" by no means confirmed the King's right to nominate bishops which was given in the Concordat of 1516 but claimed back the right to hold elections as an indispensable condition for the restoration of the spiritual estate in its purity. But it was the court (with its functionaries intervening, sometimes quite suddenly, to influence the decisions of the institutions) which was the real conductor of the Gallican concert.

In 1614, Cardinal du Perron, a pupil of Bellarmine, managed to win the day against the Richerists, when he got the Etats Généraux to hold up a "statute of the realm" which the King had enacted and which declared that the King held his crown from God alone and that no power in the world, be it spiritual or temporal, had any rights over his kingdom. Yet the move towards absolutism, with its claim that no intermediary stood between God and the crown, was not to be halted. In 1631 Morin furthered its advance with arguments from history: when Pepin took the place of Childeric it had certainly not been because Pope Zacharias had commanded it.

It was Pierre Dupuy who propagated the idea that Ultramontane maxims owed their origin to the flattery of the benefice-hunters who flocked to Rome and worshipped the Pope like a Great Mogul.[2]

When Louis XIV extended his "régales", he was only drawing the consequences of the claim that no intermediary stood between God and the crown. For absolutism, the right to nominate bishops was a fundamental right of the King. At Trent, in view of the opposition of the Spanish and French ambassadors, this question had not been touched upon, far less resolved in the way the Curia would have wished. Could not the Pope's participation in the investiture of those who were nominated by the King

---

[1] According to Pithou, there was a list of eighty-three Gallican points of grievance to be presented in Parlement. These included the struggle against exemptions enjoyed by the orders, dispensations for which application to Rome had to be made, and the judical and administrative apparatus of the Curia. Too many cases were removed from jurisdiction of the Crown merely because there was a religious element in them, e.g. oaths, marriage, religious foundations.

[2] Préclin/Jarry, op. cit., I, 149, 153 (Lit.).

be dispensed with altogether? After all, the Uniate churches of the East had their patriarchs, who ratified the appointment of bishops quite independently of the Pope. In 1639 Richelieu was thinking of solving the problem by creating a Gallican Patriarch.

During the Portuguese War of Independence the Portuguese Prior, Nicolas Monteiro, also claimed for Juan IV of Braganza the right to nominate Portuguese bishops. But the Pope hesitated to recognize a rebel leader as king, and filled the vacant sees of Guardia, Miranda and Viseu by *motu proprio*. Juan IV retaliated by calling a national council and installing his own bishops in Lisbon, Evora and Bragha, whereupon Rome withheld confirmation. The dispute that followed led to the situation that in 1649 there was only *one* regularly appointed bishop in Portugal. Not until 1669 was a solution arrived at, and then Clement IX agreed to share the right of nomination with the Portuguese king.

It would be wrong to assume that any deliberate movement in France brought about the conflict of 1682. What happened was rather that the parties concerned were taken by surprise by isolated events. In January 1663 a young Breton, Gabriel Drouet, who was a Jesuit student, presented the following theses in his doctoral disputation at the Sorbonne:

"1. Christ has endowed Peter and his successors with supreme authority in the Church.

"2. The popes have, on legitimate grounds, conceded certain privileges to individual churches, e.g. the Gallican church.

"3. Ecumenical Councils are certainly very useful for rooting out heresies and for putting an end to schisms and other disorders, but they are not absolutely necessary."

In this doctoral disputation Parlement intervened, apparently at the instigation of the Court, which had been alerted by friends of Antoine Arnauld. The Faculty was too submissive and recorded the anti-infallibility decree of 22nd January, thus depriving itself of any room to manoeuvre.

In July 1665 the Faculty censured the Ultramontane teaching of the Portuguese Jesuit, de Moya (Guimenius) and of Jacques Vernant, but France was then taken by surprise by a counter-stroke on the part of the Pope. The nuncio in Paris disseminated a bull ("Cum ad aures") which enjoined every bishop to disregard the Paris censure. For the first time pressure from Rome was to be detected in the controversy going on inside France between the Ultramontanists and the Paris party. Guimenius had called those who disputed the infallibility of the Pope heretics. Was this opinion justified, now that their censure had been annulled by the Pope? Did Rome want to impose silence now so as to be able later to interpret this silence as silent assent? The Gallicans decided to forestall such a development. The Avocat-Général forbade all His Majesty's subjects to observe or publish the papal bull. The Faculty got a commission of doctors to resolve on the nullity of the bull on the ground that it had been published *motu proprio*, therefore without the concurrence of the cardinals, and could thus never be recognized in France.[1]

Gallican discontent also found a target in the exemptions enjoyed by religious orders. Interference in monastic affairs was really always aimed at Rome, which used the exemptions to undermine the actual power of the episcopate. The anonymous work by "Petrus Aurelius", which Arnauld was behind, was reprinted at the expense of the Assemblée du Clergé in 1635 and 1641, so as to give currency to the idea that the orders should be subordinated to the episcopate. In 1669 an edict of the French Council of State did, in fact, bring the exempted orders under the jurisdiction of bishops. Rome tried to set aside this measure, so obviously designed to further absolutism, with the constitution, "Superna magni patris familias", of 21st June 1670, a carefully weighed regulation subjecting members of the orders to the jurisdiction of the local bishops only when they preached and heard confession outside their orders' own churches.

Louis XIV extended his "political régales" by asserting the right to receive revenues from vacant bishoprics, such revenues to be used for the benefit of the royal treasury or for religious activities (such as the conversion of the Huguenots). At the same time, he gave himself new, hitherto unrecognized "religious régales" by claiming, in the event of a bishopric being vacant, the right of nomination to nunneries other than those expressly listed in the Concordat, and to benefices without pastoral responsibility. In this way the King appropriated rights which previously belonged to the Vicar-General. The royal proclamation of 10th February 1673 extended the application of the political régales to the southern provinces and substantiated the religious régales.[2]

Opposition to the exercise of these rights of régale first came from Bishop Pavillon d'Alet, and his friend, Caulet of Pamiers. These bishops, who up till then had been Richerists, called in the Pope. The internal dispute in France was reported to Innocent XI by the Dominican Mailhat.[3] Caulet wrote a letter expressing his concern: "Unless the popes and all the prelates oppose this from the very start, eventually nothing will be secure from the princes' grasp." Innocent XI took his stand with the brief

[1] Ibid., I, 153ff. Le Vayer prepared at the King's request the "Traité de l'autorité du roi" (frequently reissued with new titles).

[2] Ibid., I, 153 (Lit.) D. Dubruel has come upon hints of the excommunication of Louis XIV: "Les nonces de France et l'église gallicane", in *Revue d'Histoire Ecclésiastique*, 1955.

[3] Préclin/Jarry, op. cit., I, 156. Another of Rome's informants was N. de Pontchateau.

"Binis iam litteris", dated December 1679.[1] The King was threatened with spiritual sanctions. On 7th August 1680 the Pope annulled the King's nomination of the Prioress de Grandchamp as head of the Cistercian convent at Charonne.

In an attempt to bring this dispute to an end, the King's Council sent Cardinal César d'Estrée to Rome to negotiate. In order to get the Curia to negotiate, d'Estrée suggested a method which had proved successful in the circumstances of 1657. This was to make preparations, which would be far from secret, to get the clergy in France to make a declaration which the Pope would be bound to resist. When Innocent XI refused to be intimidated by an assembly of French bishops held on 19th March 1681, d'Estrée counselled more drastic measures.

The two Le Telliers, the Lord Chancellor of France and his son, the Archbishop of Rheims, were bent on peace, and since 1680 had been advocating a novel solution to the question of the régales. Since the Pope and the King were too committed to be able to make concessions, the Clergé de France should assume the role of mediator. The Assemblée should persist in this role in the hope that the Pope would be won over. Bossuet's[2] inaugural sermon on 9th November 1681, one of the masterpieces of French literature, was a gesture of conciliation. Paul, who had laboured more than the other apostles, had founded the Church of Rome jointly with Peter, but nevertheless had allowed Peter to occupy the episcopal see. This might be seen as an analogy for the solution of the present conflict between Rome and France. The faith of Rome, which had never known heresy, remained the faith of the Church. As for the case of Honorius, which Combéfis had made it impossible to overlook, this had left no more trace behind it than a ship gliding through the water. The authority the French bishops possessed was certainly the same as the Pope's, and came, indeed, from the same source. Why then should the one be abased that the other might be exalted? It was obviously Christ's intention in the beginning to give power to an individual which he subsequently wished to give to a number. But this did not mean that the first individual was thereby dislodged. That the two jurisdictions should be jealous of each other constituted a sore in Christendom.

[1] Ibid, I, 157. Favorati and Dorat tried to bring Innocent XI to the point of declaring rights of régales to be heretical.

[2] Bossuet's ecclesiology already came to the fore in his doctoral disputation of 5th July 1651, in which five of the eight theses dealt with ecclesiology, in definitive formulae. His ecclesiology was developed in connection with his controversy with the Protestants, and in it he ignored Bellarmine and returned to the Fathers, for whom the érudits had the greatest respect. The Pope stood not at the beginning of Bossuet's ecclesiology but at its end. Möhler later took over this method from Bossuet. According to Bossuet, the power to determine orthodox belief was to be ascribed not to the Pope alone, but to the entire episcopate.

On 19th March 1682 the Four Articles "Cleri gallicani de ecclesiastica potestate declaratio", which Bossuet had drawn up, were unanimously adopted by the Assemblée, and were recommended as an edict to the King. This idea, which the Le Telliers had advocated for the sake of peace, was interpreted by the Pope as a gesture of defiance.[1]

Innocent XI's first step was to protest with the brief "Patronae caritati" of 11th April 1682, hoping that refutations would be forthcoming from the theologians. But the works which came from Spain (by Aguirre, with his *Defensio cathedrae Sancti Petri* of 1683, and by Thyrsus Gonzales, S.J.) and a declaration by the Hungarian Archbishop Szelepesny of Gran failed to carry the day.[2] So the Pope resorted to more drastic tactics: he refused the *institutio canonica* to all newly appointed French bishops, inasmuch as they had signed the Four Articles. The first to be affected were the bishops nominated to Castres and Clermont in the Auvergnes, and by 1688 there were thirty-five episcopal sees without bishops.

A settlement with France only became possible when Alexander VIII succeeded to the throne of Peter. His brief of 4th August 1690, "Inter multiplices", renewed the censure of the Gallican Declaratio on the ground that its signatories lacked canonical competence. On 14th September 1693 Louis XIV renounced the imposition of the Four Articles on the Church of France, and all the French signatories of 1682 were obliged to send a letter of apology to the Pope.[3]

3. SICILY AND THE "LEGAZIA APOSTOLICA"

One of the most favourable territories for exploiting the régales to further absolutist ecclesiastical policies was obviously Sicily. There, by virtue of the bull, "Quia propter prudentiam tuam" of 1097, the Crown could avail itself of the Legazia Apostolica, which had been granted in the exceptional circumstances of the Norman war against the Arabs. The Sicilian kings exercised their authority over the Church of the island as "legati nati" of the Pope, and the canonists could not classify this as royal usurpation in any way. Ancient rights were interpreted by the absolute monarchs of the eighteenth century to fit in with their ideas for independent state churches:

[1] Préclin/Jarry, op. cit., I, 157 (Lit.) Bossuet's subsequent "Defensio" departed from the negative lines which the "Four Articles" had represented. Although affirmation of the superiority of councils and of the historical fact of popes being in error is retained, there are positive utterances concerning the Pope. Patristic influences had now served to thrust into the background the ideas which stemmed from Gerson and Almain. Bossuet avoided in his ecclesiology analogies to secular communities. His concern was to provide a theological rehabilitation of the episcopate. The Church was always a plurality, to which the Holy Ghost was present.

[2] Préclin/Jarry, op. cit., I, 159f. Pastor, op. cit., E.T., xxxii, 309ff.

[3] Pastor, op. cit., E.T., xxxii, 599ff. For a later assessment of Rome's controversy with Gallicanism, see Manning, *The true story of the Vatican Council*, London 1877.

the royal Exequatur, without which no papal pronouncement could be published, the *jus spolii*, which applied in the case of vacant benefices, and royal patronage were all involved.

In 1711 trouble arose over the appointment of a bishop to the see of the Liparian Islands, the situation being aggravated by the fact that Philip V, King of Spain and Lord of the Isle of Sicily, was resentful that the Pope had recognized the Hapsburg Pretender to the Spanish throne. This was the only Sicilian see in the filling of which Rome had any rights, for Lipari had belonged to Naples since 1610. Rome lost no time in sending out a suitable person, a prince of the Church, Mgr Nicolo Maria Tedeschi, who till then had been Secretary of the Congregation of Rites. Scarcely had Tedeschi reached the Aeolian Islands than he was called upon to pay local taxes; he thereupon excommunicated the responsible officials as infringing the immunity of the Church within the meaning of "Coena Domini". When the "Judge of the Royal Monarchy", who claimed to hold office in virtue of the Legazia, lifted the excommunication, the Bishop of Lipari got his Sicilian colleagues to prepare for an attack on the Legazia itself. The Roman Congregatio dell' Immunità declared that the absolution granted to the offenders of Lipari lacked jurisdiction and was therefore invalid. The papal communication to the Sicilian episcopate of 16th January 1712 did not receive the royal Exequatur, but the Bishops of Catania and Girgenti were nevertheless ready to publish it.

The dispute was only resolved when Rome gave way—with the "Concordia" of Benedict XIII in 1728. In thirty-five articles, the area of jurisdiction of the Tribunal of the Royal Monarchy (based on the Legazia Apostolica) was defined. A settlement with Rome became possible when it was agreed that, in future, "causae majores" which came before the bishops would be referred to the Holy See. Further, the changing of the name "Judge of the Royal Monarchy" to "Iudex ecclesiasticus delegatus" gave the impression that it was no longer a question of the old Legazia, but rather a new privilege, and that the judge derived his authority from the Holy See. Mention was made only of the office of judge, as if no other rights were involved. With this arrangement, the Emperor was disposed to end the struggle.

The first real demonstration, however, of the state's authority over the Church came in 1735 when the Spanish Bourbons, who were already lords of Naples, invaded the Isle of Sicily and ousted the Austrian garrisons. The fact that the Bourbon courts took part in the campaign against the Jesuits, as well as their inclination towards Italian Jansenism, are a tribute to the systematic labours of the Minister, Tanucci, and his ability to exert influence beyond the bounds of Neapolitan territories. The anticlericalism which he taught the next generation (under Pietro Giannone's influence) was the fulcrum from which ideas of reform were directed into the civil sphere as well.

As long as Benedict XV (1750–8) was Pope it was possible to maintain a balance of power, because he understood how to make generous concessions to these forces and to the practical needs of the absolutist states. But the reactionary politics of Clement XIII provoked a precipitate attack on the privileges of the Curia. Naples was the centre of the storm, but after a short time (1769) Parma became involved as well. In Venice, anti-curialist politics seemed to be flourishing again, and Lugano became the focus of the anti-Jesuit press.

In Naples, it was a question of anti-curial practices only: in Milan, an 'Enlightenment' world of culture was developing (Academia Dei pugni). When the new ideas stemming from Kaunitz began to affect individuals brought up in the spirit of the Enlightenment, the combination of absolutism and enlightenment proved to be surprisingly fruitful. Disputes with Rome then led to the formation in 1756 of the "Giunta economale" to take over the entire ecclesiastical administration. Reorganization of studies and censorship, in which functions formerly belonging to the Inquisition were transferred to state functionaries, served to increase the opposition. The Inquisition was bereft of its authority and eventually was entirely suppressed (1775).

Sicily thereupon threw caution to the winds and in 1778 communications between the monasteries and Rome were suspended and the King's right to nominate his own representatives on cathedral chapters was affirmed.

4. FEBRONIANISM

The political Gallicanism of the Paris Parlement was to dominate the eithteenth century and was not to be countered from the Roman side. Theological Gallicanism now found expression only in connection with the Jansenist movement, its most effective advocate being the Louvain canonist, van Espen. ("Jus ecclesiasticum universum", 1700; placed on the Index in 1704, but it still went to ten further editions.) No Jansenist himself, van Espen nevertheless saw in Jansenist opposition a chance to exploit his canonistic ideas of the limitation of papal power through the power of the state, through Councils and through episcopal prerogatives.[1] It was he who was responsible for introducing Gallican theories into the episcopal movement in the German Empire.

"Gallican" influences were at work when the Elector, Franz Georg of

[1] In 1778 Abbé Lucet made an analysis of van Espen's works, adapted to fit the requirements of the French monarchy. On Gallicanism in France in the eighteenth century, see Préclin/Jarry, op. cit., I, 220–33 (Lit.).

Schönborn, Archbishop of Trier, started a dispute among the metro-politans of the Rhine over the preservation of the so-called powers of Nuntiature, i.e. the rights of dispensation and abolution claimed by the Curia. The Suffragan Bishop of Trier, Nikolaus von Hontheim, who was a pupil of van Espen, took this opportunity of putting forward a new interpretation of the Church's constitution in his book, *De Statu Ecclesiae*, which he published in 1763 under the pseudonym "Febronius". In this, Hontheim drew on the particular themes of German history which had been treated in contemporary works on canon and civil law in Germany, but which had hitherto not been brought together in a system. The grievances of the German nation and the Concordat of Vienna of 1448 replaced the specific historical arguments which French Gallicanism had highlighted. While van Espen had been concerned with the relation between ecclesiastical and civil power, which did not actually exist in the ecclesiastical territories of Germany, Hontheim concentrated on the judicial activity of the nuncios, something which was obviously on the increase and which was a phenomenon accompanying the expansion of the Curia's machinery—carried out in a manner analagous to the building up of the machinery of the absolutist state.

According to the *De Statu Ecclesiae*, if the pattern of the "ecclesia primitiva" is followed, the Church is not monarchical in constitution. The power of the keys belongs to the whole Church and the whole Church transmits it to all the apostles (i.e. bishops). Here one can detect the influence of the current Lutheran theory of the state church, the system of col-legiality, which looked upon the Church as a union, in which the exercise of authority belongs to all members but—in terms of the well-known "unhistorical construction of the Enlightenment"—is nevertheless given by tacit assent to the holders of office (the bishops, according to Febronius).

Compared with Gallican theories, this "Multitudinism" of Febronius was something new. The Roman pope was denied all jurisdiction over the bishops and his primacy merely provided the whole Church with an indispensable 'centrum unitatis'. The rights which the pope required to enable him to exercise this function were limited to supervision of ec-clesiastical laws, the protection of the bishops' jurisdiction, decision of disputes in matters of faith and the calling of ecumenical councils. Any rights over and above these, which the papacy had usurped since the Decretals of Pseudo-Isidore, were to be restored to the episcopate by national councils, which the civil power and enlightened people would alike support, or by an ecumenical council. The ecumenical council was the highest forum of the whole Church because it was the best representa-tion of the faithful in their entirety, but its decisions had to be received by the state churches.

Febronius was placed on the Index in 1764 and Clement XIII expressed his disapproval in a brief to the Bishop of Regensburg.[1] Nevertheless, his influence was far-reaching, not least through Italian and Portugese translations and a summary in French (published in Würzburg in 1766 by the Premonstratensian Jean Remacle Lissoir). In 1769 representatives of the three Rhineland archbishops held a consultation at Coblenz and drew upon Febronius in compiling in thirty-one articles a list of their grievances against all the reservations and exemptions which the Curia had usurped (the Avisamento of Coblenz). In 1763 the censorship authorities in Vienna cleared this dangerous book, a prelude to the growth in absolutist Austria at the time of the Enlightenment of that particular state-church system which was later to be known as "Josephinism".

5. JOSEPHINISM[2]

What had happened to the composition of the Vienna College of Censors that they were able to clear Febronius? Jansenism and Gallican theories of church law had been exercising an influence in Vienna through contacts with the Netherlands, in particular through the activities of Maria Theresa's Dutch physician, van Swieten. In 1749 van Swieten had managed to wrest control of censorship from the hands of the Jesuits.

Other intellectual forces were at work at this time. Karl Heinrich Seibt had been responsible for spreading German Enlightenment philosophy, as practised in Leipzig, to nearby Prague;[3] and it was from Seibt's circle that the men came who were later to devote themselves to the work of reform in Vienna: Freiherr von Kressl, head of the "Royal Ecclesiastical Commission", and Rautenstrauch, the Benedictine Abbot. In 1774 a programme of studies which Rautenstrauch had prepared, and which was to replace the Jesuits' educational system, was made compulsory for those studying philosophy and theology at the University of Vienna. The Italian Enlightenment, represented by men like Muratori, gained an entrance into the Hapsburg Empire through Austrian students studying in Italy. It was from Muratori that Joseph II got his enthusiasm for a "purified Catholic Christendom", and there was a Muratori circle in Salzburg as early as 1740.

[1] Previous students of Febronius, including Cardauns, were unable to explain how the Nuncio Oddi managed to identify the pseudonym. Now H. Raab has made it clear that it was Canon Dumeiz of Frankfurt, the middle man between Hontheim and the Frankfurt publisher, who betrayed the secret, for reasons unknown.

[2] M. C. Goodwin, *The Papal Conflict with Josephism*, New York 1938.

[3] The case brought against Seibt in 1779, which, however, was unable to shake his position, demonstrated the power of baroque Catholic resistance to reform. The pro-Augustinian Premonstratensians, the Piarists and the Augustinian hermits in Bohemia and Austria formed an alliance to support Seibt and his circle against the Jesuits.

Documents in the archives of palace, court and state in Vienna prove that it was Chancellor Kaunitz himself who was the actual author of the new scheme for a state church. The first measures were concerned with Lombardy. In 1760 Clement XIII had filled the episcopal see of Como without waiting for a recommendation from the Emperor. Shortly after, the see of Mantua was also filled. Vienna thought it could be proved that the Emperor had the power of appointment in this Duchy and that this should have been exercised. Austria thereupon followed the example of Spain and Sicily and introduced the "Placet" as a necessity before Roman decrees became effective in Austrian Lombardy. This made an inroad into an area of law which had hitherto been untouched, and marks the beginning of 'Josephinist' legislation. Chancellor Kaunitz's letter of 17th September 1764 to the Governor of Milan is its earliest expression.[1] Relying on documents discovered by the Registrar, Ilario Corti, concerning the implementation of the Milan amortization laws, Kaunitz gave the clergy one year to dispossess themselves of their recent acquisitions.

Conflicts soon broke out in Swabian districts of Austria. Maria Theresa had reached an agreement with Benedict XIV to the effect that if subjects in these parts appealed to the nuncio's court in Lucerne they would not be summoned abroad for hearing, but instead would receive justice on the spot from delegated judges. This arrangement, dating from 9th May 1755, was understood to apply to the laity. After 1761, however, the Swabian clergy had used it to evade the jurisdiction of the nuncio and had been supported in this practice by the government of Western Austria in Freiburg. In the Bohemian-Austrian Chancellory, the supreme court of the Western government, the problem was tackled by Councillor Heinke, who had recently been promoted from Prague to Vienna. Heinke laid down the following principle: every sovereign, without requiring any special privilege, had the right to prevent a subject being summoned abroad. If the Chancellor were to give way, then that would be tantamount to "declaring that the clergy are not subjects". So Kaunitz made the first act of defiance against ecclesiastical tradition.

The excommunication of Duke Ferdinand of Parma, the Empress's future son-in-law, on 30th June 1768, had the effect of removing restraints which held Maria Theresa back and which stood in the way of the Enlightenment ideal of a state church being realized.

When the Empress died (1780), Joseph II found that there was already in existence a state church structure together with a body of fellow workers trained to administer it. The Emperor now issued a series of hasty measures which were designed to create a Catholic state church with new dioceses

[1] In 1783 Lombardy was again the decisive area, when the Emperor for his part made the Provost, Visconti, Archbishop of Milan.

and so to assist the conversion of Austria from a conglomeration of patrimonial dominions and crown lands into a bureaucratic, centralized state. All kinds of regulations were necessary to bring the new system into being, and no fewer than 6,206 royal decrees were issued. With the suppression of the Jesuits a rapprochement between the Pope and the Jansenists became possible and Vienna negotiated the attempt of the little church in Utrecht to return to the sort of Catholicism which could comprehend a territorial church. Through a relative of Hontheim who lived in Vienna, Andreas Adolf von Krufft, a permanent association was set up between Vienna and Trier.

One opponent of the reform of the Austrian Church was the nuncio, Garampi, who, under the pretence of fostering "scholarly" contacts, set up a net-work of confidential agents whose task was to keep him informed. He also installed an observer in Trier to watch Hontheim, and it was a measure of Garampi's skill that he managed to contrive the recall of the ageing Honthem. On 19th December 1781 the Emperor informed the nuncio through Chancellor Kaunitz that he would tolerate no foreign interference in matters which must be regarded as the sole concern of himself as the sovereign authority in the land. Redress of abuses in no way depended on the Holy See, since it had no power in the state at all.

Consistently with this attitude, on 15th March 1781 communication between the orders and their generals in "foreign" Rome was stopped, and on 4th May the bull "Unigenitus", which condemned Jansenism, was annulled as an illegal extension of papal power. On 4th September 1781 an order was made prohibiting petitions to Rome or to the nuncio in Vienna for dispensations in matrimonial causes.

Josephinist reforms were directed particularly against the monasteries, except in so far as these were useful for educational or charitable purposes. On 12th January 1782, 700 convents given over to the devotional life were closed. From then on, no-one under the age of 24 and who had not completed his studies in school was allowed to take the habit. Civil rights of monks were curtailed: they could not witness wills, and the amount which a monk entering a monastery could donate or which a monastery could accept as a legacy was restricted to 1,500 florins. The authority of the prior was diminished by the suppression of monastery prisons. The assets of the suppressed monasteries were consigned to a Fund for Religion, which, although not at first administered with great skill, was, in fact, devoted to the work of the Church—as well as providing stipends for priests from the orders who had become seculars.[1] Joseph recognized that secular priests could be useful servants of the state, and their education was standardized

[1] The fund for religion lasted till the downfall of the Austro-Hungarian Empire in 1918.

by the establishment of nine general seminaries, under state supervision and outside the control of the bishops.[1]

The Josephinist toleration was commended by Bishop Herberstein of Laibach in his pastoral letter of 1782, whereupon Pius VI declared his teaching heretical. At this point, with the attempt at "sinceration" of the bishop, the Josephinist system and its measures were in danger of going beyond the sphere of "res mixtae" and persisting in something that was a deviation in doctrine from Rome. The consequences were only prevented by the premature death of the Bishop of Laibach.[2]

When the Emperor attacked "superstition" as being incompatible with the purity of the original teaching of the Church, when, on 25th February 1783, he issued a new service book simplified in accordance with the ideas of the Enlightenment, when he forbade weekday services "to save expenses of church music and staff", when he ordered the removal of the drapery with which images of the saints had been bedecked, when he cut down processions, and directed that burials should be in funeral bags instead of in coffins with wood, nails and shroud—all this served to make him lose popularity with the people. Pius VI made personal contact in 1782 when he visited Vienna, but this led to nothing more than a concordat sanctioning the reorganization of dioceses, which Joseph had previously undertaken himself.[3] In Belgium, the bishops rallied round Cardinal Frankenberg of Malines and held out so effectively against the Josephinist measures that the country rose up in revolt and put an end to Hapsburg domination.

In 1786, at the Congress of the German bishops at Ems, it looked once again as if co-operation between the Emperor and the metropolitans of the Rhine might succeed in bringing into being a national German Church

[1] A decisive factor in the historical evaluation of the general seminaries is whether two letters containing reports ("Lettre d'un évêque Autrichien à un évêque Belge", May 1789, and "Lettre d'un religieux de St. François, nommé professeur dans une académie du Tirol", 17th September 1788, in Receuil des représentations, protestations et rcélamations des Pays-Bas Autrichiens, xiii, 193-7, 199-214), are to be considered genuine or fabrications to stir up revolt in Belgium. The main reason for opposition to the general seminaries at the time of their foundation was the level of the taxes which had to be paid into the Fund for Religion so that they could be opened.

[2] The Josephinist principle of tolerance first appeared in 1777, when there was a mass movement of the Moravian peasants into the Evangelical Church and Maria Theresa forced them to return. This led to an exchange of letters between mother and son, which brought conflicting ideas of tolerance to a head. During his visit to Rome in December 1783 there was an unfortunate hitch in negotiations and the Emperor was only prevented from going into schism by the efforts of Azara, the Spanish ambassador.

[3] The papal visit was determined by the desire to prevent the Emperor from imposing his own solution on the question of the Lombardy benefices. In conversations between Emperor and Pope on this and return visits, it is noteworthy that there was a certain glossing over of religious questions.

based on Febronian principles. The German bishops were roused by the growing network of nunciatures for which the Elector, Karl Theodor, of Bavaria had been responsible. Despairing of the possibility of integrating his territories of Bavaria, the Palatinate, Jülich and Berg in a territorial bishopric, he had at last in 1785 got Rome to establish a nunciature in Munich for the whole of Bavaria. (This was held by Zoglio, in addition to Vienna, Cologne and Lucerne.) Archbishop Colloredo of Salzburg prevailed upon the Electors of Mainz, Trier and Cologne to join in a complaint to Joseph II, and, encouraged by a rescript from the Emperor, in the "Punktation" of Ems of 21st August 1786, which referred to the thirty-one Articles of Coblenz, they called on the Pope to renounce the privileges that were based on the Pseudo-Isidorian decretals. The bishops protested against rights of appeal to Rome, papal reservations of dispensations, exemptions granted to the orders, quinquennial powers, and, above all, against the judicial powers of nuncios. Here the bishops showed their perspicacity at the time which saw that duplication in ecclesiastical government which began with the development of the nunciature system. Communications from the Curia would in future require the bishop's "placet". Nevertheless, a number of suffragan bishops went into opposition under the leadership of Prince Bishop Limburg-Stierum of Speyer, and since the advantages the temporal magnates of the Empire were hoping for from their absolutist territorial churches were not the same as those of their spiritual neighbours, there was no real community of interest and the Emperor refrained from calling a national council. The German episcopal front quickly crumbled: the Elector of Mainz, von Erthal, began, with Prussian help, to enter into secret negotiations with Rome, and in 1790 the Elector of Trier, Clement Wenzel of Saxony, withdrew.

Tuscany, which had been ruled since 1737 under the Austrian Law of Secundogenitur, became another centre of Josephinist influence under Leopold II, the Emperor's brother. With the support of Bishop Scipione Ricci, the Synod of Pistoia carried out thorough-going reforms of a Josephinist, Enlightenment nature (anathematized by the Bull, "Auctorem fidei", in 1794).[1]

[1] The synod of Pistoia accepted the four Gallican articles of 1682, commended Quesnel, rejected devotion to the Heart of Jesus, indulgences, the holding of benefices in absentia, surplice taxes, fixed devotional exercises and popular missions, and called for a reform of the orders, which would integrate them into one order, modelled on Port Royal. At the national synod of Tuscany in Florence in 1787 a majority of bishops could not be found to support these reforms, so Leopold dissolved it and set about introducing reforms on his own. When Leopold became Emperor in 1790 Ricci could not remain in the country. There was a popular revolt in Pistoia, when orders were given to remove the mantillini placed on the Madonnas on feast days (Daniel-Rops, op. cit., II, 299: E.T. *Church in the Eighteenth century*, p. 237). Ricci did not submit until 1805.

6. SPANISH AND PORTUGUESE MISSIONARY RIGHTS AND "PROPAGANDA"

In 1622 the *Congregatio de propaganda fide* was given the task of centralizing foreign missions administration in Rome. This meant not only making a break with the particular methods of individual missionary orders, but also replacing the rights of patronage enjoyed by Spain and Portugal in the realm of the foreign missions. Now it was for Propaganda to approve the appointment of missionary superiors; to it, annual reports had to be submitted; and no missionary might start work without its letters patent. In 1640 Propaganda was given jurisdiction over all missions,[1] and this made a clash inevitable between two completely different conceptions of mission, between that of the absolutist colonial powers and that of Rome. The reasoning of the absolutist states demanded the exclusion of missionaries of other foreign nationalities, and the result was that missionary monks often had to assume Spanish or Portuguese names if they wanted to enter colonial territories. Propaganda, on the other hand, had since 1630 insisted on the advantages of training an indigenous clergy. Their instructions to their missionaries in the Far East in 1659 recommended that they should desist from the "Europeanization" of catechumens.

At this point a royalist move started in Madrid and was taken up in Lisbon, strengthening the exercise of the Spanish and Portuguese rights of patronage. Juan Sollorzano Pereira's *De Indiarum iure*—which had been placed on the Index in 1642, an act of law which was not published by the colonial powers outside Europe—remained an authority in the colonial courts.[2] Basing his arguments on the papal bulls of the fifteenth century, Pereira maintained that the head of the Church in the colonies was the King. In addition to rights of nomination, the traditional privilege of patronage, Pereira claimed that other rights were included: the right to discipline and expel secular clergy and members of the orders, the requirement that commissioners of the orders should have visas endorsed in their letters patent, and the right to start new missions even without the consent of any bishop.

When it became clear that centralization in Rome was going to be impossible as far as the Spanish and Portuguese patronage was concerned, Propaganda tried a different method. Charge of missions was given to Apostolic Vicars of episcopal rank, who were to be responsible solely to Propaganda. France, which had no right of patronage itself, came forward with timely support.[3] In the course of his travels, a Jesuit missionary

---

[1] Préclin/Jarry, op. cit., II, 539.
[2] Ibid., I, 66.
[3] In 1644 an anonymous work appeared, *Mémoires et instructions chrétiennes sur le*

from Avignon, Father de Rhodes, came across a group of young men associated with the Compagnie du Saint-Sacrement, "les bons amis", as they were called, former students of Jesuit colleges. Convinced that he had discovered the ideal men to beome the Apostolic Vicars of the future, he put first the nuncio and then Propaganda in touch with them (7th March 1653). The "bons amis" discussed their missionary ideals with Alexander VII himself in Rome. In fact, Propaganda delayed until 1658 the appointment of Pallus and Lambert de la Motte as the first Apostolic Vicars. But the instructions which were issued to them in 1659 have long remained a veritable charter of Catholic missions.

In order to avoid premature reprisals by the absolutist colonial powers, Propaganda ordered the Apostolic Vicars not to use Portuguese transport on their journey out to India. Only after their arrival in the mission field were they to announce their appointment to the new office that had been created for them.

The Apostolic Vicars went into retreat at Couarde to prepare themselves for their task, and there they were joined by twenty future missionaries. Thus a new development took shape: the setting up of a first missionary seminary. In 1663 agents in France purchased a block of buildings in the Rue du Bac for the Paris Missionary Seminary. The Compagnie du Saint-Sacrement helped in their own unostentatious way, and Bossuet preached at the opening.

In 1661 the Portuguese government voiced its objections to the sending of the Apostolic Vicars to the Far East, and took counter-measures. From the other side, Lambert de la Motte made a voluminous report from Siam, and sent a colleague to Rome to strengthen his position. In the event, a papal brief dated 4th July 1669 extended the jurisdiction of the Vicars to Siam, and another dated 13th September ordered the missionaries from the orders to present their letters patent to the Vicars and to get their authorization before taking up their missionary service. The Vicars were also given the right to allot pastoral duties to the missionaries from the orders and to deal with disputes between rival orders. Local catechists, whatever order had installed them, were to be subject to the control of the Vicars. Between 1670 and 1674 the last attempts to subordinate the Vicars to bishops appointed under the patronage of the national powers came to an end. A brief of Innocent XI, dated 10th October 1678, went the length of imposing an oath of obedience to the Apostolic Vicars on all missionaries.

---

sujet des Missions étrangères, setting out a comprehensive missionary stategy. Here it is already stated that it seemed that God had withdrawn many of his blessings from Spain since she had begun to abuse them. Préclin/Jarry, op cit., II, 545f. The Curia was, in fact, concerned lest a third claimant to rights of patronage should emerge, namely France (A. S. Rosso, *Apostolic Legations to China*, South Passadena 1947).

This aroused opposition among the Jesuits, but the Roman Congregation exerted so much pressure on Oliva, the General of the Order, that on 26th June 1680 he instructed his missionaries in the Far East to comply with Propaganda's demands.[1] Louis XIV informed Pallu, who was staying in France in 1680 prior to setting out on a further missionary tour, that he would not tolerate the exaction of oaths from French missionaries. Behind the King's attitude on this point stood Père de la Chaise, S.J., who on this occasion was exploiting Gallican arguments to protect the interests of his order. Here again, Oliva had to put matters right.[2] The Spanish Dominicans, who had gone to Fukien from the Philippines, and the Franciscans and Augustinians from Canton all lodged protests with the King of Spain against the oath. At this point, the conflict remained unresolved.

[1] Préclin/Jarry, op cit., II, 554f. Since the Curia omitted to give Portugal the opportunity of approving the decisions of Propaganda, Portugal systematically ignored the Apostolic Vicars.

[2] Ibid., 556. In 1686 there were difficulties in France as well. The doctors of the Sorbonne declared the oath to be incompatible with the liberties of the Gallican Church.

CHAPTER II

TOWARDS A CATHOLIC UNIFICATION OF THE DIVIDED CHURCHES

The termination of the Thirty Years War had destroyed any prospect of restoring the unity of the Church by means of "the temporal arm". The Protestants had established themselves in a compact, geographical block. Leibniz's judgment of Rome was: "Even in Rome they now see that nothing is to be gained by wars of religion." Only irenic moves could now further prospects of a European society with a united Church.

It is to the credit of the Roman Church that she refused to abandon the idea of integrating Christendom in a living whole. The critical question was how far this was to be a matter of diplomacy and how far it was also to involve spiritual devotion and acute theological thinking. In the period that was beginning, both are to be encountered.

I. MASEN, S.J., EMPEROR LEOPOLD I, PRINCE BISHOP JOHANN PHILIPP OF SCHÖNBORN AND SPINOLA

A Jesuit at the Court of Vienna, Jacob Masen, worked out a plan of union, which soon received the active support of Emperor Leopold I and of the Prince Bishop of Mainz, Johann Philipp of Schonborn, whose electoral court had attracted a group of gifted converts. In 1673, Christopher Rojas de Spinola, Bishop of Tina in Dalmatia, with Leopold I's backing, spent eight months visiting the courts of the Protestant princes of North Germany. At this time church union was actually only one point in a more comprehensive programme which was also concerned with defence against the attack the Turks were expected to make and with a coalition against Louis XIV. Pope Clement X lent his support to this policy. Spinola's first report to the Curia, on 14th May 1674, had more to say at this stage on financial and military problems than on religious questions.

On a second journey, Spinola tried to get agreements in Hanover, Brandenburg, Saxony, Brunswick and the Palatinate. This time Spinola was peddling Roman concessions. If his report to Innocent XI in 1677 is to be believed, the Protestants he was in touch with were indicating that they were prepared to accept numerous Catholic points: mass, purgatory, invocation of the saints, veneration of images, the authority of the Councils. But protests were immediately voiced in Berlin, Königsberg and Frankfurt, contesting these alleged concessions. So the Pope and Buonvisi, the nuncio, then sent an instruction to Spinola[1] setting out their conditions.

In his report of his third tour, which Spinola sent off to Rome on 28th May 1679—and this was perhaps the most reliable of his utterances—Spinola claimed victory. A close examination, however, reveals that Spinola could not, in fact, point to any real signs of reconciliation, but only the readiness of certain merchant princes to make a political deal. Ernst August of Hanover was aiming at the secularization of Osnabrück. In view of the influence of the Protestant Abbess of Herford on the Grand Elector, his conversion could be counted on. In Saxony, Johann Georg was already fasting on Fridays and went to confession, allowed his soldiers to go to mass and had texts attacking the Pope struck out of the Protestant prayer-books. Spinola thought that all that was now necessary to bring about the conversion of the Germans was to allow them communion in both kinds. The Curia tried to verify the possibilities Spinola had indicated and tended to back his scheme. The nuncio, Buonvisi, however, went forthwith to consult the Emperor, Leopold I.

Two and a half years later, Spinola, at his own expense, again set off on a ten months' journey to the Protestant courts. In Hanover, in particular, negotiations were taken up once more. In December 1682 the nuncio Buonvisi reported that meetings had taken place between Spinola and a group of irenic Lutheran pastors, who included Molanus, the Abbot of Loccum, the younger Calixtus and Theodore Mayer, and who had drawn up a definite plan. Concessions on the part of the Romans included the use of German in worship and communion in both kinds, and on the part of the Protestants, celibacy of the priesthood (subject, of course, to the rights of pastors who were already married), recognition of the Pope as visible head of the Church, optional invocation of saints, and re-ordination of pastors by Catholic bishops. Although the Curia were uneasy about the extent of Spinola's concessions, they refrained from censuring him and gave him a favourable reception in 1683. However, the three irenic papers which Molanus published in 1683 intimated further Lutheran demands: no public recantation, recognition of Lutheran ordination, retention by the princes of confiscated Church property, and suspending of the decisions of the Council of Trent until a new Council met. Innocent XI had been ignorant of these conditions when he authorized the bishop to continue his negotiations, but when he got more accurate information he immediately changed his tune.[2]

[1] Préclin/Jarry, op. cit., II, 664.
[2] In 1661 Molanus had taken part in a theological discussion in Kassel with the Marburg theologians, and there for the first time it was emphatically agreed that differences in teaching must not lead to division in the Church (R. Rouse and S. C. Neill, *A History of the Ecumenical Movement*, London 1954, 97).

2. BOSSUET

In the meantime, Roman Catholicism in France had demonstrated its ability to deal with its Protestant counterpart in a completely new way. In Charenton the Jesuit François Veronius (1575–1649) had abandoned that fruitless type of polemic which foisted on the other side opinions which they could not recognize as their own. Veronius realized that the real problem was to distinguish dogmas from their subjective interpretation, and he laid down principles which would enable dogma to be presented in its objectivity (*"Règle générale de la foy catholique séparé de toutes autres doctrines"*). The criteria of dogma were revelation and what had been pronounced by the magisterium as binding on the whole Church (*"propositio ecclesiae"*). The "propositio" could never exhaust the content of revelation. This was the basis of dogmatic development.[1]

Jacques Bénigne Bossuet, from 1669 Bishop of Condom and tutor to the Dauphin, carried Veronius's objective approach further in his *"Exposition de la doctrine catholique sur les matières de controverse"* of 1671. Bossuet expressed agreement with Dallaeus, the Reformed theologian: "Only official propositions which were required to be believed and followed by all" were to be considered as suitable subjects of theological discussion in the controversy. Bossuet accordingly confined himself to the decrees of the Council of Trent.[2]

Bossuet presented Catholic doctrines in a way which was so free from scholastic trappings that new insight into them became possible. Many Protestants even doubted that this really was authentic Catholic doctrine, and were astounded when the "Exposition" received episcopal and ultimately papal approval. In the light of the Protestants' reactions, Bossuet came to realize that the really decisive question at issue between the confessions was the problem of the Church.

In 1682 he discussed this point with the evangelical pastor, Claude, in a memorable series of meetings. In their discussion, they managed to overcome the old-style Jesuitical polemical methods which tended to proceed in far too fragmentary a way, dealing with individual points of doctrine. In order to show that the authority of scripture required the support of a

---

[1] Apart from German idealism, Möhler's Symbolics was strongly influenced by Veronius. Veronius produced his Symbolics from antitheses, Möhler his Symbolics of antitheses. Döllinger said of Veronius, "He was the first to grasp the idea of separating the basic teaching of the Church from all the theological additions and opinions of the schools. Veronius has very often been reprinted, is short and to the point and still as useful as it was two hundred years ago."

[2] Döllinger called Bossuet (in a letter in the possession of the Old Catholic congregation in Münich) "the greatest theologian in the episcopate for four or five hundred years", and his work, "a masterpiece, but it takes up only those teachings of the Catholic Church which have been rejected, distorted or misunderstood by Protestants".

"testificatio ecclesiae", Bellarmine, arguing against the Lutheran doctrine of the *testimonium spiritus*, had already drawn attention to the wealth of different Protestant interpretations which had accompanied the subjective appropriation of scripture.[1] Bossuet devoted a complete work to the subject of these differing interpretations: *"Histoire des variations des Eglises protestantes"* (1688). In this he appealed to pre-Reformation times when the Church was still undivided. This unity continued to exist in the Roman Church, while the Protestants were constantly changing and produced so many versions of doctrine that it was impossible to decide which of them was the true one. Bossuet supported this assessment of the Protestant Churches by quoting from their Confessions.[2] In this study, a new dimension of historical understanding was introduced by Bosseut to throw light on the confessional situation.

In 1678 the Hanoverian statesman, Leibniz, entered into correspondence with Bossuet on the question of reunion. When this exchange broke down it was the turn of the ladies to pick up the threads—in particular, Benedikte, the Dowager Duchess of Hanover, who had moved to Paris, Anna Gonzaga, the Abbess of Maubuisson (Louise Hollandine) and her secretary, Mme de Brinon. Leibniz had a vision of the role that Europe must play in the world. He realized that a united Christendom was a presupposition of the new position of dominance Europe was to occupy, and of world-wide mission, which, Voltaire's contempt for the Church notwithstanding, he considered as something which could not be renounced. Leibniz was striving for a universal Church sufficiently broadly based to include all varieties of Christianity and not to be identified with any of the existing churches.[3] With his mathematical training he sought to find a precise method of settling religious controversies and for securing an area of ground common to all confessions. His desire was to draw on all the sciences to construct a logic in comparison with which Aristotelian logic would appear but a crude affair.[4]

In a letter dated 6th July 1691, Leibniz informed Mme de Brinon that

---

[1] J. Gerhard, Loci communes 50, discussion of the theory of variation of the Jesuits: "Qui ex interno spiritus sancti testimonio iudicant de scriptura, sententiis invicem variant." Gerhard replied that the Church itself has also produced contradictory interpretations of scripture. Therefore its testificatio could furnish no proof for the canonical authority of scripture. The Holy Spirit does not impart his gifts alike to all men in the same measure. Even those who receive the gifts of the Spirit do not always follow its dictates, or in the same way.

[2] Bossuet defended himself against Protestant attacks in two writings: *Défense de l'Histoire des variations* and *Avertissements aux protestants*, in which he opposed Jurieu in particular, who pointed to the variations of Protestantism as a proof of its truth.

[3] When he was 17, Leibniz had been rummaging about in his father's library, and discovered documents on the controversy. From then on he was especially interested in this area.

[4] Bossuet, *Correspondance*, II, 167–9.

the Protestants might be expected to grant certain concessions in questions of discipline. When Bossuet expressed great hopes in his reply of 10th January 1692, the correspondence entered its most intensive phase.[1] In this exchange of letters the following positions were arrived at: according to Bossuet, if Protestants examined the dogmas, they would reach a consensus with the Roman Church and could then reunite. That was the method which had been tried since the start of the division in the Church, but which was meantime being discarded. According to Leibniz, the procedure should be reversed: that is to say, first reunion, then resolution of the dogmatic questions. That had not been tried. Leibniz supported his proposal with an argument from ecclesiastical history: the Council of Basel had received the Bohemian champions of communion in two kinds into the Church and only then required them on their side to recognize Catholics who communicated in *one* kind. Should it not be possible to proceed in the same way in the seventeenth century with the Lutherans? When, on 7th May 1692, Bossuet indicated his refusal to see here any proper analogy or to study this question further, a point was reached beyond which Leibniz would not go.[2]

Leibniz's analysis of the interconfessional situation was to the effect that the authority of the Council of Trent was the main reason why a bridge could not be built between the opposing sides. He denied that Trent was truly ecumenical in character and hoped that, taking into account the Gallican reservations and the refusal of Catherine of Medici and Henry IV to ratify the Council, it might be done away with. On 23rd October 1693 he wrote to Mme de Brinon: "Si l'on croit obtenir un parfait consentement sur toutes les decisions de Trente—Adieu la réunion."

Here, however, Bosseut's demand that discussion should be confined to the objective texts of the various confessions was relevant—a tendency he had inherited from Veronius. Even though, as a Gallican, he saw the hooks of national Church jurisdiction on which the recognition of the Council of Trent in Catholic states hung, he contended against Leibniz for the actual statements of faith contained in the Tridentine formulae. "Can it be doubted that in matters relating to faith the decrees are accepted by Catholics in France as in Germany, in Spain and in Italy? Has one single Catholic ever been heard of who has thought himself free to accept or not to accept the faith of the Council?" (10th January 1692). Bossuet opposed the Leibnizian procedure of re-examining the historical decisions taken by the Church at Trent. He envisaged the possibility that all the traditional dogmatic pronouncements would then have to be scrutinized anew. On 29th March 1693 Leibniz retorted that the believer would in any event

[1] Ibid., V, 8–11.   [2] Ibid., V, 10.

have to carry out his own personal scrutiny and arrive at his own convictions. When Leibniz continued his attack on Trent by observing that this Council was an Italian affair only and therefore not truly representative, all Bossuet's hopes of agreement crumbled.[1]

3. CATHOLICIZING IN FRANCE

A new campaign against the Huguenots was initiated by Richelieu because he considered that their political organization was hindering the adoption of a great national policy in France. Since 1632 consolidation of distinctively Catholic forces had been taking place, and under the spiritual sway of Berulle, the Compagnie du St Sacrement had set about curbing the Huguenots' influence in society. This they did by getting their members who were doctors, master craftsmen or officers in the militia to take over appointments held by Huguenots. After 1638, by virtue of the position they themselves occupied in place of the Huguenots, they began getting public recognition for a Catholic interpretation of the Edict of Nantes. After 1649 the Assembly of the French Clergy was also prevailed upon to work for the extermination of the Huguenots, and their sanction of fiscal measures was accompanied by calls for action. In 1656, the government began taking the same line (Revocation of the Edict of Nantes, 1685).

After the capture of Strasbourg, the obvious next move was to try to win over the Protestants of Alsace to the Catholic faith. The Jesuit Dez was sent for. With the backing of the faculty of the Collegium he addressed public meetings in the cathedral at Strasbourg at which he sought to show

[1] Ibid., V, 428-445. When peace was restored in Europe in 1698, and conditions seemed more favourable, the correspondence was renewed. Leibniz asked Bossuet to bring in a layman on his side. The correspondence got bogged down in disagreement over the Tridentine canon which included the Apocrypha. Guhrauer, the Leibniz scholar of the nineteenth century, has represented Leibniz' policy on reunion as ancillary to the dynastic policies of the Court. (*Biographie*, II, 33, 56). O. Klopp thinks it was the Electress Sophia who was behind it. The French editors of Bossuet's works have likewise emphasized the political aspect. Préclin, too, emphasizes that Leibniz's work for reunion was made possible because the Hanoverian Court wanted to take over the lands of the bishopric of Onsabrück, and, in a second phase, aspired to become an electorate. The irenic overtures were to be begun at the moment when, in a third political phase, the prospect of occupying the British throne appeared. Préclin/Jarry, op. cit., 668. Kiefl has presented a convincing argument to disprove this. Lambinet emphasizes a corresponding non-political orientation in Bossuet. "The things of religion cannot be treated like temporal things. Temporal things are dealt with by mutual meeting together. For these are things of which men indeed are masters. But the things of faith are dependent on revelation, upon which only mutual declaration can be made, for the sake of clear understanding. If the difficulties seem to increase rather than decrease, and if God does not yet open men's hearts to the proposals of peace which were so admirably begun, then it is up to us to wait for the opportunities which our heavenly Father has ordained" (*Correspondance*, XIII, 2085).

that the Augustana could, in fact, be reconciled with Trent. The Protestant pastors wanted these claims printed. Although written for a special situation, the book which appeared in 1687 did indicate a new theological approach. When he was attacked by two Lutheran theologians, Dez replied in 1689 with a second, expanded edition, in which he maintained that a detailed examination of the Augustana disclosed nothing un-Catholic in it. Therefore the Lutherans were wrong to continue in separation from the Catholic Church.

4. RELATIONS BETWEEN ANGLICANS AND CATHOLICS

After the Great Revolution of 1637–8 in England and the victory of the army over the gentry, many Anglican bishops moved to Paris as émigrés. They lived under the shadow of the dissolution of the Anglican Church government (1645), the execution of Laud, their Archbishop (1645) and of King Charles I, the "Head" of their Church (1649). Among the émigrés, all efforts were directed to working out a plan for the future of the Church in England. In this connection, Charles II's chaplain, the Reverend Richard Steward, and Sir George Ratcliffe, took up discussion of the possibility of reunion with the Roman Church.[1] Hammond, the theologian who was associated with them, began translating Gallican and Jansenist writings into English, since he reckoned that the Anglican conception of a national Church could most easily be reconciled with Catholicism of a Gallican and Jansenist kind.[2] Since the question of the true constitution of the Church had become crucial for consideration of the nature of the English Church, the discussion was opened up at its most interesting point.

Just how profoundly the English Catholics themselves were influenced by Gallicanism was to appear later. After 1631 the only ecclesiastical authority in England acting as a means of communication between the English Catholic clergy and "Propaganda" was the Chapter, and its was the Chapter which allowed a protest to be made to James II against the installation of an Apostolic Delegate in England. The English Catholic clergy, so it was said here, valued diocesan bishops who served the interests of the king, whereas an Apostolic Delegate would be entirely dependent on the Pope. The very title of Apostolic Delegate was a real obstacle to reunion for the

[1] Préclin/Jarry, op. cit., II, 670f. (Lit.).

[2] The Jansenist professors at the Sorbonne presented a plan of union to Peter the Great during his visit in 1717. The relative independence of the Gallican Church would show the Tsar that it was possible to belong to the Roman Church without agreeing with the Pope in everything. The struggle of the Jansenists against the Society of Jesus was to be seen as reflected in the expulsion of the Imperial Jesuit Mission from Moscow in 1719. In the period 1728–31 the French Jansenist Jubé was working for union, on the mandate of the "Little Church" of Utrecht.

Anglicans, since it merely added force to the view that Catholics were subjects under foreign jurisdiction.

A second link was formed among the émigrés in Paris when the Anglican bishop, Bishop Cosin, met Father Robinson, the prior of one of the English Benedictine settlements which had withdrawn to the Continent at the beginning of the century. Their talks on reunion concentrated on two main subjects which were thereafter to assume decisive importance for Anglican-Catholic relations. These were the question of the Real Presence in the Anglican Lord's Supper and the question of validity of Anglican ordination. Drawing on his extensive knowledge of patristics, Cosin opposed Father Robinson's arguments; he also published a history of the doctrine of transubstantiation (which was translated into French by Durel) and planned to write a study to demonstrate the validity of Anglican ordination. Thereupon, in 1695, the Prior of Frossay, Eusèbe Renaudot, wrote his "Memorial on Confirmation and Ordination in the Anglican Church", the negative findings of which were suppressed. When, however, Bishop Gordon, the Anglican Bishop of Galloway, was converted, a Roman Congregation declared that he was not a true bishop, as he had only been consecrated in accordance with the Anglican rite. At this point two Anglicans, Stephens Daniel ("The Authority of Bishops") and Daniel Williams ("England's Reformation"), appeared on the scene to defend their orders. In 1708 Hickes wrote "The Divine Right of Bishops Asserted".

When Charles II returned to the English throne in 1660 and the Conference of Savoy of 1661 restored the Anglican conception of the Church, leadership passed to the theologians returning from their exile in France. It was they who occupied the episcopal sees. This brought the Anglicans closer than they had ever been to the Gallican Church. In October 1662 a plan for the reunion of the churches was conveyed to Rome by the Irishman, Bellings, claiming the same privileges for a Catholic "United Church of England" as those enjoyed by the Gallican Church. There was a lack of caution, and the plan became public knowledge. When that happened, it was completely disowned by the King.

Parliament, and particularly his Minister, Hyde, forced a policy of uniformity on the King. Nevertheless, Charles, who since the time of his emigration had remained in constant touch with Catholic circles, tried by means of indulgence (royal dispensation from the law) to procure more freedom for dissenters, especially for Catholics. When the King saw how Catholic France had been bolstered by its victory over the Netherlands, he at least became bold enough in 1672 to abrogate the Penal Laws against dissenters and recusants.

Parliament, however, was sufficiently powerful to be able to force through the Test Act on 29th March 1673. Under this, everyone engaged in academic work or holding office in the state or at Court, or in the army or Navy, was obliged to take the oath of loyalty and supremacy, to receive the sacrament in the national Church and to renounce transubstantiation.[1]

The suspicions of the Protestant population flared up into "national hysteria" in 1678 when Titus Oates uncovered a "popish plot" to assassinate the King. In this plot Louis XIV's confessor, Père la Chaise, also appeared to be implicated and was alleged already to have paid out £10,000 in London. On the Catholic side, the disclosures were declared to be entirely fictitious. There was a wave of arrests of Jesuits in London and an Irish bishop, seven priests and a layman, William, Viscount Stafford, were executed.[2]

With the accession of James II in 1685, there was once again a Catholic on the English throne. Rome counselled moderation, but this advice was disregarded and James II chose a Jesuit, Father Petre, as his consultant. The Test Act notwithstanding, Catholic officials were installed in office. Also, diplomatic relations were resumed with the Pope and publicly celebrated. The people had already been disturbed by the Revocation of the Edict of Nantes, and became even more restless in 1687 when the King issued his Declaration of Indulgence revoking the Penal Laws and the Test Act and when Anglican bishops who refused to allow these measures to be read out in public were arrested. This started the development which led to the crowning of William of Orange in 1688 and, as a result, to a period of Catholic impotence.[3]

Under Archbishop Wake (who became Archbishop of Canterbury in 1716), fresh negotiations towards reunion became possible. In 1686, when Wake was chaplain to the English embassy in Paris, he had entered into

[1] T. Macaulay, *History of England since the accession of James II*, London 1849–61; W. Hunt and R. L. Poole, *The Political History of England*, Vol. VIII, London 1905; R. Lodge, *The History of England from the Restoration to the death of William II 1660/1702*, London 1910. On the convert Davenport, who worked for union with the Anglicans, cf. J. Berchmans Dockery, O.F.M., *Christopher Davenport, Friar and Diplomat*, London 1960.

[2] G. Guitton, "Titus Oates, le Père de la Chaise et las grand Arnauld 1678/1681", in *R.H.E.*, 1958, 69ff. Guitton places the story of Oates on a par with the books of satire on Father la Chaise during the last thirty-four years of his life, when he was Louis XIV's confessor. With regard to his office as confessor, the Father always maintained silence, at most giving a report to the superior of his order (E. I. Watkin, *Roman Catholicism in England*, London 1957, p. 96).

[3] Watkin, op. cit., 98f. M. Wall, *The Penal Laws 1691–1700*, Dundalk 1961, elucidates the meaning of the laws and shows the efforts Catholic bishops made to maintain discipline. C. Giblin, *Catalogue of Irish interest in the collection Nunziatura di Fiandra, Vatican Archives*, Dublin 1961, gives an insight into the attempts of Catholic Confederates in Britain to gain moderation in the application of the laws (1691–1709).

debate with Bossuet ("Exposition of the doctrine of the Church of England" to which he added a first and then a second "Defence"). Wake was now so impressed by Gallican and Jansenist opposition to the bull "Ungenitus" that he went the length of suggesting a kind of organic union in which the national Anglican Church would acknowledge obedience to a French Gallican primate and enter into practical inter-communion. He knew from first-hand experience the part which the chaplain to the embassy in Paris could play, and to this post he appointed the Reverend Dr Osmond Beauvoir, whom he got to negotiate with Ellies du Pin. In the correspondence between Wake and du Pin, the Archbishop of Canterbury expressed himself as being opposed to the idea of a common confession and a common liturgy but in favour of a common system of Church government. Du Pin had the Anglican Thirty-nine Articles examined in a "Commonitorium". Of the thirty-nine, twenty-three were declared acceptable, eleven were subject to debate and five were rejected. From the Catholic side, du Pin was prepared to give up insistence upon the celibacy of the priesthood, communion in one kind, and objections to Anglican ordination. Cardinal Noailles and Joly de Fleury approved the Commonitorium. Nevertheless, Wake saw that in it equality of status for Anglicanism was really denied. This particular attempt at reunion came to an end with the seizure of du Pin's papers at the time of a rapprochement between the Regent and Rome in 1719. Pierre François le Courayer of Geneva took this opportunity of making a historical study of the validity of Anglican ordination. He got Wake to supply him with material for his researches, and as a result the two became friends. In 1725 Courayer published his dissertation "Sur la validité des ordres des Anglais". He was thereupon censured, and fled to England.[1]

---

[1] Courayer's thorough research destroyed the story of the consecration of Bishop Parker by the Elizabethan Archbishop Barlow in the Nag's Head Inn. He concentrated on demonstrating the sacramental efficacy of the Anglican ritual of Edward VI, which had been disputed by the Roman Congregations. The right of the churches to provide their own forms for the ritual was extended to include the abolition of the practice of anointing and placing the Gospel upon the head of a bishop-elect. The ritual included the laying on of hands and a prayer of invocation of the Holy Spirit. This thesis was criticized by the Jesuits Clerophilus Alethes of Hougnan, Abbé Gervaise, P. Hardouin, and the Dominican, Le Quien. But its historical argumentation remains valid. Roman criticism today, however, maintains that what Anglicans intend with the laying on of hands is not enough to constitute a sacramental act. With Anglican co-operation, Courayer prepared a careful defence. This appeared in four volumes in 1726, when a union of the Anglican and Gallican Church through contacts between the Seminary of the "33" and the "S.P.C.K." seemed assured. But this defence only served to alert English and French Catholics. Le Pelletier denounced the man from Geneva. On August 22nd 1727 he was censured in St Germain des Prés; cf. Préclin/Jarry, op. cit., II, 675ff.

5. ROYAL CONVERSIONS

In the age of absolutism it was only the reigning heads who had enough social freedom to change their faith. In their case, conversion could carry with it far-reaching consequences. The earliest and most obvious success took place when Queen Christina of Sweden went over to the Catholic Church. A daughter of Gustavus Adolphus, she had been encouraged in this step by the French minister, by Descartes, who visited Stockholm in 1649–50, and by Jesuits who managed to gain access in secret. The new convert's residence in the Eternal City gave the Roman Church great satisfaction. Her carelessness in financial matters and her political aspirations to the throne of Naples caused some embarrassment, however, and she also remained critical of legends and relics.

In the royal conversions which followed, political motives predominated. The first member of the electoral house of Saxony to go over to the Catholic Church was Christian Augustus, who was converted in 1689. He became Archbishop of Gran, and a cardinal, and arranged the conversion of his religiously indifferent cousin, the Elector Augustus the Strong. Soon, a wave of conversions swept the royal households of Germany. In 1705 Duke Christian Augustus of Holstein was converted, in 1710 Duke Anton Ulrich of Brunswick-Lüneburg, and in 1712 Duke Karl Alexander of Württemberg. The royal conversions now proved, however, inadequate as a means of solving the question of church unity in a manner acceptable to Rome.

6. THE CATHOLIC ENLIGHTENMENT AND PLANS FOR UNION

Catholic Enlightenment theology in Germany made its own contribution to the union question by virtue of the new positions it adopted. Febronius saw an opportunity to bring about the unification of the divided churches by working out an episcopal and national church structure. His thesis— only the whole body of believers possess authority in the Church *secundum originem et virtutem*—was to be of help in opening up ecumenical possibilities. Boehm, a Benedictine from Fulda, drew up a plan of union, which was discussed and criticized in an exchange of letters between him and Martin Gerbert of St Blasien. Benedikt Stattler gave expression to his ecumenical ideas in his "Anakephalaiosis ad DD protestantes in Germania", and sought further support for them in Augsburg and Münster in 1781 with his "Plan for a general and practicable unification of the Protestants with the Catholic Church". As Stattler saw it, Christianity must fall to ruins if personal opinion alone was to be the final arbiter of scripture. To check this, he formulated conditions for peace called "Canons of Union".

These were placed on the Index in Rome as early as September 1781. But his bishop, Bishop Strasoldo of Eichstätt, defended his vice-chancellor so successfully that proceedings dragged on until 1796. Stattler's condemnation was published because he was unwilling to retract twelve of his theses. Enlightenment understanding of reason and revelation indeed carried implications of an irenic nature, and how far these could go is well illustrated by the case of the Catholic, Mutschelle.

Mutschelle drew a distinction between the "external" Word of God, which comes to us as "alien command" and the "internal" Word of God (reason), and emphasized the ecumenical opportunity presented by the fact that the inner voice was everywhere the same. "Over the Word of God as preached to us or passed off to us by other men, how much dissension and difference of opinion, how much splitting into sects and churches; how much mutual hatred, persecution and condemnation, how much carping, time-wasting, brain-consuming polemical rubbish, how much fighting with pen and sword, how much murder and slaughter! But over God's Word as presented to us by our own reason, is there here too dissension, strife and battle? Here only *one* voice speaks. Here is only *one* community, one universal Church comprehending all reasoning peoples—one Shepherd, one fold and one flock."

Enlightenment irenics did not go unchallenged. For example, the Salzburg pastoral letter of 1782, which commended "peace, concord and toleration to brethren who think other than we on one point of religion or another", provoked opposition.

The sermon on toleration which the Franciscan Eulogius Schneider preached at Augsburg on 25th November 1785 created such a stir that the preacher had to flee the town. Nevertheless, the outcome of this period was significant: common participation by both Catholics and Protestants in the cultural life of Germany, which was to become characteristic of the Romantic period, was made possible by the compromise which the men of the Enlightenment achieved between the confessions.

One consequence of the levelling process of the Enlightenment was that it enabled the Princess Gallitzin to place great reliance on the prayer of the Protestant Matthias Claudius. The association between Count Stolberg, a Lutheran, and the Münster circle was formed on the basis of the unimportance of confessional differences.

On the same basis, Radowitz wanted a confederal association between Protestants and Catholics "in the political realm". Where a dialectical view of history is taken, as it was, for example, by Franz von Baader, confessional divisions are to be considered as forming a transitional stage leading to a higher unity. Baader declared in 1838 that it was folly on the part of popish Catholics simply to expect non-Catholics suddenly to become papists again.

CHAPTER III

THE APOSTOLATE OF THE ORDERS

The orders founded at the beginning of the sixteenth century came into being at the moment when the Catholic Church was being faced with the challenge of the Reformation. They were motivated by the desire to dedicate themselves to the serious pursuit of spirituality in the midst of all the secularization of Renaissance culture. The new type of monasticism devoted itself with something like military mobility to the *vita activa*. Its aims were to promote renewal of the clergy, popular preaching, missionary service, education of the young, care of the sick and of the poor. In the interests of these tasks, monastic seclusion had to be renounced.

In the seventeenth century, there was a second wave of monastic foundations. Now, however, it was a question of discovering a new kind of apostolate, having particular regard to the new structures which had developed in society, especially in France. This apostolate could only be safeguarded if those who were called to it united in religious orders.

I. CHARITY

In 1617 Vincent de Paul[1] was temporarily in charge of the Parish of Chatillon. One Sunday at mass, a woman stopped him on his way to the chancel and told him in a whisper of her desperate straits. In his sermon Vincent recounted what he had just heard. The congregation accepted its responsibility at once, and fifty of them hurried to the forsaken cottage to help.[2] This event led to the discovery that only organized action could meet current social needs which, as a result of the tax laws, were assuming the proportions of a mass phenomenon, especially in rural France. When Vincent returned to Paris and to Madame de Gondi's circle he translated his Chatillon experience into action on a wider scale. His "Dames de Charité" were the first expression of organized Charity.[3]

---

[1] Vincent de Paul, Works (ed. P. Coste), 14 vols, Paris 1924-6. After 1610 an "invasion of holiness" was to be observed in the fashionable Abbé Vincent, Court preacher to Queen Margaret, and financially well endowed by virtue of his position as abbot. What caused him to abandon his career remains unknown. He was trained by Francis de Sales and Bérulle.

[2] Daniel-Rops, *L'église des temps classiques*, Paris 1958, 8f. (E. T. *The Church in the Seventeenth Century*, London 1963, 1ff.)

[3] Ibid., 39f. (E.T., 30f.).

One of the ladies, Louise de Marillac, took note that people of high society preferred handing over their gifts rather than actually serving the needy. She accordingly decided to go further and to found the "Filles de la Charité", who first met at a little gathering in the Quartier St Victor in 1633.[1]

The institution of the "Filles de la Charité" really represented a social revolution. Up to now, the practice of charity had been the privilege of the clergy, the religious orders and the upper classes. Now, simple girls of the people, whose worth Vincent had discovered, were to be seen working alongside the most exalted names of France. Vincent transformed the lowliest tasks into duties to be respected. He used his authority to include everyone in the same kind of Christian humility. The "Soeurs grises," as they were called, visited the poor of the parish in their homes, thus becoming the prototype of "parish sisters". When Queen Anne of Austria asked for help for wounded soldiers, the "Filles de la Charité" dispatched four Sisters to the army, and they became the first army nursing sisters. In 1634 Mme Goussault was shocked to discover the wretched state of the sick in the Hotel-Dieu. It was Vincent's Sisters who then took over the nursing.

At the same time, however, the two-level nature of the Grand Siècle charity was also introduced. The great preachers made an exhortation to almsgiving a standard feature of their sermon. Fléchier said: "God's intention in creating the rich is that they might be disposed to charity. He chooses them as instruments of his goodness, as channels through which the external tokens of His grace must flow." Bourdaloue cried: "You are rich, but for whom? For the poor."[2] With the contributions that resulted, Catholic charity became institutionalized. This was the age in which the "institute" originated, which those like the "Filles de la Charité" were prepared to run,[3] e.g. in Paris, the Hospice Saint-Nom-de-Jésus and Enfants Trouvés, the Hôpital Général, and those of the Val-de-Grace and the Invalides. In the French provinces twenty-seven hospitals were opened between 1661 and 1715. The Royal Chambre de la Charité Chrétienne, which had been founded by Henry IV in 1606, exercised the state's right to inspect hospitals. In the territories annexed by Louis XIV, the bishop's first task when he arrived was to build a hospital. The movement spread well beyond the borders of France: Turin built three hospitals, Milan two, Venice two and Vienna four.[4]

[1] C. K. Murphy, *The Spirit of the Society of St. Vincent*, 1940.

[2] Daniel-Rops, op. cit., 327 (E.T., 282).

[3] The brothers of St Jean de Dieu were also at the disposal of the charitable institutions (especially in Rome). Daniel-Rops, op. cit., 108 (E.T., 92, 281, 282). The Order of the Merciful Sisters of St Charles Borromaeus began in 1652 in Nancy.

[4] Daniel-Rops, op. cit., 108, 328 (E.T., 92, 283). The Council of Trent had charged the Church with the administration of hosptials, but realization of this came later. In Germany the movement took hold especially in the Julius Hospital in Würzburg, founded in March 1579 by Julius Echter of Mespelbrunn.

2. MISSIONS

Absolutism led to the elaborate development of official residences, but this was at the expense of the rest of the country. Hence the challenge of mission in the rural districts. Father Veron now worked away in the area round Caën, and Michel de Nobletz in Brittany. In Corsica the Barnabite Alexander Sauli was at work, and in the villages of Italy the Jesuit Segneri.

The Electoral Princess Anna Maria Louise of the Palatinate, who resided at Düsseldorf, got a group of Jesuits from the Lower Rhine province to make a journey home to Italy so that they might study the preaching techniques used by Segneri in his mission campaigns and which seemed to be so successful in rousing the people. Self-castigation by the preacher now became the order of the day in the pulpit.

Following the ravages of the Thirty Years War, the Archbishop of Cologne made it a matter of priority to have Jesuits conducting missions throughout the country, in village after village.[1] In Spain, preaching missions were conducted by Lopez and Gonzalez. In Paris, it was Mme de Gondi who pressed Vincent de Paul, as priest to her estates, to apply himself to the needs of the country districts. Vincent had (unintentionally, at the start) discovered at Folleville how receptive a neglected country parish could be to the gospel. Now he went on to hold parish missions in Paillart and Sèrevilliers in Picardy, then in Villepreux, Joigny and Macon in Burgundy. Vincent was soon convinced that his missions could only be of lasting effect if they were followed up by others. The methods which had been proved successful in a single campaign would have to be extended and this meant forming a team of priests for mission. A £30,000 endowment, which Mme de Gondi had been putting aside for a period of seven years expressly for rural missions, made a beginning possible. In 1633 Urban VIII gave official sanction to the work of this mission. Since they had the use of the property of the monastery of St Lazare, the fathers engaged on this work were given the name "Lazarists".[2]

One point Vincent always impressed upon his missionaries: if they were going to speak of Christ in a way which would be understood, they would have to be simple. "Enough of this *'Bibus'* and *'coeli coelorum'*!" Strutting like a peacock through "finely-turned discourses is blasphemy".

---

[1] In 1651 two Jesuits were sent on missions to Westphalia to restore Catholic worship and found brotherhoods and schools. The same thing took place in the Duchy of Jülich-Berg. These, and visitations of the kind envisaged at Trent, were the Archbishop's main contributions. Reports were made by Bishop Max Heinrich (1650–88) for the years 1651, 1654, 1659, 1668, 1675, and by his successors in 1692, 1701, 1755, which are in the archives of the Roman Congregation of the Council. In missions conducted from 1669 to 1692 the Jesuit Mayenberg converted the mountain districts of Valais in Switzerland.

[2] Préclin/Jarry, op. cit., II, 510 (Lit). Daniel-Rops, 27ff. (E.T., 17ff.).

So, at a time when classical culture was blossoming in France, a mission of the Lazarists was a real event for those who stood outside the world of culture. It became clear that Vincent's charity did not represent an isolated and specialized phenomenon, but was only a part of a many-sided enterprise.

At Laon, the market was closed so as to give everyone a chance to hear the missionaries. From Poitiers, one of them wrote: "Souls which seemed hard as stone have been filled with a holy fire." Even towns like Arles, Angoulême, Cahors and Annecy insisted on having the men of St Lazare. By the time of Vincent's death in 1660, 840 missions had been held.[1]

3. SEMINARY TRAINING FOR THE PRIESTHOOD

Vincent was highly critical of the contemporary generation of priests: "The depravity of the priestly estate is the chief cause of the Church's downfall. Priests who live the way most of them do to-day are the greatest enemies of the Church of God. Everything must therefore be done to help the clergy to acquire the virtues necessary for their position."[2] A pointer to a practical solution came from the Bishop of Beauvais, when Vincent was accompanying him in July 1628 on a visitation of his diocese. Suddenly awaking out of a dream, the bishop opened his eyes and called out: "At last I see a short and realistic way of preparing priests for ordination. I shall have them to stay with us for a few days. They will devote themselves to pious exercises and will be instructed in their tasks." Vincent was convinced that this idea had come from God and took it upon himself to arrange the subjects to be worked at in this time of preparation. This was the origin of ordinands' exercises. On the following Ember Days, Vincent held the first exercises in Beauvais and compiled a manual, "Entretiens des Ordinands". Soon the Archbishop of Paris wanted similar exercises. Troyes, Noyon, Savoy and Rome followed. One of the participants asked that the course should be extended in a similar milieu: twenty days of the exercises had not been enough for him. So on 24th June 1633 Vincent started the "Conférences du Mardi", weekly meetings for the further education of priests.[3]

Yet this could not be the whole answer. Session XXIII of the Council of Trent had instructed the setting up of seminaries, and Pallavicini had declared that thanks to this idea the Council of Trent had already justified

---

[1] Daniel-Rops, op. cit., 29ff. (E.T., 18f.). In 1782 a new commission suddenly fell to the Lazarists. The Jesuit missionary settlements in the Ottoman Empire, endangered as a result of the dissolution of the Order, became their responsibility.

[2] According to Daniel-Rops, II, 442, there is no modern study of the history of the seminaries. Only histories of individual seminaries exist.

[3] Daniel-Rops, op. cit., 35 (E.T., 23).

itself. Nevertheless, in practice no suitable form of seminary had yet been devised. The seminaries founded by Charles Borromeo in Milan and by Cardinal von Lothringen in Rheims, following the Tridentine directive, had not produced encouraging results. Berulle, who had been inspired by the example of Philip Neri, had, with the help of the French Oratory, founded in 1611–13 a community of priests, who saw it as their calling to get back to the ideal of a priesthood which "had no other spirit than the spirit of the Church itself, no other rules than the canons" (Bossuet).[1] However, the seminaries started by the Oratory in Lyon, Macon, Langres and St Magloire failed to flourish. Between 1612 and 1638, Adrian Bourdoise founded communities of priests in twenty dioceses, but then confined himself to setting up a model seminary in St Nicolas du Chardonnet. In this he debated a long time whether concentration on the practical aims of training for the priesthood was not the point most urgently requiring attention.[2]

Then suddenly, between March 1641 and October 1644, a practicable formula was arrived at. It was the discovery of no single individual. Vincent, Olier and Eudes all went into action at practically the same time. Thereafter, Lazarist, Sulpician and Eudist seminaries were to flourish.

It was Richelieu himself who, in a memorable audience, encouraged Vincent to start a seminary. At the Collège des Bons Enfants, which he founded in 1642, a division was made for the first time between schoolboys (in the "little seminary") and the actual seminarists in the "great seminary", thereby correcting the weakness which had more than anything else been responsible for the failure of the "Trent" seminaries.[3]

John Eudes had been convinced during his mission in Caën in 1632 that it was essential to have a seminary there. "Just what are so many doctors and wise men doing in Paris whilst souls are perishing by the thousand?" He plunged into action "to raise up the dead". First he got a group of priests "into shape" at a retreat. Then he went with them from parish to parish, staying twelve weeks in each, according to the method which he prescribed in his "Prédicateur apostolique", published posthumously. Eudes got a response from the people of Normandy. Now they were converted—but for how long? "What can you expect of them when they are led by the kind of pastors we see all around? Is it not inevitable that they will forget the great truths by which they were moved during the mission, and fall back into their original state?" Eudes concluded that if

---

[1] Ibid., 83 (E.T., 69f.).
[2] Ibid., 36 (E.T., 24).
[3] Richelieu supported all attempts to set up seminaries. He offered Olier the castle of Rueil, sent 1,000 thalers to Vincent and 3,000 to the new General of the Oratorians, Bourgoing (since 1641), for the training of priests, and commissioned the Duchess of Aiguillon to help Jean Eudes (Daniel-Rops, op. cit., 89; E.T., 75).

his missionary work was to be of lasting value the training of priests would have to be put on a new basis.

In the course of a mission in 1641 in Remilly-sur-Lozon, near Coutances, Eudes called the priests of the district together to discuss the duties of a pastor. He was impressed by the fact that there were so many of them. But would it not be better to start a proper seminary? Among those who encouraged Eudes at this time was Marie des Vallées, the visionary of Coutances.

But when John Eudes laid his plan before his superiors at the Oratory he was rebuffed. They said he was better qualified for mission preaching than for directing seminaries. This decision forced Eudes to leave the Oratory. Richelieu now helped him with letters patent and Vincent de Paul with advice. On 25th March 1643 Eudes, with five companions, founded his Society of Jesus and Mary in Caën and with them opened his seminary, which was to be in the closest possible touch with the mission. Here the emphasis was to be more on an apostolate to the masses than on theological education. It was true that Rome slowed things down, having been startled by four applications in eighteen months to establish similar institutions; and the local church authorities carried their opposition to the extent of placing the chapel of the seminary of Caën under interdict. Nevertheless, the seminary flourished. The Assemblée du Clergé de France sent congratulations to its founder and the bishops of the province appealed to Eudes to start up similar seminaries: at Coutances in 1650, at Lisieux in 1653, at Rouen in 1658, at Evreux in 1667 and in Brittany in 1670.[1]

It was Jean-Jacques Olier at Saint Sulpice[2] who succeeded in finding the most viable solution to the problem of seminary training. After much anxious questioning, Olier had, under Vincent's guidance, come to recognize his priestly calling and entered into missionary work. When, on 29th December 1641, he founded his modest seminary in the village of Vaugirard, he had not yet made the discovery that was to be so characteristic of his work, namely, his recognition of the need to set up a special community to be concerned with the training of future professors and directors of seminaries. This came about almost spontaneously. When he took charge of the Parish of Saint-Sulpice, which was right in the midst of the poorest section of the population, Olier moved his seminary to the parish church, and even, to begin with, to the rectory. The future priests were to be trained in the context of the exercise of pastoral duties. Olier,

---

[1] Sources, J. Eudes, *Works*, 12 vols; Vannes, 1905-11; Préclin/Jarry, op. cit., 513; Daniel-Rops, op. cit., 89 (E.T., 73). Eudes was not canonized until 1925, probably because of his connection with Marie des Vallées.

[2] Préclin-Jarry, op. cit., II, 511f. (Lit.). Daniel-Rops, op cit., 92ff. (E.T., 76ff.).

however, did not hold with the idea of mixing theory and practice and sending young priests out on missions in the villages and suburbs before their training was complete. Their theoretical training lasted five years and was intended to be at the same time a school of holiness. Out of this idea another grew: to train priests in this way required good professors. Olier therefore took his best students out of the ordinary course and put them into an inner seminary, in which he trained those who were to be the teachers of the future. This was the origin of those educators of the clergy who still bear the name of "Sulpicians". By 1700 ten seminaries had been founded and manned by Sulpicians in France. In 1652, outside the capital, at Issy, Olier built the complex of buildings which serves to this day as the "Great Seminary" of Paris. The first foundation of this kind outside France was the seminary in Montreal for the training of the Canadian clergy.[1]

The setting up of seminaries marked the beginning of a radical transformation of those uneducated and untrained Catholic clerics who were so much the object of the Reformers' criticisms.[2]

The bishops also joined in the seminary movement. If one or two hesitated, it was simply because it was a far-reaching decision to entrust the training of priests to societies which were not directly under their control. In 1640, in Germany, which after the Thirty Years War badly needed a new kind of training for its priests, the Dean of Salzburg, Bartholomäus Holzhauser, formed a union of secular priests living in Community, sharing their goods. These "Bartholomites" were at their most effective under their fifth Superior General, Johann Appelius, training future priests in "great" and "little" seminaries. At that time, the community drew its recruits mainly from the electoral bishopric of Mainz, but they also set up centres of revival in Bavaria, Austria, Poland, Bohemia and Hungary. After the death of the tenth Superior General (1770) this work came to an end.

4. LAY ACTIVITY

The growth of societies, making an impact on the whole of social life, was not confined to the clergy. At this time, also, as an early kind of "actio catholica", an association of laymen was formed in 1629 at the instigation of the young Henri de Levis, Duc de Ventadour, the King's Lieutenant-General in Languedoc and Viceroy of Canada. These men were moved to action by seeing what Vincent de Paul was doing. Father de

---

[1] Daniel-Rops, op. cit., 95 (E.T., 80).
[2] Because the pupils of St Sulpice were recruited exclusively from the upper classes the Order went into decline on the eve of the Revolution. It was Emery's achievement to put a stop to the decline.

Condren advised them and approved their aims. They met as a brother-hood every Thursday, the day dedicated to the sacrament, to give account of the week's activities, hence the name, Compagnie du Saint-Sacrement. Article 15 of their statute listed their duties: charitable work in hospitals and prisons, bringing influence to bear on municipal authorities to uphold Christian morality and to carry out the edicts against the Huguenots, supporting everything in secular society which took place to the honour of God—and each member was to do all this either personally himself or through people whom he had commissioned. All were subject to the discipline of secrecy. This was not merely an expression of humility, by which the members wished to emulate the hiddenness of Christ's presence in the sacrament (Article 9); tactical considerations were also involved. Soon, all sorts of important people, including priests, were to be found in the ranks of the Compagnie du Saint-Sacrement: Vincent de Paul, Olier, Eudes, de Condren, Bossuet, members of the nobility. The King and Richelieu were kept informed of the progress of their activities.[1]

Yet the working classes, too, were not without their own apostolate. Henri Buch was a simple cobbler who had come to Paris from Luxem-burg, but his sole aim in life was to look after the welfare of the members of his guild, to wean them away from the wine shops and from vice, and to lead them back to the sacrament. Through his efforts, the pious societies of the Frères Cordonniers and the Frères Tailleurs came into existence. In Dijon, Father Bénigne Joly founded the Frères des Oeuvres Fortes. These were attempts by members of specific social groups to "rechristianize" the group to which they belonged.[2]

5. THE CHRISTIAN SCHOOL

The Counter-Reformation congregations had been concerned about education, and this concern was reflected in the emergence of senior schools and in girls' education. It was mainly for the benefit of the upper classes. In 1700 the Jesuits alone were running about 100 collegia in each of

[1] Detailed information about the Compagnie du Saint-Sacrement only became available at the end of the nineteenth century, when Le Lasseur, S.J., discovered MS. 14489 of the National Library in Paris, which provided a rich documentation. In 1900 the MS. was published by Dom Beauchet-Filleau. Two pamphlets directed against the society in 1660 diminished its influence ("Conspiracy against the King") Daniel-Rops, op. cit., 117; (E.T., 98).

[2] Ibid., 116 (E.T., 97). It was through Baron Gaston de Renty that Buch came into contact with the Compagnie. His struggle was aimed at the suppression of the secret craftsmen's guilds, the so-called Compagnonnages. He succeeded in having them publicly condemned by municipal and church authorities. The date of the foundation of the Frères cordonniers was 1645, that of the "tailleurs" 1647. Buch's efforts produced results beyond the frontiers of France.

France, Germany and Spain, and 133 in Italy.[1] The Ursulines maintained 320 institutions in France for daughters of good families.[2]

Meanwhile, however, concern for popular education had come to the fore. At Autun, Bishop Gabriel de Roquette drew up a plan for elementary schools, and his successor, Colbert—son of the Minister—made the parish priests bring in from the fields children who absented themselves from the parish schools. Bishop Pavillon of Alet allocated for his schools 7,000 livres out of his annual budget of 20,000. But this was all to no avail as long as the question of teacher training was left unsettled. Boys' schools were not the exclusive concern of any one congregation. Of the thirty schools which had come into existence in the Quartier St Sulpice in Olier's time, only one, the school in Rue Princesse, survived, and it was grossly deficient in staff.[3]

Then in Lyon, in 1666, a young priest, Charles Démia, issued his "Remonstrances" to the merchants and officials of Lyon on the need to set up schools for the poor. This appeal failed to lead to anything, so he began opening free schools with the support of the Compagnie du Saint-Sacrement. By 1689 there were twenty-six of them, financed by a section of the Bureau des Écoles. In 1672 the Archbishop appointed Démia director of the diocesan schools. For the training of teachers, he founded the Communauté de St Charles, which soon also had a women's branch.[4] Here, instruction was concentrated on teaching method.

In Rouen, Father Barré[5] worked on similar lines with his free schools of the Frères du Saint-Enfant-Jésus. Although the practical results were meagre, his "Statuts et Règlements" laid foundations for the future. One of Barré's pupils, Nicolas Roland, a canon, tried to found a free school for girls and a community for schoolmistresses in Rheims, but on his death-bed he had to hand over this work to someone else. Another of Barré's pupils, Adrien Nyel, who had travelled all over France as a humble teacher, founding schools, was looking for a situation in Rheims. This all prepared the way for the brief for education falling to Jean Baptiste de la Salle, a man of the highest rank, educated at St Sulpice, a canon at Rheims.

In 1678 de la Salle[6] took over the direction of the institutions which

[1] Daniel-Rops, op. cit., 336 (E.T., 289).

[2] Ibid., 337 (E.T., 290). The most influential of the Ursuline Congregations in France are those of Paris (founded in 1610 by Mme de Sainte-Beuve) and of Bordeaux, which spread to Flanders and, through a niece of Mazarin, to Rome. When Ursulines from Flanders left the cloister and travelled abroad between 1684 and 1732 they helped to promote the adoption of their rules by other houses (Préclin/Jarry, op. cit., II 514f. (Lit.)). In Germany there were eleven foundations between 1648 and 1720.

[3] Daniel-Rops, op. cit., 338 (E.T., 291). Préclin/Jarry, op. cit., II, 529.

[4] Daniel-Rops, op. cit., 339 (E.T., 292).

[5] Most recent biography by Cardonnier, Paris, 1938; the best is by H. des Grèses, Bar-le-Duc, 1892.

[6] W. J. Battersby, Lettres et Documents, London 1952: also his Bibliography, London 1949.

Roland had founded, in 1679 he offered Adrien Nyel a job and helped him to open the first free school for boys in the Parish of St Mauritius. His insistence on living in community with teachers who were thought to be in no way his social equals led to a quarrel with his own family. In 1684, in face of the famine in Champagne, he divested himself of his fortune and took vows with twelve teachers to form the congregation of "The Brothers of the Christian Schools".[1] The new congregation of teachers quickly assumed responsibility for new elementary schools and founded a teachers' seminary in Rheims, the first of its kind known to history.

In the spring of 1688 Paris experienced a real sensation in the realm of education, in the sole remaining school in St Sulpice, the one in the Rue Princesse. Here Jean Baptiste de la Salle put into practice the new ideas in elementary school-teaching which he had worked out at home: for beginners, lessons in the vernacular and the giving up of Latin, instruction in classes instead of individual tuition, the use of schoolbooks to make it easier to follow the lessons, no compulsory manual work. The influx of pupils was so great that soon a new school had to be opened in the Rue du Bac. By 1691 more than 1,000 pupils were attending school in five institutions. For those already employed, and for adults, too, de la Salle started special courses, as he did for "backward pupils". Out of his own unique experience grew de la Salle's theoretical work: "Conduite des Écoles".[2]

Naturally, all this did not go unopposed. The Paris guild of "master writers" had been impoverished when books began to be printed and had, for their part, secured the privilege of giving paid instruction in writing. They got the police to intervene and stop the Brothers of the Christian Schools forming themselves into a community before they had obtained letters patent from the King. De la Salle then withdrew to Rouen.

Under the leadership of Brother Timothée, the congregation got its royal letters patent in 1724, and in 1725 it was sanctioned by Benedict XIII.[3] In 1750 a school was founded in Dole and this served as a model for Switzerland.

---

[1] Daniel-Rops, op. cit., 343 (E.T., 296). In 1694 a further phase in the founding of orders began.

[2] Ibid., 342ff. (E.T., 294ff.).

[3] Préclin/Jarry, op. cit., 532. W. J. Battersby, *History of the Institute of the Brothers of the Christian Schools in the Eighteenth Century, 1719–1798*, London 1960, also *Brother Salomon, Martyr of the French Revolution*, London 1960. (At the time of the outbreak of the Revolution there were 116 settlements and *c.* 1,000 members, only a few of whom were abroad. Not being ordained as priests, the brothers were not required to take the constitutional oath.)

6. HISTORICAL RESEARCH

The Benedictine Order in France was divided into three congregations, Cluny, Saint-Vannes (1604) and Saint-Maur (1618). Saint-Germain des Prés, the sacred shrine of the Merovingians, had been steeped in the spirit of the humanities by Chezal-Benoit in the sixteenth century and was now linked with Saint-Maur. After 1650 it became the centre of literary and historical research.[1] The Maurists can be acquitted of the charge that they were simply pursuing their own interest in their study of diplomacy and palaeography. The monks of Saint-Germain proceeded rather in accordance with the Benedictine rule, which prescribed the reading of sacred texts to provide liberation from base ignorance and to combat idleness, "the enemy of the soul".[2] Mabillon wrote: "In our studies we should have no other aim than Jesus Christ. (The six subjects of study) have their limits in the fact that they should create in us and in others the new man, of whom the Saviour in His person has given us the image." No arbitrary choice, therefore, determined the subjects of research. Rather the monks searched the Order's libraries for texts which could serve as historical examples of belief in action and so increase the ardour of faith. An order circulated to all the monasteries of the congregation on 13th November 1647 called for a systematic examination of texts and sought to publish hitherto unknown or inaccessible manuscripts. This was to be done according to strict rules. The consequence was that they decided to compile the newly discovered texts in a collection which became known by the name of "Spicilegium." Dom Luc d'Achery completed this task in twenty-two years. That was their starting-point. The publication of the Spicilegium had only reached its eighth volume when in 1668 Dom Mabillon produced the first volume of his history of the Benedictine Order. This, too, was not the outcome of the research of an individual pursuing his own interests and developing his own special themes; it was rather the fulfilment of a plan which the superiors of the Order had had in mind when the congregation was founded. In nine volumes the lives of the saints "(vitae")" of the Order were subjected to a critical examination and were presented chronologically, a task which Mabillon had worked at between 1668 and 1701 in collaboration with Germain and Ruinart. Six centuries of monastic history, from the sixth to the twelfth century, were here presented in a

[1] Préclin/Jarry, op. cit., I, 78. Fruitful research in church history at this time was not limited to St Maur. The Italian Oratorian, Rinaldi, succeeded in producing the first new outline of church history on the basis of the works of the Fathers published between 1646 and 1679.

[2] Tarisse wanted to foster the piety of his monks by providing them with new texts to read.

manner unique in its methodical rigour and in its comprehensiveness. But this did not exhaust Mabillon's labours. After a critical illness, between 1675 and 1686 he compiled in four printed volumes of Vetera Analecta the by-products of his researches, hitherto unknown studies on different subjects. Because the Maurists included foreign literature in their study, their historical writings acquired a European character.[1] France, however, is indebted to the Maurists for the first collection of documents of its national history.

In 1643 two Jesuits from Antwerp, Bolland and Henschenius, brought to fruition a project which their fellow Jesuit, Rosweyde, had announced in 1603, and published the first two volumes of the Acta Sanctorum. At the invitation of Rome, Henschenius and van Papenbroek went to visit the libraries there, and also between 1660 and 1662 the Greek monastery of Grotta Ferrata. As a result of this visit, the "Bollandists" came to realize that they had not left enough room in their original plan for Byzantine hagiography. For the first time European scholarship was being broadened to include Greek patristics—a tendency which was to be fully developed later in the work of the Bollandist Delahaye. The exposure of legendary material by the use of historical criticism uncovered a sensitive spot when the Acts of the Saint Albert showed that the traditions of the Carmelites by no means went back to the prophet Elijah, but that St Albert had given them the rule which had received papal sanction in 1226. The principle involved here became the subject of a controversy which was fought out over fifteen years, and in 1693 the Belgian provincial of the Carmelites set about getting the Bollandists condemned by the Pope. In 1695 they were censured by the Spanish Inquisition. Then, as a result of two years' activity by the Bollandist Janninck in Rome, the threatened danger was averted at least to the extent that only one single volume of the Bollandists was actually placed on the Index. Among those who came out on the side of the Bollandists in their hour of danger was Mabillon, the Maurist.[2]

In the work of another Maurist, Dom Gabriel Gerberon, interest in patristics gave rise to the attempt to replace scholastic theology with the theology of the Fathers. Consequently, his superiors suspected him of Jansenist tendencies. Nevertheless, he was called to Saint-Germain des Près in 1666, and there Gerberon launched his fellow monks on a study of St Augustine's work, a great undertaking which was entrusted to Dom Delfau. In 1682 Dom Gerberon was accused of Jansenism, and fled to Brussels. In 1703, at the command of the King of Spain, Gerberon was

---

[1] The "Iter germanicum" is contained in the Vetera Analecta. On Mabillon's German travels cf. Préclin/Jarry, op. cit., 469.

[2] The work was only struck off the Index by Leo XXII 200 years later.

arrested, and committed to Louis XIV's prisons, where he languished until his death in 1711.[1]

The Jansenist controversy went on inside St Maur and destroyed the congregation's sense of community. In 1727 Dom Thibaud made an attempt in the chapter to force compulsory subscription to the bull, "Ungenitus". For hundred monks opposed this and the plan was thwarted. When, in 1733, the chapter nevertheless went ahead with the subscription of the bull, this was such a violation of the monastic spirit that signs of unrest soon began to appear. Twenty-eight Maurists renounced their rule and demanded release from the habit, nocturnal service and fasting. An increase in these trends led the French Assembly of the Clergy in 1765 to set up the Commission des Réguliers which in some measure anticipated the solution to the monastic question which the Revolution supplied.[2]

7. ASCETICISM

Of all the trends towards reform at work in the old orders,[3] the renewal

[1] Gerberon's works run to fifty-five titles. Of the Jansenist pamphlets, the one which attracted most attention was "Les avis salutaires de la V. Marie à ses dévots indiscrets", 1673. In Brussels he edited the *Acta Marii Mercatoris* (a student of Augustine).

[2] Préclin/Jarry, op. cit., 469, 231. The Commission des Réguliers drafted the edict of 24th March 1768, which forbade the taking of monastic vows by men under 21, and by girls under 18—a decision which caused the supply of vocations to dry up (D'Alembert). No congregation was to have more than two settlements in Paris or more than one in any provincial town. Houses which could not show a minimum number of inmates (nine to fifteen monks) should be closed. Clement XIII protested in vain. In France 400 monasteries were closed in fifteen years. Nine congregations entirely disappeared. In 1784, when the bishops managed to bring an end to the commission's work, the number of monks in France had been reduced by a third (Daniel-Rops, op. cit., II, 288f.; E.T. *The Church in the Eighteenth Century*, London 1964, 229).

[3] On the Benedictines, see Préclin/Jarry, op. cit., II, 464f. In Italy the philosopher Benaglia adorned the monastery of Monte Cassino. Pannonhalma in Hungary opposed Josephinism. The Observance of Melk was adopted by eleven abbots in 1625, but its extension was affected by the Thirty Years War. Among the Cistercians, the La Trappe reforms were not the only ones. Dom E. de Beaufort, Abbot from 1656 to 1700, reformed Sept-Fons in the diocese of Moulin. The Carthusians, who suffered from the burning of Chartreuse (for the eighth time) in 1676, were revitalized through the new statutes of 1682. The Superior General, Le Masson, carried out reconstruction in 1688. Josephinism was to cost the Carthusians forty-four monasteries in Austria. The Augustinians, who had a large number of very small monasteries particularly in Italy, were affected by the decree of Innocent X in 1652, which dissolved houses with less than ten monks and this cost the order 344 monasteries (Préclin/Jarry, op. cit., II. 484). The Capuchins, as a new Italian order which had impressed the Fathers of the Council of Trent and which became naturalized in France through Cardinal von Lothringen, were exactly suited to the age of absolutism. Charles Joseph de Troyes, the anti-Jansenist expert on Augustine, was their great theologian in the seventeenth century. Among the three orders, Picpus flourished in France, because it enjoyed the

of the Cistercian abbey of La Trappe[1] after 1662 provided the most radical answer as well as the one which made the most extreme demands on human nature. The "in commendam" principle allowed the revenues of a monastery to fall to an "abbé commendataire", someone unconnected with the monastic community, preferably someone acceptable to Paris society. Under this system Richelieu's nephew, Armand Jean Bouthillier de Rancé (1626-1700), had from the age of 10 received 15,000 livres from ecclesiastical revenues. In 1657 de Rancé was so shattered by the death of Madame de Montbazon, to whom he was deeply attached, that, straightway kneeling down on the stone flags of the castle steps, he broke with his previous way of life, his fashionable connections, his coaches, his footmen and his hunting. He also renounced all his "in commendam" revenues except those from the Abbey of La Trappe, of which he assumed practical control himself as abbot in 1662. The six monks who were there at the time found it impossible to adjust themselves to the new régime and left the monastery of their own free will. Cistercians of the strict observance came in their place, and even though when de Rancé went to Rome in 1664, he failed to persuade the Pope to grant a really strict rule,[2] he nevertheless went ahead on his own with the reformation of La Trappe. No fish, eggs, butter or spices, not even a palliasse at night! The monastery silver was sold, the monks were withdrawn from preaching and confession duties, in 1667 perpetual silence was introduced and letters and visits were prohibited. From 1673 the rule of St Bernard was observed unmodified. The monks were required to fast for seven months in the year, during which they were allowed only one meal a day. On Good Friday they had to sing psalms barefoot for twelve hours! It was not unknown for the monks' health to break down. The challenge to the spirit of the age which all this represented was further emphasized by literary onslaughts, which, however infelicitous in composition, nevertheless made it impossible to

---

favour of Louis XIV. In this way the Mercedarians acquired great significance in the seventeenth century because of their collections to ransom Europeans who had fallen into the hands of the North African privateers and become slaves (Préclin/Jarry, op. cit., II, 496). The history of Spanish and Portuguese monasticism lacks an index of sources. The material in archives is scattered and difficult of access. Up till now there have been only local studies. A "Week of Monastic Studies" was held from 29th September to 4th October 1958 in the monastery of Montserrat and set as the task of the next "Week" the production of an index of sources and the freeing of the history of Iberian monasticism from the misrepresentations and legends which have overlaid it. In Hungary the Franciscans, who had been identified with the people under the Turkish yoke, came to the fore, and, being also chosen by Leopold I as his favourite order, became bastions of the Counter-reformation, which had been delayed by the Turkish War.

[1] Préclin/Jarry, op. cit., II, 473ff. Daniel-Rops, op. cit., 317f. (E.T., 278f.).
[2] The Trappist reform was only ratified in 1678, by Innocent XI.

ignore the call to repentance. Naturally, many of the other monastic groups defended themselves against de Rancé's polemics. Innocent Le Masson, the Superior General of the Carthusians, spoke of a "slander" on his monks by the "abbé Tempête".[1] The Maurist, Jean Mabillon, challenged de Rancé's claim that scholarly work was destructive of humility, the spirit of prayer and asceticism. On the contrary, no one was more disposed to humility than the man who had learned from his studies how ill-equipped he was to engage in them. Anyway, who would support de Rancé's criticisms of Saint-Maur when even de Rancé's own monks were falling away from his ideals? Eventually, in 1693, out of the goodness of his heart, Mabillon went to see the Abbot of La Trappe again to effect a reconciliation.

8. DISSOLUTION OF THE JESUITS

The Jesuits—with 16,000 members in 1650 and 22,000 in 1750—functioned as a unit. They were highly skilled, bearing the stamp of the bygone age of Counter-Reformation. But times changed. Their anniversary book, *Imago primi saeculi*, had already been criticized. As fathers confessor to the absolutist princes, obedient to the instructions of Aquaviva in 1608, they exercized great influence in high places: Father Masen at the Court of Leopold I, Father Vota in Warsaw, Fathers Neidhac, Daubenton and Ravago in Madrid, Father Gaspard in Lisbon, with de la Chaise and Tellier at the Court of Louis XIV. General Vitelleschi had, of course, forbidden the fathers confessor to take part themselves in the councils of state.[2] But it was not without good reason that the Order met with increasing criticism, incurring the rivalry of the Oratorians in France and of the missionary orders in the foreign field, the hatred of the Jansenists and unpopularity among the bishops, finally being persecuted wherever the Bourbon family was in power,[3] and, in 1773, being dissolved.

The Order held the key positions in education, in the universities and colleges, and this turned into a kind of tyranny when the educational principles of the Order became antiquated. Jesuit emphasis on the humanities held back the timely acceptance of new branches of scientific learning. The spirit of the age was having its influence even on the study of the humanities and turned the study of classics into philology. Jesuit colleges bitterly resisted this change. Descartes, who had himself been a student at the Jesuit college of La Flèche, but who soon found himself in conflict with the order, was banned from Jesuit establishments, even though current

[1] Préclin/Jarry, op. cit., II, 474, 482.
[2] Préclin/Jarry, op. cit., II, 682f.
[3] The Minister, Choiseul, brought about the alliance of the Bourbon courts in 1761. The attempt to bring in Vienna, too, by bribing Count Christiani, failed.

opinion was on the side of the philosopher. In their educational programme the Order resisted going as far with specialization as was now
generally deemed necessary. Reform of the old plan of studies which
Aquaviva had devised remained a constant item on the agenda of the
General Congregation, but one which never received a solution which
did justice to modern thinking.

The Order's moral teaching and confessional practice had been
developed for the typical Renaissance man. Jesuit school drama brought
on to the stage the "fair soul", the man who took his stance in the world,
in well-balanced possession of all his faculties. The Jesuit conception of
holiness involved practical consequences for the things of God in the
world. Taking account of the increasingly complicated relationships in the
world, the Order had tried to solve ethical questions by providing model
answers to the most widely varying cases. There was no lack of discussion
of problems such as whether one might take communion after dancing all
night at a ball. If a rule was made for an individual case, then abuse would
not be extensive. But the mood of the age was changing. The Christian
began to see himself as one standing aloof from the world. To contemporary ethical rigorists, the moral teaching of the Jesuits appeared lax. The
unity of the Order, which in any case had suffered structurally in 1648
when Innocent X had forced General Congregations on it, was further
threatened when Thyrsus Gonzales championed the strict moral teaching
of the "Probabiliorists", and, presuming upon his office of General, broke
the Order's rules of censorship by having his work on moral theology
printed in Dillingen in 1691. In view of the fact that the courts of Madrid
and Vienna were supporting Gonzalez, Innocent XI did not withhold
papal permission to the publication.[1]

It became clear that an organization as firmly united behind the Pope
as the Jesuit order was did not fit in with the absolutists' authoritarian ideas
of state churches. The Catholic national powers tried to influence the
election of Generals, as the Spanish minister did in the case of Gonzalez.
In 1682 the newly elected General, de Noyelle, called upon the Spanish
ambassador before calling on the French one, and this so exasperated Louis
XIV that he wanted to put the French fathers under the control of a
separate Commissioner-General. The provincials of the French provinces
had to prostrate themselves before the King before this danger was
averted.

In 1699 Charmot began to campaign in Rome and France for an

---

[1] Probabilism, which began in Spain, had also its critics in Spain. The way was
open for Equiprobabilism, normative for later Catholicism, and this was advocated
by the Spaniard Ignatius de Camargo (1699–1722) before it found its definitive
exposition in Alphonsus Liguori.

inquiry into the missionary practice of the Jesuits and this led educated circles in Europe to take a special interest in the question of the Chinese and Malabar rites. The Order's missionary activity was intense: in 1653 there were 780 Jesuit missionaries, in 1710 the Fathers had 200 mission stations, and in 1749 there were 273. Their technique was one of adaptation to the existing local culture. With some difficulty, Robert de Nobili, who went to India in 1604, had persuaded Aquaviva, his uncle Robert Bellarmine and eventually Pope Gregory XV to give him permission to live like a Brahmin, to all outward appearance separated from the other Jesuits. He was followed in this by Beschi and Bouchet in 1700. Others lived like Pariahs, and threw themselves in the dust from afar before their fellow priests. In China, the practice of ancestor worship had to be examined. Since the wise men of the country declared that they themselves drew a distinction between these ceremonies and true religion, they did not scruple, despite the use of incense and the practice of genuflection, to pay homage to Confucius and to ancestors. In addition to the question of traditional Chinese ceremonies, there was also the question of whether Chinese expressions should be used to translate the theological terms of Christianity. Or should foreign, European words be brought into the vocabulary of the Chinese Christians? On the question of "Termini", Father Ricci decided in favour of legalizing a Chinese vocabulary.

In 1631 Dominicans and Franciscans began to appear on the Chinese mission field and took note of the special relationship which the Jesuits enjoyed with the Emperor, Kang-Chi, a relationship they owed to their methods of adaptation and to the scientific and technical assistance they were able to give. This gave rise to criticism—though at first it was confined to a small circle. The first to object was a Dominican, Morales, who in 1645 challenged Propaganda to express an opinion. Counter-representations were made on behalf of the Jesuits by Father Martini, and, in fact, in 1656 were given a favourable reception in Rome. They nevertheless raised the question as to how conflicting Roman positions were to be reconciled. In 1693, when Mgr Maigrot was Apostolic Vicar for China, the question of the Chinese rites flared up again. He was behind Charmot in raising the alarm throughout Europe. In 1704 Rome decided against the Jesuits (Tournon's Action) and when, in spite of this, the Emperor Kang-Chi and the Jesuits submitted a joint defence, Europe got the impression that the Order was playing its own power game in the Far East. From post-Tridentine Catholicism, which attached such importance to external uniformity as a bond of unity, a deeper understanding of the path being taken by the Jesuits was hardly to be expected.

The first blows against the Order were struck by Pombal in Portugal in 1757 and by the Parlement in Paris in 1761. What was it that led to state action? Jesuit missionaries in Paraguay had founded villages for Indian Christians, the so-called "Reductions", to protect them from warring tribes. In 1731 there were 138,934 indigenous Christians there. Between 1700 and 1767, 120 Germans came to join in this missionary work, including, in particular, a number of qualified master craftsmen. Spurred on by the suspicion that rare metals were to be found in the Reductions, Portugal concluded a treaty of delimitation with Spain in 1750. Under this treaty, the territories of the Indian Reductions came under Portuguese sovereignty: but armed opposition on the part of the Indians prevented the Portuguese from occupying these territories until 1756.[1] The Marquis de Pombal saw the Jesuits as accomplices of the Indians, accused them of the political enslavement of the natives and of pursuing their own political ends, and in 1757 expelled the Fathers from the Portuguese Court. After an attempt on the King's life, Pombal declared in 1759 that Jesuit intrigues were at the back of it and ordered the execution of Malagrida, a Jesuit missionary from Italy who was famous for his stirring appeals on behalf of the Indians. Pombal also got the Pope to annul the privileges of jurisdiction which the Order enjoyed. The Order's properties were confiscated and eighty Fathers were severely punished. Cardinal Saldanha, whom Benedict XIV had sent to Portugal as Apostolic Visitor, submissive as ever to the court, pronounced the Fathers guilty. When the nuncio, Acciajuoli, on the instructions of Clement XIII, made a cautious request for a further inquiry, he was hustled over the border under military escort.[2] The expulsion of the missionaries from the Portuguese colonies and their shipment back to Italy lasted up to 1769. Fathers from abroad were detained in Portuguese jails and were only released after protracted negotiations by the ambassadors.

In France the conflict was brought to a head by the Order's participation in trading ventures, which they engaged in to raise their missionary income. The Superior of the Mission in the Antilles, Antoine La Valette, S.J., had been particularly successful in reviving the depressed sugar and coffee trade of the mission plantations and in appeasing the Antilles mission's creditors by negotiating credit with the Frères Lioncy in Marseilles. In 1753 he was summoned by Rouillé, the Secretary of State, to give an account of his activities. From then on La Valette had his opponents in Paris, and even some of the Jesuits, such as Father Frey de Neuville, sided with Rouillé against him. The public, who as yet knew little of the standards of colonial trading, were naturally amazed to find a monk in the company of reckless traders. There was considerable reaction, when La Valette suffered economic setbacks: the slaves on his plantations died in an epidemic; his merchant ships were seized by English pirates

[1] Préclin/Jarry, op. cit., II, 689.   [2] Ibid., II, 690.

even before the outbreak of war. The Frères Lioncy were threatened with bankruptcy. The French Provincial, now Frey de Neuville, refused to accept liability on behalf of the Order. However, one of La Valette's flock, the widow Grou, succeeded in getting a judgment from the consular court of Paris on 30th January 1760 which declared the Order liable. If the Order was going to extricate itself from this affair, it would have to lodge an appeal. It could have gone to the Grand Conseil, as the court of second instance. That it chose instead to appeal to the Parlement was its undoing. That body was dominated by Jansenists and Gallicans and they were now determined to take the matter further. In its judgment of 8th May 1761, Parlement forced the Order to make good the losses. This they managed without too much difficulty by selling off land and taking up an English loan. The Visitor of the Order summoned the bold La Valette back to Europe and placed him under interdict. That might have been the end of the affair. But, with public opinion behind him, Chauvelin, clerk of the Council, now demanded that the Order's constitution be laid before Parlement.[1] On 17th April 1761 he drew attention to specific points in the constitution which contravened the discipline of the Church and the constitutional principles of the kingdom. Orders issued by the General were said to take precedence over those issued by pope, king or episcopate. On 6th August 1761 came the first pronouncements against the Order, condemning twenty-four Jesuit publications, forbidding the acceptance of novices and banning teaching in Jesuit colleges as from 1st October 1761. Certainly there were plenty of efforts to halt this disastrous development. An extraordinary meeting of the Assembly of the Clergy of France, which the King had summoned for 3rd November 1761, declared itself by an overwhelming majority in favour of the Order. The Paris Provincial was prepared to accept the four Gallican Articles and only his General prevented him from doing so. In Rome, Choiseul renewed the suggestion that a French Vicar General should be appointed, but Clement XIII and the General, Ricci, refused to countenance a solution of this kind. In an edict of 9th March 1762 Louis XV decreed that the Jesuit General must delegate his powers to the five French Provincials, that they must be bound by oath to the law of the kingdom, that before orders of the General or of the General Congregation became binding on the French Fathers they must be submitted to Parlement for examination, and that the Fathers were subject to the jurisdiction of the appropriate ordinaries and magistrates. Yet this attempt on the part of the royal government to reach a satisfactory compromise was swept aside by the actions of Parlement and on 26th November 1764 the Order was dissolved in France.[2]

[1] Ibid., II, 692f.
[2] Ibid., II, 695. In Spain the Jesuits' opponents managed to win over Charles III,

The Jesuit question overshadowed the conclave at which Cardinal Ganganelli was elected as Pope Clement XIV.[1] The brief "Dominus ac Redemptor", dated 21st July 1773, contained the Pope's dissolution of the Order.[2] In the educational field the activity of the Enlightenment prevented the extinction of the Order leaving too great a gap in Europe. But the damage which was done to the work of overseas missions of Christendom cannot be overestimated.

9. ALPHONSUS LIGUORI

The spirit of the eighteenth century was opposed to the monastic life. But when the Neapolitan nobleman and advocate Alphonsus Liguori discovered he had in the course of a successful suit wrongly interpreted a document and got a verdict contrary to justice, his alarm led to an inner conversion which expressed itself in the foundation of an order of a very special kind. Liguori's plan was to serve in foreign missions, and he joined

---

who banished the Jesuit confessor Ravago and blamed the Jesuits for the revolt of 1766. Count Aronda got the secret council of 29th January 1767 to issue a decree expelling the fathers for treason. Since Clement XIII did not wish to receive the Jesuits into the Papal States (!), an uncomfortable sojourn in Corsica ensued. While being transported across the sea 600 American fathers are said to have died. The abolition of the Order led to the uprooting of 2,617 missionaries from territories overseas. In Naples and Sicily the "enlightenment" Minister, Tanucci, who had been active as an opponent of the Jesuits in Spain, took action on the basis of an edict dated 5th November 1767, under which the fathers were ejected from six Neapolitan institutes and expelled over the borders into the Papal States. In Germany, French anti-Jesuit influences were effective as a result of political contacts between the Bavarian royal household and Savoy, and through contacts which Count Kaunitz formed between Vienna and Paris, though this influence was somewhat counteracted by Maria Theresa. The question of who was to fill university chairs was involved. In Bavaria, Lori proposed the foundation of an Academy of Sciences, to do something against the Jesuits.

[1] The extent to which the long conclave from 25th February to 19th May 1769, which ended in the choice of Ganganelli as Pope (Clement XIV), was dominated by the intrigues of the Bourbon ambassadors, determined that only a candidate who approved of the abolition of the Society of Jesus would be elected, is the subject of academic controversy. Crétinau-Joly (Clement XIV et les Jésuites, Paris 1847, and Histoire de la Compagnie de Jésus, IV, 275) posited secret negotiations between Ganganelli and the Spanish ambassador Soli, in which the papal candidate had given a declaration for the Spanish King, that the Pope had the right to execute canonical dissolution of the Order, and that it was his wish to fulfil the desire of the courts. F. Masson, Carayon and V. Pastor deny any such intrigues (cf. Préclin/Jarry, op. cit., II, 697f.). H. Becher develops the contrary thesis that Ganganelli, who owed his cardinalate to the decision of the Jesuits and had approved of the steps Clement XIII had taken to protect the Order, now let himself be swayed by the wishes of the powers out of his ambition to become Pope.

[2] The General, Lorenzo Ricci, suffered continually in the prison on the Engelsburg. On the role of the Spanish ambassador Moninos, cf. Préclin/Jarry, op. cit., 699. The Bank of England kept Jesuit funds on deposit until the Order was re-instituted.

a college for the training of an indigenous Chinese clergy. However, the Rector, Falcoja, directed him to an area of need lying much closer to hand, namely the misery and distress of the masses in and around Naples. The mission Liguori set up there was given an unexpected welcome. His confessional was thronged. A nunnery was re-formed and in 1731 this formed the basis of a new congregation of nuns. In 1732 he organized his fellow mission workers into a male branch. The Order of "Redemptorists", as they were called, was infused with Alphonsus Liguori's own spirit which was focused on the contemplation of the Cross and the Eucharist. The mysticism of Crostarosa, a Visitandine whom the founder had met, also made its influence felt.

Liguori's literary activity, which began in 1728 with a collection of meditations, developed rapidly after 1745. In championing Liguori's Theologia Moralis, which first appeared in 1748 in the form of notes on the Medulla of the Jesuit Busenbaum, the Redemptorists provided effective opposition to Jansenism, which was spreading in Italy.[1] The rigour of the Jansenists seemed to Alphonsus Liguori to make impossible the proper use of the sacrament of penance and the Eucharist. He himself on the one hand extended the scope of moral teaching, and on the other hand, with his "equiprobabilism", developed a comprehensive casuistry. For this reason Alphonsus Liguori became the authoritative moral teacher for the nineteenth century on the question of confessional practice, his influence spreading from Rome to Ultramontane circles everywhere. The new-found piety of the Restoration period was coloured by Liguori's writings on the Glories of Mary (1750), Great Means to Prayer (1759) and Visits to the Blessed Sacrament (1768).[2]

The advance of the Order of Redemptorists was soon halted by the Bourbon royalists of Naples. The Order withdrew from the capital to Scala, Ciorani and Nocera. Yet even this was not enough to enable it to escape persecution by the Minister, Tanucci. A split inside the Order between a royalist, Neapolitan faction, and a papalist, Roman one, forced the founder himself out of his own houses.[3] But the two rival factions

---

[1] Liguori's written work amounts to almost 200 titles. The controversy with Jansenism was inevitable, since Liguori had a Jansenist moralist, Canonicus Torni, as a teacher.

[2] Kierkegaard studied the writings of Liguori in 1848–50, after the attack of the "Corsairs" while he was writing Sickness unto Death. Hugues had (in 1842–6) produced the first German edition of Liguori and selected from this an anthology which was sent to Kierkegaard in 1849. Hence his sharpened interest in ethics. "Il distaccio", i.e "Separation from the world", was taken over from Liguori. In 1871, to Döllinger's disgust, Liguori was declared a doctor ecclesiae, and in 1950 patron of confessors and moralists.

[3] Préclin/Jarry, op. cit., II, 534. Préclin's interpretation has been contested by the Redemptorists.

united, and when two young Germans, Thaddäus Hubl and Clemens Maria Hofbauer, who had joined in 1784, opened up new territories for the Order through their preaching and their conversions among the Protestants and Orthodox in Warsaw, Stralsund and Kurland, it began to be almost a substitute for the Jesuits.[1]

[1] Carr (an Irish Redemptorist) on Najella and Hofbauer. Hofbauer was expelled in 1808 when the duchy of Warsaw was founded and paved the way for Napoleonic reforms. Thereafter he worked in Vienna.

CHAPTER IV

TRENDS IN THEOLOGY AND PIETY

The seventeenth century in France saw the beginning of two religious movements which were really signs of a profound, questioning concern not catered for within the framework of uniformity envisaged by the Council of Trent. They led to a split in the edifice of Catholicism, and the Catholic Church is still debating whether it was, in fact, inevitable that these movements should have been quashed as heretical. In the struggle against Jansenism and Quietism there was too much rivalry either on the part of the Jesuits or on the part of the hierarchy; and the tendency in current Catholic scholarship is to give these movements more sympathetic consideration.[1]

Under the impact of the Copernican revolution, man's traditional understanding of the world he lived in collapsed, and people were forced to think of God more in terms of His omnipotence and of isolated man more in terms of his individuality. Jansenism, with its individualistic piety, complemented this view; and Quietism can be understood as a reaction against the external standards imposed by the Counter-Reformation, as the expression of a longing for the real emotional experience of a mystical union with God.

In assessing the Catholic piety of the Age of Enlightenment, it is as well to reject the ciriticisms which the period immediately following the Enlightenment made of it and which were given their first reliable expression in the work of Brück. These "movements" were something new, something truly comparable with the Reformation movements. But by this

---

[1] A. Gazier, *L'histoire générale du mouvement janséniste*, Paris 1924, has begun to moderate the Catholic condemnation of Jansenism. There never was a "Jansenism". This was an invention of the enemies of Port Royal. Belgian students see here a tragic conflict between two schools within Catholicism, namely between the humanistic tendency of the Jesuits and the Augustinian doctrine of grace. But this interpretation has been contested, e.g. Daniel-Rops, op. cit., 395 (E.T., 345) underlines the inordinate self-confidence of Jansen and Saint-Cyran: "Who is to add the final touch to the theological controversy over free will and divine grace?" Jansen replied, "I, I am the only true interpreter of Augustine." Port Royal started Catholic, but was finally led into deviations by the interpolations of Saint-Cyran (ibid., 390f.; E.T., 337f.). The thesis first mooted by Veronius that Jansenism was a species of Protestantism gained ground. Prosper Guéranger advocated it. Daniel-Rops sees the Protestant element in the restriction of the gift of saving grace solely to the predestined. Here, a "Christ with short arms" is preached. The rehabilitation of Fénélon and Quietism in general began with Bremond half a century ago.

time there had been a considerable expansion in the educated classes of European society, able to appreciate literary works of merit and capable of identifying consciously with one party or the other. For this reason, these movements were in no way confined to the theological "schools", nor were they to be checked in new exclusive monastic foundations, but reached far into the total structure of society.

I. THE JANSENISM OF PORT ROYAL AND ANTOINE ARNAULD

Jansenism grew out of the association, which began in 1619, between the Louvain theologian, Cornelius Jansen, and the Frenchman, Jean Duvergier de Hauranne (Saint-Cyran). These two men were concerned to find a synthesis of doctrines which appeared to be contradictory: it all depended upon whether one concentrated on the *liberum arbitrium* of man or on the grace of God. Jansen was convinced that the necessary synthesis was to be found in Augustine, so he dedicated himself to the production of his *"Augustinus"*, which eventually appeared in 1640 (two years after his death) and was sold at the Frankfurt Book Fair. Saint-Cyran found at Port Royal a power-house for the dissemination of this newly discovered truth. The Abbess of this Bernardine Abbey was Mère Angélique Arnauld, who had experienced a spiritual awakening as a girl of 17, following the Lenten preaching of a Capuchin Father, and it was she who was responsible for leading her community of nuns away from their worldly ways. On 25th September 1609 the Journée du Guichet (Day of the Grating), she refused her own father entrance and started to reform the convent in a manner which was to inspire the "Grand siècle des âmes".[1]

As Port Royal lay in a valley which was far from healthy, Mère Angélique looked for a new settlement in Paris in the Faubourg St Jacques. There an association grew up between the Abbey and the Compagnie du Sacrement, and this helped to increase its influence.[2]

Saint-Cyran was the Lenten preacher in 1635, and from then on acted as spiritual director of Port Royal. Spiritually minded men occupying important positions began to attach themselves as *"solitaires"*, and Saint-Cyran took advantage of their presence at Port Royal to set up the *"petites écoles"*, which put into practice a new kind of teaching, with the emphasis on character development.[3] Richelieu was suspicious and on 14th May 1638 had Saint-Cyran taken into custody. In 1641, with his bull *"In Eminenti"*, Urban VIII was obliged to put his signature to the first

[1] Daniel-Rops, op. cit., 385ff. (E.T. *The Church in the Seventeenth Century*, London 1963, 333ff.). J. Orcibal states that the history of Port Royal has still to be written.
[2] Ibid., 391 (E.T., 336).
[3] Ibid., 392 (E.T., 339).

condemnation of Jansenism. In 1643 Mazarin released Saint-Cyran, but shortly afterwards Saint-Cyran died, a Jansenist martyr.[1]

Now Antoine Arnauld, the youngest of the family, succeeded Saint-Cyran, to whom he had pledged himself while Saint-Cyran was in prison. On 1st February 1643 Saint-Cyran had written to Arnauld from the prison of Vincennes: "The time to speak has come. To be silent would be a crime." In his writings Arnauld set about storming the Jesuit positions, expounding the close connection that existed between receiving the sacrament and the practice of asceticism. The Jesuit Sesmaisons supplied Arnauld with an excellent opportunity for action by giving certain spiritual advice to the Marquise de Sablé: he instructed her that she might go to a dance with a clear conscience on a day on which she had communicated. This instruction stood in direct contrast to the prohibition which Saint-Cyran had pronounced in his capacity as the Princesse Guémené's spiritual director. On 25th August 1643 Arnauld's *"De la fréquente communion"* appeared, with its claim to get back to the authentic practice of the sacrament according to the Fathers, papal decisions and councils, after the Jesuits' perversion and all their laxness. In this, Arnauld expressed the view that the blessing of the sacrament was only to be had at the cost of an extra, self-mortifying asceticism. One feature of Arnauld's work which stemmed from Jansenist ideas was that only those should come to communion who felt the call of grace upon them declaring their predestination. To abstain from communion thus became a sign of exemplary humility, and before confessors permitted their penitents to approach the sacrament they should impose upon them long periods of penance.

Reaction was lively and was not confined to the Jesuits. Vincent de Paul asked if there was a man anywhere in the world who had such a high opinion of his own virtue as to think himself worthy to receive communion. When, as a result of Arnauld's influence, the number of ordinary parishioners taking communion declined, Monsieur Vincent declared: "If perhaps a hundred Parisians using this (Arnauld's book) have become more reverent in their use of the sacrament, there are at least ten thousand to whom it has done nothing but harm."[2]

While bishops like Caulet and Pavillon expressed their approval of *"De la fréquente communion"* and Rome seemed disposed to regard it with favour, the Jesuit Pétau attacked it in a thorough-going polemical treatise and at St Sulpice, Olier intervened to oppose Arnauld. While these disputes were going on Jansenism was struck at—and, for the first time, effectively

[1] Ibid., 396 (E.T., 346).
[2] Ibid., 402f. (E.T., 348f.). H. Bremond, *Histoire littéraire du sentiment religieux en France*, III, Paris 1921 (E.T., *A Literary History of Religious Thought*, 3 vols, London 1928–36).

—by papal condemnation. What led to this act on the part of Rome?

A young Jesuit, Dechamps, had discovered the similarity between Jansen's *"Augustinus"* and the theses of Bajus, who had been condemned by the Sorbonne in 1560—and in Paris condemnation by the Sorbonne carried more weight than any number of condemnations by the Pope. Thereafter, when the Jesuit Veronius equated Jansenism with the heresy of Calvinism, Arnauld felt obliged to take a step which was to have momentous consequences: he lodged a complaint with the Sorbonne against the equation of his work with heresies. But Nicolas Cornet, the Syndicus of the Theological Faculty, following the current manner of scholarship, abstracted from the work a number of *"propositiones"* intended to set forth the *"Augustinus"* in comprehensive fashion, and these he presented to the Sorbonne on 1st July 1649. Arnauld, alarmed by this development, got Parlement to prohibit the University from dealing with this question. This so roused the doctors' hostility that they referred the propositions to the Assemblée du Clergé and recommended that they be submitted to Rome. Vincent de Paul feared the danger of heresy which appeared to be round the corner and, largely by his own personal efforts, collected the signatures of bishops for an appeal to Rome. This resulted in a grouping of eighty-five French bishops against eleven, which so impressed Rome that with the bull *"Cum Occasione"* of 31st May 1653 the five *propositiones* were rejected as heretical.[1]

At this time Arnauld was getting encouragement from the new blossoms on the trees at Port Royal des Champs, which had recently been drained, from the increased spiritual strength of the *solitaires* and from the flow of supporters into the Jansenist party. He resisted submission to the papal judgment by drawing the exonerating[2] distinction between the *"question du droit"* and the *"question du fait"*. It was true that the Pope had condemned the five *propositiones* which rightly had to be rejected as heresy; but these *propositiones* were not contained in the *"Augustinus"*.[3] In 1654 the Assemblée du Clergé and, later, a papal brief endeavoured to have it confirmed that the *"propositiones"* were represented in the *"Augustinus"*. But Arnauld then claimed that the competence of Pope and bishops was restricted to the plane of right doctrine, apart from which the hierarchy had no special competence to make authoritative pronouncements on questions of fact, since every reasonable man was capable of doing this for himself. Infallibility, indeed, was hardly to be attributed to the Pope if he chose to constitute himself judge in the question whether something was or was not a fact.

[1] Daniel-Rops, op. cit., 405 (E.T., 350). Préclin/Jarry, op. cit., I, 194f.
[2] Described by Catholics as "hair-splitting" (Tüchle).
[3] Préclin/Jarry, op. cit., I, 195. Daniel-Rops, op. cit., 407f. (E.T., 352f.).

The struggle in the Church, now in full swing, was raised to such a pitch that anti-Jansenist confessors made absolution conditional on repudiation of Jansenism and on the acceptance of the papal bull. When, on these grounds, the Sulpician Picoté denied absolution to a parishioner of high social rank, the Duc de Liancourt, Arnauld intervened with two inflammatory letters attacking St Sulpice. The opposition's reaction to these letters was vicious: on 23rd January 1656 the doctors of the Sorbonne expelled Dr Arnauld from their midst, while the friends of Port Royal walked out in protest.[1]

On that very day a pamphlet appeared in Paris attacking the laxity of the Jesuits with ethical rigour as well as biting logic, and once again questioning the successes of the anti-Jansenist front. This was the *"Lettre écrite à un Provincial et aux RR. PP. Jésuites sur la morale et la pratique de ces Pères"*. Further anonymous letters, eighteen in all, continued to appear at irregular intervals up to the middle of 1657. The mathematician, Blaise Pascal, after his shattering encounter with God, on the night of 23rd November 1654 (described in his Memorial: Fire, fire. . . God of Abraham, of Isaac and of Jacob, not of the philosophers!) had taken as his spiritual adviser Monsieur Singlin of Port Royal and was soon numbered among the *solitaires*. To Pascal, Arnauld had entrusted the task of writing the sequel to his two letters to the Sulpicians, since he wanted them to have a better and more pointed literary form. Pascal had finished composing the first letter in ten days.[2]

In August 1656 the Assemblée du Clergé introduced a formula which Pierre de Marca, the Archbishop of Toulouse, had drafted and which Alexander VII ratified forthwith. Subscription to this formula was to be obligatory on all French bishops. In it the five propositions were to be condemned without any distinction between law and fact.[3] In fact, Arnauld succeeded in persuading Parlement to refuse to register Alexander VII's constitution and he got the Vicar General of Paris to make a declaration taking up again the distinction between law and fact. He had, however, made an enemy of Mazarin, who had not forgotten the "Te Deum" the Jansenists had sung on the occasion of the successful escape of his rival,

---

[1] Préclin/Jarry, op. cit., 196.

[2] H. S. Stewart, *Les lettres au provincial de Pascal*, Manchester 1920. It is a question for Catholic study whether Pascal shared in the Jansenist heresy. Bremond, *inter alia*, did much to vindicate Pascal as a Catholic. ('Au dessous de ce Pascal plus au moins intoxiqué par la théologie de ses maîtres il y a un autre, qui échappe à ces maîtres et dont l'influence doit un jour ramener au catholicisme intègral des âmes sans nombre'; op. cit., IV, Paris 1923; E.T., London 1936). An example of Catholic argument: if Pascal allows Christ to say, 'Je pensais à toi dans mon agonie', then he directly contradicts Jansenius, who, according to the fifth condemned proposition, does not allow that Christ died for all.

[3] Daniel-Rops, op. cit., 416 (E.T., 359f.). Préclin/Jarry, op. cit., I, 200.

Cardinal Retz,[1] and who was inciting the young Louis XIV to wipe out Jansenism altogether. Soon, opponents of Jansenism like Pierre de Marca and Annat, S.J., entered the Conseil de Conscience and Port Royal was ordered to dismiss its novices and boarders. The royal offensive encountered resistance. The nuns of Port Royal in Paris, led by Mère Angléique de St Jean, refused the new archbishop, Hardouin de Péréfixe, when he asked them to sign the declaration demanded by the Court, and thus started a conflict scarcely comprehensible within Catholicism, the conflict of Church against conscience. On 26th August 1664 Péréfixe appeared with the police and designated twelve nuns to be separated and removed to other convents. When it appeared that the ladies were prepared to resist to the point of martyrdom, there remained only one solution, namely, to gather the nuns in Port Royal des Champs and in their isolation to deprive them of sacramental life.

In 1664 Louis XIV got Parlement to register a declaration under which the entire clergy were obliged to sign the formula under pain of loss of benefice, but the "four bishops" claimed that the King had no right to legislate for the Church. These were Pavillon of Alet, Caulet of Pamiers, Choart de Buzenval of Beauvais, and Henri Arnauld of Angers. Alexander VII acceded to the King's request on this matter and in his bull "Regiminis Apostolici" made the signing of the new formula obligatory. But the "four bishops" persisted in their dioceses in maintaining the validity of the distinction between law and fact, and the situation became even more critical. It was the next occupant of the See of Peter, Clement IX, who called a halt to this hopeless dispute in 1669 with the "Pax Clementina".[2]

However, after ten years of peace, the King's suspicions led to a new confrontation between the two sides. Louis XIV now had to take issue with Bishops Pavillon and Caulet in connection with the dispute over the "régales". Was it perhaps Jansenist opposition which was now causing the bishops to resist any extension of the King's jurisdiction over the Church in France? Was not Innocent XI, who was resisting the King over the "régales", a Jansenist Pope? The strict nature of his criticisms of the pro-babilism of the Jesuits seemed to indicate this.

There was now spreading all over Europe, and especially in the Netherlands and Italy,[3] a form of Jansenism which was characterized less by its teaching on grace than by its ethical rigour. Through Père de la Chaise, the Jesuits had the ear of Louis XIV. Archbishop Harlay of Paris, thinking to gain the King's favour, took the first coercive measures on 17th May 1679, in the course of a visitation of Port Royal. The number of nuns was

---

[1] Daniel-Rops, op. cit., 417 (E.T., 360).
[2] Ibid., 419 (E.T., 362f.). Préclin/Jarry, op. cit., I, 203f.
[3] Daniel-Rops, op. cit., 454 (E.T., 394).

reduced to fifty and all the novices were compelled to leave. Arnauld himself fled to the Netherlands. In Paris, it was now Racine, the dramatist, the most talented pupil of the "petites écoles", who, in his poetry and in his *Histoire de Port Royal*, faithfully reflected the Jansenist cause.

2. THE JANSENISM OF QUESNEL

In 1681 anti-Jansenist action struck the French Oratory. It had been in constant rivalry with the Society of Jesus and its ethical outlook was not unconnected with Jansenism. Its General, Abel de Sainte-Marthe, now had to give up his office because of his association with Arnauld. His friend, Pasquier Quesnel, who was the Director of the Oratory in Paris, having been exposed as a Jansenist sympathizer following the indiscreet publication of some personal papers, had to leave, too, and went to join Arnauld in Brussels.[1]

At this point, one of Quesnel's earlier literary works, "Réflexions morales sur le Nouveau Testament", a spiritual treatise written in 1671, began to be seen in a different light. The first edition contained no Jansenist features and had been publicly commended by important bishops, such as Bishop Vialart de Herse of Châlons-sur-Marne and, even more enthusiastically, his successor, Noailles. Bossuet and Père de la Chaise had praised the book, and the Pope had read it. But with each new edition, Quesnel expanded his "Réflexions morales" and its Jansenist elements began to emerge. He retained, however, unaltered the original commendations of the Catholic bishops. Could these still be valid for later editions? The anti-Jansenists seized on this point in their campaign against Quesnel. In 1694 complaints against the "Reflexions morales" were lodged at the Sorbonne and in the Holy Office.

The calling of Noailles from Châlons-sur-Marne to the See of Paris was hailed as a triumph by the Jansenists in view of his eulogy of Quesnel. But the Jesuits compelled Noailles ("Notre reculante Eminence") to censor a recently published edition of a work by the Jansenist author Bartos on the theology of grace. Noailles found himself in the embarrassing position of condoning Quesnel and condemning Bartos, a position which was exploited in an anonymous Maurist satire which held up Noailles to the ridicule of the Parisians. Bossuet tried to find a way out of the difficulty by the expedient of producing a new edition of the "Reflexions morales". He himself went through the text, purging it of passages which might be capable of a Jansenist interpretation, and sent it to Quesnel in Brussels. Bossuet was at that time full of indignation: "Is it not manifest calumny to bring an action against the author of the 'Reflexions' for having said

[1] Ibid., 456ff. (E.T. 396ff.). Préclin/Jarry, op. cit., I, 209ff.

no more than a multitude of saints have done before him? If this language is suspect, we shall have to be continually on our guard against the words of the Gospel lest some quibbler comes along and says, 'You are a Jansenist'."

The way out of the difficulty which the Bishop of Meaux was hoping for was blocked when Quesnel returned Bossuet's version of his text and himself set about preparing a new edition of the "Réflexions", which turned out to be more Jansenist in tone than ever. This gave Fénélon the chance to get his own back on Bossuet and Noailles for the humiliation he had suffered as champion of Quietism and at the same time to restore his reputation in the eyes of the King and the Pope. Assuming the role of anti-Jansenist spokesman, Fénélon outmanoeuvred the Bishops of Meaux and Paris at the Assemblée du Clergé of 1700. The Jansenists, counting (not without reason) on Noailles's vacillating ways, now tried to force the Cardinal to make a stand on their behalf. As the appropriate means, they chose to submit to him a *"cas de conscience"*. The facts seemed to be that the leader of the Seminary of Clérmont-Ferrand had refused absolution to Fréhel, the priest of Notre Dame du Port, on the grounds that Fréhel had given absolution to the Jansenist Abbé Perier, a nephew of Pascal. Had Fréhel not done the right thing? Forty doctors of the Sorbonne said that he had. The *"cas de conscience"* now became an affair involving the whole of France.[1]

The ageing Louis XIV was by this time weary of Jansenist non-conformity and short-circuited the whole affair. He put the blame on Quesnel, got his grandson, Philip V, the new Bourbon King of Spain, to arrest him in Brussels, and took possession of the papers which had been confiscated when Quesnel's lodgings had been searched. He persuaded Clement XI to publish the bull *"Vineam Domini"* in 1703, which compelled subscription of the anti-Jansenist formula in such unequivocal terms, without the possibility of the escape route of the *"silentium obsequiosum"*, that even Noailles was unable to find any means of evasion.

Only the nuns of Port Royal des Champs remained firm in their refusal to sign unless they were allowed to add the proviso *"sans préjudice à la paix de Clement XI"*. The result was the Noailles found himself in as awkward a position as his opponents could have wished for him: if he had to resort to violence against Port Royal he would become an object of loathing to the Jansenists.

Louis XIV asked the Pope to suppress the convent. On 29th October 1709 the Chief of Police, D'Argenson, organized the compulsory removal of the twenty-two elderly nuns who had stayed on, long after the time when it had been possible for them to receive novices. Because the deserted

[1] Daniel-Rops, op. cit., 457ff. (E.T., 396ff.).

building still remained a place of pilgrimage for the Jansenists, the King had the convent destroyed in January 1710. As the Jansenists continued to come to pray in the cemetery there, the corpses were disinterred and thrown into a communal grave.

But despite all this, the King's actions in no way succeeded in bringing Jansenism to an end. The three parishes in Paris to which the bodies of the most famous Jansenists were taken were to form a triangle of future resistance in the capital. Quesnel, who had escaped from prison in the Netherlands, made a daring attack on the Roman censure of 1708 with his *"Entretiens sur le décret de Rome"*. When Louis XIV demanded that the Pope should issue a formal condemnation of Quesnel, Clement XI did not miss the opportunity which the King thus gave him to assert his authority as Pope. On 8th September 1713 he published the bull "Unigenitus", and among the 101 propositions here condemned he was able to slip in a number which were not Jansenist but Gallican.[1]

Though the bull was intended to close the subject, its actual effect was to divide the French clergy and eventually the whole of Europe once again. Fénélon wrote an opinion counselling acceptance of the bull, the Assemblée du Clergé declared itself of the same mind and 117 bishops acquiesced. But eight went into opposition. Cardinal Noailles's brother, who had now succeeded him as bishop in Châlons, wrote: "If the Pope is in error in straying from the tradition of his See, then it is he who is parting company with the Church". The Cardinal himself, decisive at last, forbade his priests to accept the bull, under pain of suspension from office.[2] Louis XIV wanted to settle matters by calling a national council, but even before he died this solution foundered.[3] Under the Regency, it was Dubois who succeeded in getting both "Acceptors" and "Appellants" (i.e. those who wanted to appeal to a future council against "Unigenitus" and later also against the bull, "Pastoralis Officii") including Noailles to accept the settlement of 1720, known as the "Accommodement". But Clement XI refused ratification. In 1721 a fresh appeal was made by three bishops, 1,500 others holding office in the Church, 500 Benedictines and 30 "Feuillantes".[4]

[1] Ibid., 464 (E.T. 404).
[2] This attitude led to friendly contacts being made between N. and Count Zinzendorf in December 1719. It pleased Z. that N. could say to him that the Catholic Church could find a place for his talents such as the Lutheran State Church denied. But he has to ask, "Do you wish, Mgr, that I should come over to the Church which even now is persecuting its most saintly bishops?" At the time of Noailles's resignation Z. breaks off a correspondence concerning the relation of the cardinal to the Pope and the appellants thus: "So it has come to an end, Mgr. That great courage which has defied all dangers and astounded the enemies of truth, has given way to fawning hope for an improper peace." In 1725 Z. sent his friend F. v. Wattewille to Paris with a translation of Joh. Arndt. N. was godfather of Z's eldest son.
[3] Daniel-Rops, op. cit., 466 (E.T., 406). Préclin/Jarry, op. cit., I, 239ff.
[4] Daniel-Rops, op. cit., 469f. (E.T., 408f.). Préclin/Jarry, op. cit., I, 241ff.

When the police began to make examples of them the movement of refugee "appellants" to Holland increased. The local Dutch clergy joined the refugees in their appeal against "Unigenitus". In vain, the lawfully elected Archbishop Petrus Codde attempted to prevent a breach with Rome, and after his resignation the French missionary bishop Varlet consecrated Cornelius Steenhoven as his successor in 1724. Thus began the free Church of Utrecht, separated from Rome. In the Council of Utrecht, 1763, there was a pronounced fading away of Jansenist influence; what was now noticeable was the affirmation of a new role for the Church of Utrecht, that of guardian of the old episcopal idea. After 1870 it was the Church of Utrecht which transmitted the office of bishop to the Old Catholics.[1]

3. QUIETISM

The Jansenist controversy was not the only one the Jesuit Order had to engage in. It also took issue against "Quietism",[2] at least in its beginnings. A Spanish priest, Miguel de Molinos, had been active in Rome since 1663 and became very popular as a spiritual director, even among the College of Cardinals. His main work, "Guida Spirituale", written in 1675, and based on St Teresa of Avila and Gregorio Lopez,[3] received the imprimatur of the Church and the approval of eminent theologians. It was translated into the most important European languages and soon became widely known. Its aim was "to prescribe the means which uncreated Love employs in order to lead from the wretchedness of sin to rest and quietness of heart". Molinos required that the heart should be inclined not to this or that good, but only to the highest good. According to this "quietist" type of mysticism, Christian perfection was to be attained by "contemplatio passiva infusa", in which the powers of the soul are suspended. The soul must allow God himself to replace the Ego ("I"). The desire to strive after blessedness by moral effort is bound to be thwarted.

The great Italian missionary, Paolo Segneri, S.J., came out against Molinos. Cure of souls for the Jesuits was a matter of attempting to release impulses to action and Segneri, therefore, could not but be critical of the passivity of the Quietists. But the Jesuit refutations were placed on the

---

(Bibliography on eighteenth-century Jansenism, which partly was no more than a party to keep the Gallicans in being as an opposition movement to the papacy and promote their political aims; and partly a movement sympathetic to miraculous cures and convulsions; cp. Préclin/Jarry, op. cit., I, 234f.).

[1] Ibid., I, 212ff., 242ff., 260ff.
[2] Ibid., I, 165, 168; R. A. Knox, *Enthusiasm*, Oxford 1950. On Fénelon, J. Lewis May, London 1940; K. D. Little, New York 1951.
[3] Daniel-Rops, op. cit., 430 (E.T., 372).

Index in 1681. Molinos had the favour of Innocent XI, who made the Oratorian, Pietro Matteo Petrucci, a friend of Molinos who wrote in his defence, Bishop of Jesi.

Then came a sudden reversal of fortune. Perhaps the decisive factor was the observation of Archbishop Caraciolo of Naples that nuns following "quietist" principles were neglecting to use the Church's external means of salvation; perhaps it was the pressure brought to bear by the French ambassador, Cardinal César d'Estrée, to compromise the Pope's position. Anyway, on 18th July 1685 Molinos was imprisoned by the Inquisition. With the bearing of a Christian rejoicing at being given to share the humiliation of his Lord, he accepted all that befell him, and in Santa Maria sopra Minerva, recanted everything he was asked to recant. He was condemned to imprisonment for life. The bull "Coelestis Pastor" rejected sixty-eight propositions abstracted from his writings.[1] To save Bishop Petrucci from prison, Innocent XI took him into the College of Cardinals. His case was settled by putting his writings on the Index and by his retraction of offensive theses extracted from them.[2]

The events in Rome in 1687 reverberated throughout Europe and boosted the influence of Quietism, even in Protestant pietist circles. A. H. Francke translated the "Guida Spirituale" into Latin, and Gottfried Arnold translated it into German. But the most important effects were to be found in France.

Here the stimulus which came from Molinos activated a "Quietist" movement already in existence. Malavi, the blind mystic of Marseilles, had acquired a following with his "Pratique facile pour élever l'âme à la contemplation" of 1644.[3] Father Lacombe, Superior of the Barnabites at Thonon on the Lake of Geneva, assimilated Molinos's ideas in Rome and formed a close friendship with a Quietist, Bishop Ripa of Vercelli. His two tracts did not attract much attention and, in fact, Lacombe would have had no great influence had his path not been crossed by his Provincial's sister, Mme de Guyon.

About this time Mme de Guyon had founded a house for Protestant converts at Gex on the opposite shore of Lake Geneva. Lacombe, as spiritual director of this house, grew to admire this woman, in whom

[1] Whether the complaint of Molinos's moral shortcomings is justified will not be decided until the records of his trial and his correspondence (of some 20,000 items) are made available to research. Daniel-Rops, op. cit., 429 (E.T., 371), refers to him as an "enigmatical figure", "a kind of Rasputin".
[2] Petrocchi shows that the breadth of Quietism in Italy was such that it is unnecessary to trace the whole movement back to Molinos alone. As late as 1699 two Quietists, the Augustinian Romualdo and the Benedictine Geltruda Mora Cordovana, were arrested in Sicily and executed.
[3] Daniel-Rops, op. cit., 432 (E.T., 374). When "La pratique facile" was put on the Index, M. defended himself in Lettre à M. de Foresta-Colongue, Marseilles 1695.

mystical experience was blended with hysteria. In a complete fusion of souls, these two discovered "a new land, so divine as to be utterly inexpressible".[1]

Thanks to an income of 50,000 livres which her husband had left her, Mme de Guyon was free to follow the vocation to which her inner voices called her. Accompanied by her spiritual director, Lacombe, she appeared in Marseilles, Lyons, Dijon and in the hospitals of Turin, conducting prophetic campaigns, and eventually had a whole chain of adherents with whom she shared her mystical theories through her private leaflet, "Torrents spirituels". To those of her contemporaries who were not without culture but who at the same time longed for a life in Christ, free of all doctrinal controversy, there was presented an "amour désinteressé", from which all consideration of reward and punishment were excluded, a state to rest in, not just a question of individual action, but rather accompanied by an "indifférence aux actes" ("passivité", "abandon", "marriage spirituel"). There was one point on which Mme de Guyon and Lacombe differed from Molinos: the self-detachment of the mystic could lead the soul to commit sins, indeed the most horrible of all sins. But thereby the greatest sacrifice to God was to be offered. It was on this point that later theological criticism was to settle.

During a period of tranquillity after a crisis in 1683 in which Mme de Guyon did not know whether she was bearing in her womb the child Jesus or the Great Dragon of the Apocalypse, she composed her treatise, "Moyen court et très facile de faire oraison". This was published two years later, and met with surprising success. When the prophetic couple arrived in Paris they were enthusiastically received in social circles. But this made the Archbishop uneasy. The condemnation of Molinos by Rome supplied him with good arguments and he had the Barnabite committed to the Bastille. Lacombe was to spend the rest of his life in prison. But Mme de Guyon, who for the time being was confined to the house of the Visitandines in Rue St Antoine, made a triumphant return. At the Duchess of Charost's salon she made the acquaintance of the brilliant Fénélon, and was captivated by his spirituality.[2] Between 1689 and 1694 Fénélon and Mme de Goyon lived under the spell of a common vision. Fénélon was entrusted with the education of the King's nephew, with whom he might perhaps one day rule France. For his pupil, he wrote his novel, *Télémaque*, setting forth a

---

[1] Daniel-Rops, op. cit., 434 (E.T., 376). Mme de Maintenon, Louis XIV, Bossuet and Noailles held that the relations between the two soul-mates had gone further. But Mme de Guyon always denied it. Lacombe's confessions were made after he had become insane. On "Hysteria", Catholic Church history tends to indulge in excessive spiritualization of canonized persons, and excessive psychoanalysis of condemned ones.

[2] Daniel-Rops, op. cit., 436 (E.T., 376ff.).

policy totally subordinated to the divine. In the girls' school of Saint-Cyr, which had been founded by the mighty Mme de Maintenon herself for the young ladies who would become the élite of France, Fénélon's lectures with their Quietist emphasis made a great impression. With the help of the principal, Mlle de la Maisonfort, who was a cousin of hers, Mme de Guyon also started frequenting the new school, which had no religious tradition of its own. The young ladies were now subjected to a kind of teaching which, in the interests of Quietist passivity, set little store by work, periods of prayer, practice of virtue, or punishment. Mme de Maintenon resented losing control of this school and it was her jealousy which led to the downfall of Quietism. She lodged a complaint with the Bishop of Chartres, who had jurisdiction, and suggested that Bossuet should be appointed to investigate. Mme de Guyon, who was confined during the inquiry to the convent of the Visitandines at Meaux, managed to have Tronson, the Rector of Saint-Sulpice, and Noailles appointed adjudicators to act along with Bossuet. The inquiry took place in the new Sulpician seminary at Issy and eventually issued a judgement condemning "30 Articles" from Mme de Guyon's works.[1]

At Issy, Fénélon's position had not been questioned. He was now Archbishop of Cambrai. But for reasons hard to fathom a most acrimonious dispute subsequently developed between him and Bossuet. In 1696 Bossuet again tackled the problem of Quietism in an "Instruction pastorale sur les états d'oraison", and sent the manuscript to Fénélon for his approval. Without examining it properly, and still less giving it his approval as was expected, Fénélon on his side dashed on to paper his "Maximes des Saints sur la vie intérieure", the object of which was to show how easy it was to turn true mystics into heretics by distorting their ideas. Fénélon moved so quickly that his book appeared in print one month before Bossuet's and this marked the breach between the two great bishops of France.[2] Theological argument now gave way to personal animosity. Both parties carried on the feud at Court and in Rome. Eventually, it was the King who requested that the dispute should be brought to an end by a formal judgment, and in 1699 the Pope designated twenty-three propositions from Fénélon as "offensive and rash". Nothing was said of heresy.

The death of Quietism cut off all possible outlets for mysticism as such, and this was one of the causes of the development of the Enlightenment within Catholic Christendom. As mysticism's last author, Fénélon was to exercise a second phase of influence, after the interim period in which the Enlightenment flourished. In Matthias Claudius's translation it was he who

---

[1] Préclin/Jarry, op. cit., I, 970.
[2] Daniel-Rops, op. cit., 445ff. (E.T., 385ff.).

disclosed the mystical dimension to the Romantic generation in Germany.[1]

4. BAROQUE BELIEF IN MIRACLE

In Baroque Catholicism life in heaven and the supernatural were represented in material terms as vivid scenes set on solid clouds. Its world was a world in which physical manifestations of the miraculous took place. Baroque Catholics' ideas of piety were full of fantasy on this subject, and it was just because of this that the Enlightenment had later to work out criteria for judging the validity of miracle. The *demonstratio Catholica*, in opposition to the heretics, put the emphasis on what could be seen and heard.[2] From the bishopric of Münster after the ravages of the Thirty Years War, the Archbishop, Count Galen, reported to Rome in 1660 that all the churches had been newly decorated and were radiant. In Wessobrunn there were more than six hundred craftsmen in stucco work who between them decorated almost 3,500 churches. The Baroque movement helped to establish the Tridentine reform of the liturgy, which was completed with the 1614 Rite, by introducing the instrumental Mass and by its influence in the Oratory. The task of bringing the German diocesan liturgical books into conformity with the Roman Order was begun in Mainz as early as 1551, but was not concluded until 1671. The Baroque taste for dramatization is well illustrated by the way the Feast of the Trinity was celebrated at the Graben in Vienna in 1680. Abraham à Sancta Clara concluded his sermon with an appeal to "resounding trumpets" to echo his thanksgiving. "Thereupon the entire chorus, with trumpets and loud throbbing drums, entered in, proclaiming their joy".

In particular, veneration of the miracle of transubstantiation in the sacrament took new Baroque forms. After 1634, Mgr D'Authier de Sisgaud advised his priests to practise fervent prayer after the manner of the Chapelet du Saint Sacrement. On 12th March 1654, in the choir of the Daughters of the Holy Sacrament, the Queen Mother, Anne of Austria, read a prayer of her own for the reparation of injuries which the exhibition of the sacrament would bring about. This kind of prayer was to spread. Father Epiphanius de St Louis in 1673 composed an "hour-hand" of prayers of reparation which was turned into verse anonymously and was widely used.

[1] Fénelon's Lectures contributed to the Catholicizing trend among the German Romantics. The 'Explication des maximes des saints' was particularly influential on M. Claudius, who published German translations of Fénelon in 1800, 1809 and 1811. These influenced, e.g., the poet and teacher, Johannes Falk.

[2] The Oberammergau Text dates from 1661. The baroque period was the great time for Nativity plays. The use of holy oil (which had almost become obsolete) was revived for the glorification of the confessional. Johann von Nepomuk was canonized in 1729, and the sacramental rites of consecration according to the Ritual of 1614, were widely used.

Then came the firing of salutes in honour of the sacrament, a practice followed regularly by the Theatines in Paris, at the chapel of the Château at Versailles, and at the Cathedral at Rheims.[1] The miracle was turned into something that could actually be heard.

Catholic piety of the Baroque period should receive consideration from Protestants in so far as it became more biblically based. The German Baroque Bible—the 1662 Catholic Mayntz Bible—had its beginnings in Protestantism. Its editor, Volusius, was a convert who had formerly been pastor of the French Reformed congregation of Hanau. When his archbishop, Johann Philipp of Schönborn, discovered that the translator had entered into a contract with the Frankfurt publisher, Schönwetter, before the work had been approved by his Ordinary, he insisted, under threat of loss of benefice to its translator, that it should be examined for its theology.

To a certain extent, however, Baroque biblicism did display the characteristic flourishes of the period. It was at this time, for example, that importance began to be attached to contemplation of the "secret sufferings of Christ"—unknown to the Evangelists—which had been "revealed" in visions to the Clairist nun, Magdalen Beutler, in the fifteenth century.[2]

In his Normandy missions Jean Eudes gave great impetus to the cult of the Sacred Heart of Jesus. At the Visitandines' Convent at Paray-le-Monial, on 27th December 1673, the Mistress of Novices, a woman who alternated between pangs of conscience and prophetic ecstasy, had, on withdrawing from the altar, received a vision of the Lord, taking His heart from His breast and putting it in hers. Flames shot from her heart as the Lord took it back again. Then Margaret Mary Alacoque heard His words: "Till now thou hast borne the name of My servant. Now I give to thee the name of much-beloved disciple of My Sacred Heart." Second and third visions followed in 1674 and 1675, which commanded the taking of communion following the midnight hour of meditation on the first Friday of each month for the reparation of human ingratitude towards the Sacred Heart.[3]

A Trinitarian rhythm ran through Baroque Catholicism, but Marian accents also were strong, a notable emphasis being placed on them by the ruling heads of state, who were well aware of the benefits of encouraging piety for political ends.

When the Lutheran King of Sweden, Charles X, attacked Poland and took Warsaw, the only resistance put up in the conquered territories was

---

[1] Préclin/Jarry, op. cit., I, 288ff. The practice of the prayer of reparation was also taken up in Germany, e.g. in the Redemptorists' missions.

[2] Martin von Cochem led Baroque piety along this path.

[3] Préclin/Jarry, op. cit., I, 289f. (Development of the cult of the Heart of Jesus in Dijon and by the wife of James II; Louis XIV's suspicions; positive and negative attitudes on the part of theologians.) This devotion spread through Alsace to Germany.

that of the Paulinist monastery on the Jasna Góra at Czéstochowa. After a siege lasting the symbolic period of forty days, the Swedish army had to withdraw in flight on 26th December 1655.[1] To Counter-Reformation piety, this was a miracle, and since that time Polish nationalism has been associated with the Poles' sense of standing under the protection of the black Virgin. King Jan II Casimir (1648–68) had been a Jesuit and a cardinal, but Innocent II released him from his vows so that he could succeed to the Polish crown when his brother died and thus secure gains for the Counter-Reformation. On 1st April 1656 his wife, Luise Maria Gonzaga, the friend of Vincent, at the Cathedral of Lemberg and in the presence of the nuncio, dedicated the country to the Virgin as "Queen of Poland".[2]

Ferdinand II had already given Mary the title of "Supreme Strategist", and the liberation of Vienna in 1683 was celebrated with the "Feast of Thanksgiving to the Name of Mary". In a much-quoted sentence, Abraham à Sancta Clara expressed the conviction he had formed during the Turkish wars: "Whoever bears Mary on his shield, as the protectress of Christian arms, and honours her with all zeal need not doubt the victory."[3] The frescoes of the Maria-Hilfer Church in Deutsch-Matrei (attributing to the Virgin the victories of Prince Eugen) exalted her as "auxilium christianorum".

Baroque piety was also a piety carefully controlled by the authorities.[4] If its pilgrimages flourished, it suffered from territorial limitations. At this time, for instance, Mariazell became Austrian and Alt-Ötting became Bavarian.

The ruling princes still enjoyed the privilege of receiving the chalice on their coronation day. Of Francis I it was said in 1745: "On the day of your Coronation, 4th October, Your Imperial Roman Majesty gave the people an edifying example. For when the Most Reverend Lord Consecrator said the 'Domine non sum dignus' at the altar, Your Imperial Majesty lay prostrate for the space of almost a whole Pater Noster before receiving communion, and again, before taking the chalice." The ceremonial associated with First Communion, with children dressed in "angels'

---

[1] On the changed situation brought about by Jasna Góra, cf. *The Cambridge History of Poland*, 1950; W. Tom-Rievic, *The Reign of Casimir*, 518ff.; Daniel-Rops, op. cit., 450f. (E.T., 308f.); Préclin/Jarry, op. cit., I, 172.

[2] Préclin/Jarry, op. cit., II, 407.

[3] The May devotions to the Virgin derived from baroque Italy, but spread to Germany through the book *Monat Mariae*, by Fr Peter Beck, which was immediately recommended by the Mainz "Katholik".

[4] Church orders issued by the spiritual authorities copied from those of Protestant territories and anticipated first in Eichsfeld in 1605 were supported by police regulations of the civil powers, in accordance with the Imperial Police Ordinance of 1577 (e.g. in Salzburg in 1731 the Ordinance begins with the salutation "Praise be to Jesus Christ").

attire", with wreaths on their heads and lighted candles in their hands, was originally a Baroque Jesuit institution (started in Münster in 1661).

Jansenist circles were no less open to miracle. On 24th March 1656 a healing miracle which took place in Pascal's family confirmed the great mathematician in his struggle against the Jesuits. The Pascal family had for long been custodians of a thorn from the crown of Christ, and this was now on display at Port Royal. A 10-year old niece of Marguerite Périer, suffering from a running sore, approached it with prayer. She was cured. Other cures followed, as if to indicate that the relic only released its power to Jansenists.[1] The Jansenist "appellants" set great store by the healing miracles which took place in 1727 and after in the cemetery of Saint-Médard at the grave of François de Paris, a famous Jansenist who, to mortify himself, had become an ordinary weaver. On 13th August 1731 twenty-three Paris priests asked Mgr de Vintimille to confirm five new miracles, which had been investigated by doctors. When a royal decree suddenly closed the cemetery of Saint-Médard in January 1732 and put it under police protection, the following couplet appeared:

> De par le Roi, défense à Dieu,
> de faire miracle en ce lieu.[2]

What appeared to be Enlightenment criticism of the Baroque belief in miracles was really the not unconnected emergence of a certain social differentiation within the Catholic community. The priest of Gap observed the process in his parish: "There are in my parish people who receive the Word of God in its straightforward simplicity, who believe everything that religion teaches without having to dispute it; but there are others who feel themselves called upon to debate the why and wherefore, who play the part of learned men, imagining that they know more than their priest". It is with irony that the priest of Gap addresses this new type of "bourgeois" as "Monsieur". "But you, Monsieur, have to reason interminably about religion and its mysteries."

While the Enlightenment was spreading all over the rest of Europe, Italy was unaffected by the new culture and new social developments and remained the land of miracles and saints. In 1716 a little group of Franciscans led by Leonard of Port-Maurice set out barefoot into the snow and built themselves cells at the mountain church of San Salvatore in order to live an ascetic existence as hermits. After fourteen years of trial, Leonard permitted himself to go to Rome, and his down-to-earth preaching there proved unusually powerful. Everywhere he went preaching he erected

[1] Daniel-Rops, op. cit., 413 (E.T., 357).
[2] Préclin/Jarry, op. cit., I, 249. Döllinger was so interested in the convulsionarists that he got his Paris bookseller, Abbé Delbes, to buy all available material.

Ways of the Cross, no fewer than 576 in all, and he it was who, at Christmas 1750, put up the Cross in the Colosseum.

Human terror and mystical rapture were combined in the experience of Paul of the Cross (e.g. his vision of Hell, in 1713). On Good Friday 1715, during his meditation, he experienced the pains of crucifixion in his body, and at the same time union with God in his soul. Through ecstasies without number he pressed on, until on 21st November 1723, in the isolation of his mountain hermitage at Argentaro, he had the experience of mystical marriage. After that, the meaning of life seemed to him to lie in embodying the Passion of Christ and proclaiming it. By 1720 he had already completed on paper his plans for the foundation of his new Order of Passionists. But the opposition of rival Orders did not come to an end until 1746 when Benedict XIV ratified the new foundation. His biographer, Vincent Maria Strambi, describes in moving terms Paul of the Cross's preaching to the most impoverished classes: how he told the Passion of Christ in mime; how he thrashed himself in public to the point of exhaustion in order to show exactly what the scourging was like. Crippled as he was by rheumatism, he would drag himself along showing Christ carrying the Cross, until, with tears streaming down his face, he broke out into the "Ecce lignum crucis".[1]

The common people loved an element of the spectacular in miracles. Thus, during Easter 1783, thousands streamed to the recent grave of Benedict Labre, "the Beggar of the Colosseum", in Santa Maria dei Monti. For fifteen years Labre, clad in the most wretched of rags, had wandered around as a pilgrim from sanctuary to sanctuary in Catholic Christendom, from relic to relic. In the ruins of the Colosseum, by the Cross, he had sung his nightly litanies to the memory of the martyrs. At the end of his strength, he had collapsed in the streets of Rome. The crowds which streamed into church was so great that they had to make room for the priest to say mass.[2] But the French ambassador, Cardinal de Bernis,[3] irritated by this fanaticism, reported to his Minister: "One must accept that this pious comedy will not end too quickly." Such was the distance which separated the faith of one sociological group from that of another.

5. THE CATHOLIC ENLIGHTENMENT

In his oration at the funeral of Anna Gonzaga, at Val de Grâce in August 1685, Bossuet drew attention to the rebellion that was growing on the

---

[1] Daniel-Rops, op. cit., II, 393, 396ff. (E.T. *The Church in the Eighteenth Century*, London 1964, 312, 316ff.). Préclin/Jarry, op. cit., II, 535
[2] Daniel-Rops, op. cit., 337ff. (E.T., 269ff.).
[3] M. Cheke (British Minister at the Vatican), *The Cardinal de Bernis*, London 1958.

part of the intelligentsia. At the time of the trial of Galileo the Roman Church had still been able to bring the secular arm into action against him.[1] That time was now past. Catholic apologetics, directed against Voltaire and the Encyclopaedists, was concerned to defend the divine ordering of life and to give reassurance as to the validity of the position occupied by the authorities. Pascal's apologetic work is unique in the sense that there was no other comparable attempt on the Catholic side to enter into debate with the new spirit of unbelief. According to Pascal, faith is based alike on "raisonnement" and "coeur", the unearned gift of God, and it is the example of those who witnessed to it that brings unbelievers to long for a similar faith. God Himself then supplies the necessary evidence. Pascal uses historical proofs as arguments for the existence of the God who is revealed, who, however, remains hidden and only discloses Himself to those who seek Him.[2]

From the middle of the eighteenth century, "cannon shot was pouring into the house of the Lord" (Diderot). In France, in the twenty years prior to the Revolution, there were 400 new anti-religious publications.[3] None of the Catholic apologists was particularly gifted. Apologetic tactics were responsible for many authors taking up strange positions: the Jesuit Berruyer abandoned Holy Scripture to criticism, falling back on the assertion that the dogmatic truths which could serve as a foundation had been handed on by Christ only after the Resurrection. Gabriel Gauchat declared that it was a misuse of the Bible to use it like a book of physics. Tradition was to be believed because the wholeness of humanity had never ceased to exist and therefore the handing on of tradition had never been interrupted. But many of the Catholic apologists clung like leeches to individual authors of modern unbelief; Nonnotte to Voltaire's "Essai sur les moeurs", Bergier to the "Vicaire Savoyard" and to Holbach.

Cartesian philosophy was now gaining ground and the Oratorian, Malebranche, in his "Recherche de la Vérité", was the first to try to incorporate elements of Cartesianism in a Catholic philosophical system.[4]

While literature advanced the cause of unbelief, in the Church the literature of piety was also growing. The spiritual works of the seventeenth century (Bossuet's as well as Arnauld's) and classical devotional literature went into edition after edition. (Between 1735 and 1789 the "Imitatio Christi" had no less than nineteen French editions!) When current taste changed, Father Pichon's "Esprit de Jésus-Christ", Father Girardeau's "Evangile médité", and the Abbé Clément's "Méditations sur la Passion"

[1] Daniel-Rops, op. cit., 7 (E.T., 4).
[2] R. Guardini, Pascal, 1947. M. L. Hubert, Pascal's Unfinished Apology, Oxford 1932. J. Steinmann, Pascal, 1962 (E.T. London 1965).
[3] Daniel-Rops, op. cit., 94 (E.T., 74). Préclin/Jarry, II, 730ff.
[4] Préclin/Jarry, op. cit., II, 709.

were especially admired. In this connection, the Church did not leave out of account the new divisions in society which were then taking place. For "simple people" a special literary genre was created: *"Instructions et prières à l'usage des domestiques et des personnes qui travaillent en ville"*.[1]

In the diocese of Lodève, too, a start was made in the distribution of mass books among the faithful so that they could follow the service.

In the second half of the eighteenth century efforts were made to introduce German into the liturgy, and German hymns were introduced in place of Latin chorales. This was done to stimulate the active participation of the congregation in worship and to put an end to the wretched state of Church music. In the St Blasian Hymnal of 1773 is written: "It was the proper wish of the Reverend Pastors that even in the country a sung office should be introduced on the higher Feast days. But what use to peasants is Latin singing in which their hearts and minds cannot possibly join and from which no edification is to be expected? Therefore, let our Christian people rather sing praise to the Lord in their mother tongue." The compilation of a German hymnal was also commissioned in 1785. In this the good things of old were replaced by the "contemporary".

Even in the period of faith's decline, it was still possible for new Catholic cells to grow up in Poland under August II of Saxony and Stanislaus Poniatowski; this was due more than anything else to the fact that Stanislaus Konarski of the Patres Scholarum Piarum had reformed Polish national education according to Catholic principles.[2]

In Germany there was not the falling-away from faith which satirical scepticism and materialism had brought about in France; rather, a serious Catholic Enlightenment was to be reckoned with, taking place considerably later than the Protestant Enlightenment. The dissolution of the Jesuit Order in 1773, which up to that time had monopolized the universities, suddenly opened up new possibilities in the sphere of university education, and as a result an Enlightenment movement developed among the Catholic professors. The Theresian reform of the University in Vienna provided a model for the future, and in the Universities of Maïnz,[3] Trier

---

[1] Daniel-Rops, op. cit., 366 (Lit.), 448 (E.T., 291f.). This was the beginning of special pastoral care for different professions, a development which continued until the middle of the nineteenth century. The Provincial Council of Reims considered the question of actors. Later, as regards government officials, the basic idea that it was possible to be a good public servant without any religion—a notion which the governments would have accepted—was attacked.

[2] *The Cambridge History of Poland* (*supra*), 415.

[3] The education of the beneficed clergy had not until then been laid down. After the fall of the Jesuits, Chancellor Betzel, under the Elector Emmerich Joseph, carried through Enlightenment reforms in the university. This Enlightenment period lasted for fifteen years. Only two professors sympathetic to the Enlightenment were dismissed during the French occupation by Custine.

and Bonn (here, under Maria Theresia's son in 1786), a common "Rhenish Catholic Enlightenment" flourished under the Rhineland bishops.

In general, scholasticism, being known only in its later, degenerate forms, was rejected. Engelbert Klüpfel, the Freiburg dogmatician, complained: "Things had gone so far with theological studies that, instead of good seed, all that was being cultivated was bogus corn." The Prince Abbot Martin Gerbert blamed a biased scholasticism for holding up theological advance and neglecting essential study of sources. Reform in methods of study was urgently required. Simon von Stock carried through such a reform and was commended by Klüpfel for it. In 1752 the Benedictine monk, Oliverius Legipontius, persuaded the monasteries of his order to co-ordinate their work on historical publications. The 1752 and 1774, the syllabuses adopted by University of Vienna finally provided the basis of reform, and as a result, the number of disciplines was increased.[1] The "Theologia Wirceborgensis" showed just what the Jesuit Order was capable of in the period 1766–71, despite the fact that its dissolution was so imminent. There was, however, as yet little development in exegesis or ecclesiastical history. When the Jesuits again appeared on the scene they fell into line with their "ratio studiorum" of 1832.

Benedikt Stattler of the University of Ingolstadt, an ex-Jesuit, proved

---

[1] Since the professors were bound to manuals of doctrine, the books prescribed by the Court Commission on Studies had determinative significance. *Exegesis* followed the Protestant pattern in concentrating on textual studies and criticism. For this, a knowledge of Oriental languages was required. Old Testament was entrusted to Wahn, a pupil of Seibt, and of him Migazzi claimed that Tobit, Jonah and Judith were expounded merely as doctrine in verse. *Church History* first became an independent discipline through the programme of studies devised by Rautenstrauch. In 1785 the Compendium by the Protestant Schröckh of Wittenberg was decided upon as the textbook; with an exposition of this, Dannenmayr gained first prize in an open competition: it was based on Protestant and Gallican authors, and lasted until 1834, when it was replaced by Anton Klein. Gerbert of St Blasien was enough of a historian to be able to appreciate the original scholastics. He concentrated on the field of the music of the orders and the history of liturgy and got together a scholarly organization which was to carry through the gigantic project of a Germania Sacra. Klüpfel's *Dogmatics* was introduced in 1789. There was nothing on speculation, theological controversies or scholasticism. *Moral theology* was given a new emphasis. In the open competition Wanker was outstanding. Schanza, a rigorist and Jansenist, was the first professor and used his own book. This was superseded by his successor Reyberger's book. *Pastoral theology* was reintroduced, despite the opposition of the church authorities. The demand was for the training of competent administrators. The "Pastor bonus" by the Jansenists Opstraet and Muratori was recommended. In 1782 Giftschutz's "Outlines" appeared. Because of their didactic nature, homiletics and catechetics were taught (with preaching from scripture) and help was given for the ecclesiastical bureaucrats of the future. *Canon Law* was emphasized, but as determined by Kaunitz's "Instruction", which had the approval of the Empress, and later it was removed to the Faculty of Law. The textbooks were dispensed with by Migazzi. In 1819, when the Emperor was visiting Rome, Pius VII issued a memorandum on this subject. In 1820 the books were put on the Index.

to be a German Malebranche as he sought to remodel the philosophy of Wolff so as to create a new Catholic philosophy to refute Kant and to be able to support the edifice of Catholic dogma.

Generally, however, the Catholic Enlightenment preferred to restrict itself to the field of "religion" which it clarified with arguments presented with considerable literary skill and by which was, of course, to be understood the familiar dogmatic and disciplinary structure of the Catholic Church.

In this connection, various subjects were tackled which might be called "Protestant subjects", e.g. the subject of "the Word of God". Sebastian Mutschelle argued as follows: "Through speech" what we think within is "declared without," God "does not speak directly to us but through other men and through ourselves". Reference must be made to Moses and to Jesus, but also to "a voice of conscience, a natural light of reason". "This inner voice is also a word of God". Now comes the decisive question which shows just how far the emphasis can be misplaced: "To which then, should we be especially attentive? To the external or to the inner word of God?" Answer: "It is especially good to learn from within." The word which God speaks to us through reason and conscience is the source from which the teachers Moses and Jesus also draw. In this way, revelation is reduced to reason. "Self-reflection" is always held out as superior to "alien instruction".

The act in which the insight of reason is attained is similarly identified with the gift of the Holy Spirit. "When men accept a word of God from without or read it in books, they are quite content to abide by the letter without penetrating to the spirit. But what one hears as the dictum of one's own reason is never merely a letter, but always spirit and life."

The Catholic Enlightenment replaced the contrast between reason and revelation with the contrast between reason and heart. Sailer's "The Teaching of Reason for Mankind as it is" of 1785 simply continued this development. What was wanted now was an emotional kind of religious thinking. The rejection of "Schwärmerei", on which the Enlightenment philosophers were all agreed, was resented. Thus Sailer: "Is it not an obvious offence against reason and charity to come out quite so quickly with an obituary for 'Schwärmerey'?" This was the turning-poinon the road to Romanticism. Franz von Baader adopted the typical Romantic position when, in a letter to Jacobi dated 16th June 1796, he referred to the men of the Enlightenment as "heart-thieves".

An enlightened Europe made it possible for Benedict XIV to lay down critical norms for judging the authenticity of healing miracles. A cure could be attributed to miracle only if it met certain quite specific conditions, and subject to medical confirmation. Basically, the Pope retained the

Baroque fascination for miracle, but he wanted to sift out the true and rare occurrence from a heap of dross. The Catholic Enlightenment went further and gave the concept of miracle a new meaning. It elevated the general ordering of nature itself to the status of miracle. Mutschelle writes: "Man has a passion for miracle because only what he considers to be an extraordinary miracle seems to him to be worthy of God and not that which, though ordinary, is nevertheless much more miraculous and worthier of God. He wants an isolated, special, transitory appearance from the other world; is then everything in this world that has appeared in the heavens and on earth and has continued for thousands of years, is all that nothing to him? To him, only the extraordinary, single event is miraculous. Does this mean that the ordinary course of things, preserving unaltered its measured pace in a million different combinations, is not?"

The argument for Christianity which hitherto had been drawn from the biblical framework of prophecy and fulfilment was abandoned. "Arguments which do not yield proof when subjected to scrutiny do us more harm than good." Isenbiehl was uncompromising: "As a conscientious professor and an honourable man I cannot possibly accept political counsel in matters theological." Here Enlightenment conscientiousness is evident. Isenbiehl would have nothing to do with "varnished exegesis". In the prophecy of the Virgin who was to bear a Son (Isaiah, chap. 7) he saw only a sign which the prophet gave to the King of Judah to the effect that in the short space of nine months Jerusalem's situation would change. "It is contrary to the nature of the prophetic sign that this should be an oracle of the Virgin Birth of Mary." "Are there not signs enough which are certainly not miracles?" Historical exegesis so predominates that Isenbiehl can state the rule: "Nearly all mystical interpretations are suspect and probably false."

The most significant achievement of the Catholic Enlightenment was its ability to go beyond the casuistry of the post-Tridentine period and to undertake a new moral theology. The great post-Tridentine casuistical handbooks were the practical working-out of the Council's decision (Sessn. XIV c. 5) to the effect that all sins were to be confessed according to their kind, number, and specific circumstances. The father confessor was to make a juridical judgment in each case—a debasing of morality. The "Medulla Casuum Conscientiae" by the Jesuit Busenbaum (Rector of the college at Münster) which first appeared in 1645 went through some 200 editions, a final revision being made as late as 1760. The casuistical moral systems (Probabilism, Probabiliorism, Tutiorism) differed from each other in the degree to which they laid claim to certitude as to how the law was to be kept and in the extent of the area within which a free choice of action was postulated. In this context the rigoristic criticisms which the Jansenists made were not unwarranted. By way of contrast, the Catholic Enlightenment in its ethics had something new to offer. They recognized the extent to which casuistry had regarded the human act in abstraction from the actor. Now a personalization of morality took place, action and actor being seen together. Man—as a being endowed with reason (i.e. moral capacity) and as an individual—is included in the moral judgment. Casuistry had dissolved morality into a mere matter of individual cases. Now an assessment took place which had regard to the inner unity of the moral person. In Probabilism the spirit of the market-place had been allowed to creep in. That this was changed was really the result of openness to contemporary non-Catholic influences.

The originator of the Enlightenment's brand of ethics was Eusebius Amort (1692-1775), an Augustinian canon of Polling/Bavaria, and casuistry was finally overcome in the work of Martin Gerbert, the Prince Abbot of St Blasien. Attention was paid to biblical insights, the application of which had been illustrated in the testimony of Augustine and Chrysostom. Socrates, Cicero and Juvenal had a contribution to make as authorities respected by contemporary culture. Balduin Wurzer, Aemilian Greif, Jakob Danzer, Simpert Schwarzhueber went on to develop Enlightenment ethics still further. When Augustin Zippe, Rautenstrauch's successor in Vienna, issued a challenge to the moral theologians of the Austrian Faculties to plan a new handbook of ethics, the best response was the project outlined by Wanker of Freiburg. In carrying out his plan, Wanker used the German language, and this was important because it made it easier to incorporate recent findings in anthropology and psychology.

It was at this point that the ethical theory of the Catholic Enlightenment showed its dependence on Protestant thought. Buddeus, and after him all the moral thinking of the Protestant Enlightenment, had already given ethics a psychological basis, and it was Buddeus who directly influenced Anton Josef Rosshirt, the Würzburg moral theologian.[1]

In the ethics of the Catholic Enlightenment, basic philosophical questions such as, What is man? What is he capable of? To what is he called? were in the first instance answered philosophically and only thereafter given the ological trappings.[2] The work of grace in enabling Christians to act in Christ was never given sufficient consideration. Only this might have provided valid and effective opposition to the profane Enlightenment.

They did not, however, relapse into the old Enlightenment view that moral insight automatically led to moral action. Contemporary apprecia-

---

[1] Wanker took over his "moral Physiology of Man" from the Lutheran moral theologian, Reinhard, of Wittenberg.

[2] Thus the first edition of Wanker's *Moral Teaching* of 1794. In later editions more prominence was given to the Bible and the Fathers.

tion of the enlightened understanding could "be praise for the lazy wretch who knows his Lord's will but does not do it". For Mutschelle it was a matter of doubt whether "insight passes over into action". "More energy of will" had first to be found "in the darkness of understanding".

Thus in Catholic ethics "volition" was "cultivated". The scholastic distinction between negative and positive freedom of the will (*libertas a coactione* and *a necessitate*) was thus further developed. On the basis of his freedom, man can "begin a multitude of things by himself and through himself". Nor was the fact that our freedom is limited at this point overlooked. A. K. Reyberger distinguished metaphysical freedom "as a natural basic property of all men" from "moral freedom as a property acquired by the noble among men".

The eudaemonism of the Enlightenment was taken over by the Catholic moral theologians, indeed they so stressed it that men like Wanker could describe man's ability to recognize righteousness of mind and action as the purest and most lasting of pleasures. These "moral joys" could not be touched by any power or any circumstance.

Moral theologians were not uncritical of the Enlightenment: "Everywhere moral philosophy was turned into philosophy of rapture. But whoever followed this teaching soon discovered that there was indeed nothing of rapture in it" (Mutschelle). It is "vain pretence when one promises that virtue leads to perfect rapture in this life". "Should we always have to appeal to men's inclinations in order to gain a hearing for our moral teaching?" "They are being treated like children who are promised a sweet for every good deed." Virtue therefore should not be "disfigured by artificially decking itself up in paint". "But for us everything is resolved into the loveliest harmony if indeed beyond the grave everyone is awarded his due."

A moral philosophy was developed on the basis of the dignity of man, given with his creation in the image of God. The goal was perfection. It involved a moral struggle from which one did not retire unhurt. False virtues were to be guarded against, and human instincts were now no longer the enemy. The moral philosophy of the Catholic Enlightenment recognized the ambivalence of the instincts, which were seen to nourish not sins only but virtue as well.

CHAPTER V

THE CATHOLIC CHURCH FROM THE
FRENCH REVOLUTION TO THE CONCORDATS

It is wrong to imagine that the only contribution of the French Revolution
to modern Church history was the institution of revolutionary cults.
These were only accidental groupings of people with the same sectarian
turn of mind. The real significance of the Revolution lies in the radically
new view of society to which it gave birth. Wherever this view was
accepted, it seemed impossible for the Catholic Church to become settled.
To support the ancien régime appeared to be the only solution. Thus the
problem was posed and continued throughout the nineteenth century:
how could a bridge be built between the Catholic Church and society in
its changing forms of development?

I. THE REVOLUTION OF THE PARISH CLERGY, NATIONALIZATION
OF CHURCH PROPERTY, DISSOLUTION OF THE ORDERS

The revolution of the bourgeois was preceded by the revolution of the
aristocrats. From the time of Richelieu the nobility had been excluded
from government and had been striving to regain their active role. Since
1786 they had been exploiting the financial crises and for the time being
co-operated with Parlement which was refusing to register the taxation
edicts. When the King turned to the clergy the nobles among the bishops[1]
formed an alliance with the aristocracy, insisted upon the summoning of
the Estates and thereby forced the King to capitulate. Only Mgr Emery of
St Sulpice and Mgr Thémines, Bishop of Blois, were shrewd enough to
see the danger. The revolution of the bourgeois then overtook the
revolution of the aristocrats, just as the revolution of the priests overtook
that of the nobility in the episcopate. Here the decisive factor was the
election regulations of 24th January 1789, which doubled the representation of the Third Estate and gave the parish priests an overwhelming

[1] The Concordat of 1516 gave the right to nominate bishops to the King, who
had noble families in mind. Thus while the monarchy allowed the middle classes
into the administration, noble birth remained a prerequiste for the episcopate. Bossuet,
Bourdaloue and Massillon spoke in vain against this development, which was to
prove fateful up to the time of the Restoration and the return of the émigré bishops.
Cf. J. Leflon, "La crise révolutionnaire", in *Histoire de l'Eglise* (Fliche-Martin), XX,
1951, 31.

majority in the local assemblies of clergy. Of the 296 representatives of the clergy at Versailles, there were only forty-seven bishops as against 208 parish priests.[1] On 13th May 1789 three priest delegates went over to the Third Estate, which, with its 600 delegates, was already as strong as the two others, and this opened up the way for the next step.[2] The influx of more of the clergy encouraged the delegates of the Third Estate to declare, on 17th May, that they alone constituted the National Assembly.

In the session on the night of 4th August the clergy and the nobility surrendered all their privileges. For the Catholic Church this meant also renouncing the "tithe" and relinquishing its immunity from taxation. At Talleyrand's suggestion, the Assemblée Nationale nationalized Church property in order to save the state from bankruptcy.[3]

This involved the dissolution of the Orders, since the economic basis on which the Orders rested was destroyed. Furthermore, it was not long before the monastic life was declared to be incompatible with the philosophy of the rights of man. On 28th October 1789 the Assemblée Nationale put a stop to the taking of vows, and on 13th February 1790, in terms of a scheme which Treilhard presented in the name of the Committee on Churches, it dissolved the Orders. This affected some 70,000 regular clergy.[4] Mgr de la Fare and Grégoire opposed this step by drawing attention to the services to literature which the Maurists had rendered, but

---

[1] A. Dansette, *Histoire religieuse de la France contemporaine*, I, Paris 1947, 7, begins his exposition of the Revolution with the splendid picture of the procession of 4th May 1789 to the opening of the états généraux. Here, for the last time, the ancien régime, in which the "sacral kingship" and the "Gallican Church" were united, was on display. Behind the clergy of Versailles came the members of the Third Estate, here, too, that little man, the Vicomte de Mirabeau, and the slender figure of Maximilien de Robespierre, candle in hand. After the short procession of the nobility, and as the first rank in the hierarchy, the Spirituality followed, next to the Sacrament. Behind the consecrated host, borne by the Archbishop of Paris, walked the King, weighed down by a vestment of gold brocade, which was drawn together by a blue belt, symbolizing the Holy Ghost.

[2] Bib. up to 1948, Leflon, op. cit., 7ff, 37; up to 1958, Daniel-Rops, *L'église des révolutions*, Paris 1960, 955f. (E.T. *The Church in an Age of Revolution*, London 1965, 479). The papers of the clergy and the Third Estate showed plans for reform entirely of a Gallican nature. M. G. Hutt, "The Curés and the Third Estate: the ideas of reform in the pamphlets of the French lower clergy in the period 1787–89", in *Journal of Ecclesiastical History*, VIII, 1957, 75ff; also "The rôle of the Curés in the Estate General of 1789", in *Journal of Ecclesiastical History*, VI, 1955, 190ff. Leflon, op. cit., 41f.

[3] A. Dansette traces the later distrust of the bourgeoisie of any involvement of the Church in politics back to the psychological motive that they had bought up cheaply the property of the Church and feared to lose what they had gained. On church property, cf. Leflon, 32f., 49f. Landownership by the Church was highest in Picardy (20 per cent) and lowest in the Auvergne (3.5 per cent). Scholars differ in their assessment of the economics of the sale of church property. Leflon (op. cit., 50) thinks that the sale gave the Revolution the necessary gold reserves to make the war abroad possible. Others condemn it as a pointless sale at deflated values.

[4] In comparison, France had 44,000 secular priests.

in vain. The Abbé de Montesquieu contended that it would suffice for the restoration of the rights of man if the state refused any longer to sanction the observance of vows, but in vain. The majority of monks dispersed quietly. The state's provision for penning up the remnants of the different congregations in those monasteries in which a minimum of twenty remained seemed to the monks to be less inviting. The mother Abbey of Cluny became completely deserted: of the forty monks there only two wished to hold on.[1] It was, in fact, the meditational Orders which showed the most determination to stand firm.

2. THE "CONSTITUTION CIVILE DU CLERGÉ" AND SCHISM

The action taken against the Orders was never intended to be anti-Catholic. When, however, freedom of worship was included in the Declaration of the Rights of Man, and the suggestion which a Carthusian made in April 1790 that the Catholic Church should maintain its position as the state religion was turned down, the bishops were forced to make their first protest. From 29th May to 12th July 1790 the new ordinance for the Church—called the "Constitution Civile du Clergé" because in the opinion of its author it did not affect the spiritual realm—was discussed in an unusually tedious debate.[2] When Mgr Boisgelin failed in his demand that voting on the ordinance for the Church must be preceded by negotiation with the Church, the episcopal delegates withdrew from the Assembly (i.e. The "Constituante").

The "Constitution Civile du Clergé" contained no ideas that were really new. The reforms which hitherto had been demanded of the King were now carried out by the Assemblée Nationale. The decisions were inspired by Gallicanism, and, in fact, presented a synthesis between legist and clerical Gallicanism, slanted as much towards presbyterianism as episcopalianism. Since the episcopate was drawn only from the nobility, the "Constitution Civile" refrained from setting up a national council, because this would only have brought noblemen together in a body. This was the price that now had to be paid for mistakes of old.[3]

The crucial question of the statute concerned the way in which bishops

---

[1] The abbey church was sold to building firms for demolition.

[2] The "constitution civile du clergé" was prepared in the Assemblée's "comité ecclésiastique". On 29th November 1789 Durand de Maillale had proposed a first draft, based on two principles: the joint election of bishops by cathedral chapters, two episcopal colleagues and the administrative committee of the Department, and the principle of canonical institution by the metropolitans. On 5th February 1790 the Prelates' majority on the comité ecclésiastique was broken by the co-option of fifteen further members. Now the presbyterial elements in the "constitution" could be carried through.

[3] Leflon, op. cit., 62.

were to be nominated. Appointment by the King was out of the question, the Concordat of 1516 being revoked. Therefore it would have to be by election. But who would the electors be? Cathedral chapters had fallen as victims to the new order. The intention was to follow the Early Church and to introduce election by popular vote. In accordance with the general desire for simplification and for geometric precision, new boundaries were drawn for the dioceses and these now corresponded with the civil administrative divisions of the "départements",[1] the number of historic dioceses being thereby reduced from 135 to eighty-three. The bishops were now to be elected by the same electors as delegates to the forthcoming Assemblée Législative, who, for their part, were elected by the "citoyens actifs". This meant that Protestants and Jews could also vote. The newly elected bishop would receive the "institutio canonica" from the French Metropolitan. The episcopalian Gallicans saw the advantage of this arrangement in that in this matter they would no longer be dependent on the Pope. This was thus a return to the position of the Pragmatic Sanction. Nationalist sentiment gave rise to the principle of giving jurisdiction to no episcopal see which was subjected to a foreign power.

During the discussion in the Assemblée, D'Esprémenil cried: "I ask, is the Supreme Bishop included in this anathema?" Grégoire replied that it was the Assemblée's intention that the Supreme Bishop's authority be confined within its proper bounds, but at the same time not to give rise to the schism. When it came to agreeing this article, Fréteau suggested an addition which was accepted: "Le tout sans préjudice de l'unité de foi et de la communion qui sera entretenue avec le chef visible de l'église." As far as the Pope was concerned, a newly elected bishop was required only to send him notification.

The presbyterian group within ecclesiastical Gallicanism found it easiest to accept the new order. In future the priest would no longer be dependent on the bishop for his appointment, for he would be elected by his parish in much the same way as bishops were elected. The bishop no longer had the right on his own authority to veto a priest's institution in office, his authority being limited both by the Bishops' Council, without which no exercise of jurisdiction was enforceable, and by the Synod. Thus, the demands of Richer and his school were met.

The new statute represented complete triumph for the political Gallicanism of the legists. It contained everything that had been claimed by the Parliamentarians of the ancien régime. There was no trace of separation between Church and State: the Catholic Church formed a constituent part of the national constitution. Current philosophical trends had indeed secured recognition of freedom of opinion, of the principle of

[1] Camus declared, "Nous ne faisons que changer la géographie."

toleration, and of civil rights for Jews and Protestants, but even so, there was not the least intention of allowing other religious groups their own forms of worship or of treating religious belief as a matter of individual concern with which the government had nothing to do. Exception was now taken to the fact that the état civile had been granted to Protestants in 1787.[1]

Action under the new statute made schism inevitable, in view of the Church's refusal to accept this new order. Pius VI was the authority with final jurisdiction over the new arrangement, and when tentative negotiations with him began he issued a brief calling upon Louis XVI to withhold royal sanction from the "Constitution Civile du Clergé", without which, of course, it would have been unenforceable. But the King was too weak to refuse.

The bishops, whose Gallican outlook normally made them suspicious of interventions from Rome, now, as danger mounted, turned to the Pope. In substance, this was the first Ultramontane action of modern Church history. In October 1790, Mgr Boisgelin forwarded his own "Exposition des Principes sur la Constitution Civile" to Rome, and asked Pius VI to remove canonical obstacles. Yet at this most dramatic of moments no instruction from the Pope appeared.[2]

The procedure for the election of a bishop was tried out for the first time at Quimper at the end of October. The man elected failed to find any member of the hierarchy who was prepared to consecrate him. The departmental government thereupon called upon the Assemblée to intervene. Although Maury warned against making martyrs, the "Constituante" faced the difficulties by resorting to coercion. On 27th November 1790 they accepted a law the consequences of which they could not have envisaged: within eight days bishops and priests were to take an oath of fidelity to the Constitution of which the "Constitution Civile du Clergé" was clearly a part, or else forfeit their office and stipend. This now posed a question of conscience which 130 bishops and 44,000 priests had to answer.

Mgr Boisgelin, at the King's instigation, once more made an urgent appeal to the Pope, asking him to recognize the Church statute as a fact and thereby to settle the inner conflict facing the clergy. But it was not until three months later, long after schism had broken out on this question, that the Pope issued a declaration pronouncing the "Constitution Civile"

[1] Leflon, op. cit., 59ff.
[2] Dansette is critical of the behaviour of Pius VI: the Pope believed time was on his side; the Assemblée would soon discover the difficulties involved in carrying out its schemes; Pius VI was unaware of the revolutionary ardour of the men at work in Paris. On the other hand, Leflon (op. cit., 64f.) stresses that Mgr Boisgelin's appeal was of less importance to the Pope than the news from the King. The Pope's desire was to avert schism.

heretical, and suspending from office every priest who took the oath. The Assemblée replied by ordering occupation of Avignon and Venaissin, the papal territories in France.

In a spectacular session of the Assemblée on 4th January 1791, the last day for taking the oath, the clerical delegates were called upon by name to take the oath. Only four oaths were, in fact, taken (including Grégoire and Talleyrand), despite the fact that the crowd in the street outside were yelling: "À la lanterne les rebelles!" Taking account of the representatives who assented outside Paris, 116 of the clergy took the oath, of whom seven were members of the hierarchy. When bishops of the old order then began to emigrate, they forfeited any opportunities that might have been open to them. The first to go, in January 1791, was Mgr de Machault of Amiens, and after July none of the bishops who had refused to take the oath remained on French soil. To their priests who remained they left behind admonitions to heroism.[1] The royalists began to exploit religious opposition for their political ends.[2] Talleyrand, for his part, took upon himself the colossal responsibility of consecrating a number of bishops in accordance with the new procedure.[3]

Among the parish clergy, those who were willing to take the oath formed a majority, albeit a deceptive majority.[4] Oath-taking took place on Sunday after Mass and "Club" members mingled with the worshippers. Many of the priests added pious reservations to the statutory formula.

Thereafter, the Catholic Church of France was torn between two hostile parties, the "clergé réfractaire" and the "clergé constitutionel". On 18th April the mob held up the King's carriage when he was on his way to a service to be conducted by a priest who had refused the oath. The ministers forced the monarch to declare his religious loyalty in the Assemblée and made him attend a "constitutional" service. Those who refused the oath were soon expelled from parish churches and withdrew to chapels in hospitals and monasteries. On 11th April the Directorate of the Seine issued an order forbidding the public to enter these chapels, but at the same time permitting those who wished to meet for any kind of worship to take rooms in private buildings. When on 17th April, "Club" members

---

[1] Leflon, op. cit., 69.

[2] Political and catholic reactions coincided in the Vendée rising (Leflon, 113f.).

[3] Eighty new bishops were to be elected for eighty-three new dioceses. Earlier studies expressed over-all condemnation of the new episcopate. Now the verdict is less absolute. At the consecration of Talleyrand on 24th February 1791, Mgr Emery took care to see that the exact observance of the ceremonial should ensure the validity of the consecration. Talleyrand's motive was to avoid Presbyterianism and preserve the hierarchical structure. Here the Bishop of Autun performed a liturgical function for the last time.

[4] The statistics which have been supplied concerning the "non-jurors" and "constitutionalists" (Sagnac) are disputed (Leflon, op. cit., 71).

invaded the congregation of St Sulpice, who had installed themselves in the Church of the Théatines, it became clear that whatever the government's intentions were radical groups were taking a hand in the Church matters.[1] Each of the two Church parties adopted its own methods. The constitutional priest had control of the register, as a public official, and because of this was able to gain a monopoly of baptisms and marriages. The "non-juror" priest, however, could rely on the support of the old canonical hierarchy. If he had the trust of his people he could create a vacuum round his constitutional rival in the village. Whenever possible, the latter appealed to the state for help. The new constitutional bishops were given official receptions by citizens' committees, but thereafter the administration of the diocese was no easy matter.

Shortly before it came to an end the "Constituante" took certain steps which indicated a measure of liberalization. Talleyrand came forward with the imaginative idea that religion was a private affair over which the state could exercise no control. With the support of de Siéyès and against the opposition of Treilhard, he carried through the decree of 7th May on religious freedom. The state was trying to get rid of its responsibility to settle religious issues. On 10th August 1791 the Assemblée took the Constitution Civile du Clergé out of the constitution. Thereupon the constitutional oath for the clergy became, in theory, a purely political and harmless affair. But it was a long time before there was any change in the position of those who refused the oath: they were quite unable to take advantage of this alteration in the state of affairs. It had become possible to modify the statute on religion, but nobody did anything about it. An amnesty for those who refused the oath, such as that agreed to on 13th September, on the King's initiative, could have contributed greatly towards a reconciliation.[2]

[1] Ibid., 82.

[2] Leflon (ibid., 79) shows the extent to which the theological problems at issue were championed by fiercely partisan groups in the background. For the mass of the faithful, the matters at stake were circumscription and the electoral procedure. According to reports of visitations in the Loire et Cher and in the Ardennes, it was clear that in 1799 only one thing was important for the peasants, namely that the pastor who had shared in their families' fortunes should stay. The attitude of the bishops was compounded with aristocratic prejudice. On the other hand, the diocesan letter of Mgr Philbert, Bishop of the Ardennes, dated July 1791, and the instruction of Mgr Torné, Bishop of Cher, of 30th June 1791, show the extent to which the "constitutional" bishops and the Jacobins identified the constitutional cult with revolutionary patriotism, and refusal to take the oath with counter-revolution. The Jacobins on the whole were still preoccupied by the *ancien régime*'s conception of church order, which called for one united official religion. Of the réfractaires, those who were already sympathetic to the idea of religious freedom included Mgr de La Lucerne, who adopted a judicious attitude on the question of the register of civil status, and Mgr de Langres, with his claim that the Edict of 1787 for the citizenship of Protestants and Jews should apply to "non-jurors" (Leflon, op. cit., 82f.).

3. "THE TERROR"

The Assemblée Législative, which met on 1st October, left the path of liberalization and embarked on persecution. Of the 745 delegates, there was now not one who had refused the oath, and only twenty-six priests in all. The delegates arrived in Paris in a state of agitation over Church dissension in their départements. By their decision of 29th November 1791, they authorized directors of départements to regard all priests who did not swear a new civil oath within eight days as being under suspicion[1] of revolt against the law. This time all efforts to intimidate the King into signing the decree failed.

The outbreak of war with Austria gave rise to the idea of a fateful alliance between the body of priests who refused the oath, the émigré nobility and the enemy abroad. Pius VI sent Maury[2] as his legate to Vienna, to use the French example to remind the Emperor of the consequences entailed in Josephinist principles, and to call upon his support for the defence of papal rights in Avignon and for all monarchs whose authority was being threatened. In Mainz, before a company of noble émigrés, Maury declared that the Pope needed their swords to sharpen his quills.[3]

"Rome", came the reply from the tribunes in Paris on the subject of the "réfractaires", "reprend ta funeste milice! Partez, artisans de discorde! Le sol de la liberté est fatigué de vous porter." On 26th May it was decided that everyone who had refused the oath, should, on the demand of twenty citoyens actifs, be expelled from France. The King exercised his veto against this decision, and this led to a mass demonstration. On 10th August 1792 the rebel government of the Commune came to power.[4] In the days following, the "réfractaires" were thrown into the Paris monasteries, now converted into prisons.

In the "First Terror", the "September massacres", in Paris alone

---

[1] A. Latreille, *L'Eglise Catholique et la Revolution*, I, Paris 1950, 113, considers that the concept "suspicion", introduced into this legal text, was to become the slogan for terror in the history of modern revolutions.

[2] Maury, first envoy of the Comte de Provence to Rome, went over to Napoleon in 1810. It was he who advised Napoleon, when the canonical institution of his bishops was delayed, to allow them to act as vicars capitular (Leflon, op. cit., 261).

[3] Leflon, op. cit., 95.

[4] The fall of the King, which rendered the earlier oaths meaningless, brought on a new move in connection with the oath, and on 14th August the "Legislative" decided on the following formula: "I swear to be loyal to the nation and to maintain freedom and equality." In the general uncertainty, Emery took upon himself responsibility of analysing the new oath so as to show it to be theologically permissible and proceeded with the swearing of the oath. In this he was vigorously opposed by the Royalists, by the emigré bishops and by Maury. The polemics of the time still influence historical interpretation today.

between 2nd and 6th September 1,400 victims were butchered, of whom 225 were priests. There is a problem about these murders. The statistics refer to what went on in the prisons, and therefore include the criminal inmates who were massacred, e.g. juvenile delinquents in the reformatory of Bicêtre. Of those murdered, only in the case of 354, at most 412, can it be said for certain that they were political prisoners.[1]

The "constitutional" cult had certainly wanted to remain Catholic. The best of their bishops, Grégoire, had said: "Il n'y a pas un mot de changé dans la célébration des mystères." The ideals of the Revolution, liberté, égalité and fraternité, were interpreted in "constitutional" preaching as fulfilling evangelical demands. But the fact that the "constitutional" cult was condemned by world Catholicism and eventually abandoned by the revolutionaries themselves reduced it to ridicule. Initially, "constitutional" priests could rely on the support of officials; but they soon found that they were being exploited, having to include the proclamation of new laws in their pulpit announcements and having to organize "Club" celebrations. With the introduction of the Register of Civil Status, the last act of the Assemblée Législative, any significance they had had was lost.

In March 1792 a parish priest by the name of Aubert appeared before the Assemblée Législative, accompanied by a lady, in order to be married in public. He wanted to cure all the ills that had been caused by the celibacy of the priesthood. His action was to set a precedent. Fouché, the Pro-consul of Nevers, who himself had once been a seminarist at the Oratory, ordered his priests to get married within a month. When the Paris clergy protested on the occasion of Aubert's installation in St Augustin's, they were punished with imprisonment. Thereupon, a law was passed prohibiting the removal of priests on the ground of their marriage. All married priests, even "réfractaires", were exempted from deportation.[2] After 19th July 1793 even "constitutional" clergy were

---

[1] Leflon, op. cit., 99f., speaks of a "collective psychosis". Since the archives of the Communes were destroyed, documentation of the responsibility is lacking. The "Legislative" disapproved of the massacres and instead introduced legal forms of persecution to deal with the "réfractaires". These priests were either exiled or deported. More than 30,000 went abroad. The 4,000 who asked to be taken into the Vatican had to swear an oath of loyalty to the bull Unigenitus. At a political celebration at Nantes ninety imprisoned priests were taken out on to the Loire and drowned. The report contained the comment: "Quel torrent révolutionnaire que la Loire!" Two deportation ships, Les deux associés and the Washington, were to sail for Guinea from Rochefort with interned priests. As the British were blockading the harbour, the ships lay there for a year. Les deux associés was built for 200 men, but 500 were crammed on board, and had to sleep on top of each other three deep. Three-quarters of their number lost their lives. A minority of priests, under the guise of carrying on civil occupations, continued their priestly service to a circle of the faithful. Those who were caught suffered the death penalty in accordance with the law of 21st October 1793.

[2] The constitutional episcopate did not all react in the same way to the marriage

threatened with deportation if they opposed marriage of priests or civil divorce, or kept a Catholic register.

With the "Convention", there was an increase in the number of delegations who refused to meet the costs of the "constitutional" cult in their localities any longer. In such cases, the right was given to the community to accept without debate whatever cult they pleased and to abolish any religious institutions of which they disapproved.

At the same time the destruction of the Church by the Commune was celebrated as a triumph. Archbishop Gobel, whom Hébert and Chaumette had sent for, appeared in the "Convention" with his curates, and made the following declaration: "Today, when there ought to be no other national cult but that of freedom and equality, I renounce my office as servant of the Catholic cult." Applause! "Vive la république!" With his office as priest, he surrendered his cross and ring, and, embraced by all, he accepted in exchange the red cap. Those who up to this point had conducted Catholic services were persuaded to stop.

Gobel's abjuration hastened the decline of the "constitutional" cult and accelerated total de-Christianization. On 24th November the Assemblée closed all the churches in Paris. Their president, standing before a heap of piled-up priestly vestments, candles and chalices, cried: "In this one moment of time, your eighteen centuries of folly are reduced to nothing." Of the eight-five bishops who had been elected under the "Constitution civile du clergé", twenty-four renounced their office, twenty-three fell away completely from the Catholic faith, and nine of them had married.[1] Of the 28,000 priests who took the oath, nearly 22,000 resigned. The remainder expected the same fate as the "réfractaires". Bourgeois anticlericalism found a literary genius in Hébert (Abbé Duchesne). Fouché started profaning the Catholic Church: he conducted a "Republican baptism" for his daughter, unveiled a bust of Brutus in the town church of Nevers, and on the cemetery gate hung up the motto: "Death is an eternal sleep." In a "Procession" which he headed a crucifix was dragged along, tied to a donkey's tail, and the donkey drank out of the communion chalice.

For its celebrations and services the Revolution initially used a mixture

---

of priests. Men like Grégoire and Philbert held strongly to tradition. Others demonstrated that what was involved was only a law which the Church had introduced and could revoke again. The number of those who married varies considerably. A contemporary pamphlet mentions 12,000, Consalvi 10,000, Grégoire only 2,000. On the difficulties of getting exact numbers from the diocesan archives (in which the relevant dossiers are often conspicuously absent) or the official register of status (in which the priests do not seem to be recorded with their official status), cf. Leflon, op. cit., 125.

[1] Leflon, op. cit., 119 (on the important resistance of Grégoire).

of the liturgy of the Roman Mass and its own ideological cult, but it developed its own sacral vocabulary and ceremonial, which followed the Catholic model only in the most formal sense. The Declaration of the Rights of Man was substituted for the Roman Catechism, revolutionary pageants for religious processions and national hymns for liturgical singing.[1]

4. THE CONCORDAT

Pius VI had been successful in dealing with the Josephinist reforms in Austria and Tuscany, but he failed to see the need to come to grips with the ideas of the French Revolution. His lack of insight resulted in the loss of parts of the Papal States in 1796, the harsh Peace of Tolentino[2] in 1797 and revolutionary unrest in 1798, which led to the setting up of the Roman Republic. The 80-year old Pope was carried off to prison in France and died there.[3] His successor, however, the Benedictine Chiaramonti, Pius VII,[4] who had been elected in Venice in 1800, was able to resume his seat in the Eternal City when the Neapolitans and Austrians forced the French out of Rome, and with the aid of his newly appointed cardinal Secretary of State, Ercole Consalvi, managed to take over government of the Papal States again.[5] But immediately thereafter the Italian situation was radically altered by Napoleon's victory at Marengo (July 1800).

[1] How are we to explain the progress of the Revolution from the opening Catholic procession as part of the constitutional life of the state to the substitute cults? Baruel saw here the carrying out of a plan inspired by hate, backed by the Free-masons and realized stage by stage with satanical skill. A. Aulard in 1892 was the first to contradict this theory. The state of war within and without fatefully led to the sacrifice of Catholicism. This interpretation is followed today by A. Latreille. A. Mathiez, *Les origines des cultes revolutionnaires*, 1904, 14f., agrees with Aulard that the Revolution had no anti-Christian basis. But the conflict was not exclusively political in origin: a religious controversy developed between two conflicting conceptions, those of Catholicism and patriotism. Patriotism then had a hypertrophied love of new institutions, which were valued as sources of moral and material well-being and of a world-wide renascence, and therefore attacked a Church which claimed to produce an eternal *societas perfecta*. The Marxist, D. Guérin, for his part thinks Mathiez outmoded: the revolutionary cult was a myth created by the bourgeoisie of the Revolution, disturbed by the "naked arm" of the proletariat which had assisted in the upheaval, to preserve the interests of its class, and to divert the proletariat's attention to persecution of the priests and to new festivals. Leflon advocates suspicion of all interpretations (104ff.). Daniel-Rops, op. cit., 960 (E.T., 21), approves of Abbé Sicard (*A la recherche d'une religion civile*, 1898).

[2] Leflon, op. cit., 144.

[3] Ibid., 155f.

[4] Ibid., 161 (Lit. on the conclave at Venice). Cardinal Lefèvre said to Champigny during the conclave, "You want Chiaramonti. He will be a little pope in little things. But if the issues become great, he will be as great as they are." Austria was so disappointed by this choice that it refused the Cathedral of St Mark for the celebration of his enthronement (Leflon, op. cit., 10).

[5] In the difficult negotiations of the Conclave, Consalvi had proposed and carried through the candidature of Chiaramonti (cf. Leflon, op. cit., 163).

Nevertheless, something quite unexpected happened. In Milan, on 5th June 1800, Napoleon summoned the clergy of the city to appear before him. As one who had been an atheist in Paris, a Muslim sympathizer in Cairo, what would Napoleon be now? He gave voice to the following sentences: "No society can exist without morality. But there is no good morality without religion. It is therefore only religion which can give the state firm and lasting support." The philosophers had been at pains to prove that Catholicism was an irreconcilable foe of the Republican movement. "Consequently this cruel persecution . . ." "But experience has cured the French of their delusion. France, having learned from her misfortune, has brought back the Catholic religion into her midst . . ." "I have decided to employ all necessary means to secure this religion . . ." "If I could discuss things with the new Pope . . ." Here was the perfect expression of the "religion gendarme".[1] Napoleon reckoned: if I were to change the old religion of France, it would turn against me and win. But how is the life of the Catholic Church to be organized? The "constitutional" Church is not accepted by the people. It is a monstrosity created by state legislation and can be done away with by law. The royalist bishops who have emigrated to London, Vienna and Madrid are opposing the French government from abroad. Only the Pope has authority over them. The Pope can free the Catholics of France from their royalist prelates, and "without bloodshed, reorganize them in obedience to the Republic". Napoleon therefore declared: "If there had been no Pope, it would have been necessary to invent one." Whereas the monarchy had for centuries been wrangling with the Holy See over the right to appoint the Gallican bishops, the young dictator was now prepared to hand over to Rome the question of transforming the French episcopate. He declared openly in the Council of State: "Once the Catholic really bring themselves to accept this, I shall be in a position to deal with these foreign meddlers."[2]

Church historians have so far tended to give insufficient attention to the negotiations which led to the Concordat.[3] On 22nd September Mgr Spina, the Archbishop of Corinth, was sent by Rome on a secret mission to Paris. Abbé Bernier,[4] Napoleon's representative, immediately presented

[1] Leflon, op. cit., 170. Cardinal Martiniana undertook the initial mediation between the Pope and Napoleon. As early as November 1799, Napoleon took some tentative steps towards a settlement. In place of an oath he required from the priests a declaration of loyalty, which Cardinal Maury again tried to get the Pope to forbid (cf. Leflon, op. cit., 168f.).

[2] Leflon (op. cit., 175ff.) explains Napoleon's religious position not so much in terms of political calculation as of sentimental factors harking back to his youth.

[3] Sources: *inter alia*, Leflon, op. cit., 9f., 178.

[4] B. had demonstrated his skill in diplomacy in restoring peace to the Vendée, by the Treaty of Montfaucon, 1800, which cost the local leaders their position, but which ensured freedom of worship.

himself at his hotel. Negotiations dragged on for eight months. Twenty-six drafts were prepared, one after the other. The secular state's revolutionary principles and freedom of worship were not to be revoked. To restore the Spiritual Estate to its place within the estates' framework and to provide for restitution of Church property were seen to be impossible. Napoleon needed the Church, but as an instrument of civil administration, and therefore had to secure for himself the right to appoint bishops. The secular clergy were to be paid as civic officials, and this would ensure their co-operation, for as soon as the Council of State spotted any abuse of the spiritual office it could suspend payment of stipends. Up to now, however, the French clergy had in general had no means of existence. The Vatican was not unhappy to witness the liquidation of France's past, for memories of the Gallican Church were not happy ones. Difficulties arose from the fact that the Catholic Church was to be recognized not as the "religion d'état" but only as the religion of the great majority of Frenchmen.[1] With the rescission of the divorce law, the Vatican tried to make everyday life conform once more in every way to Catholic standards. The trickiest point to be negotiated was the removal from office of the former bishops, of whom there were nearly a hundred. On this point, Consalvi declared: "You can read as much as you like in the history of the Church and you will find no comparable example. To get rid of 100 bishops is something that just cannot happen." The Curia were keen not only to regulate life in France but to rescind the points in the Treaty of Tolentino which had mutilated the Papal States.

The text of the agreement worked out on this basis was not finalized. Two powerful French politicians intervened, Talleyrand, the Foreign Minister, and Fouché, the Minister of Police. Talleyrand wanted to add a provision, soon to be called ironically, "Madame Grant's Clause", to the effect that priests of the Catholic Church who had meantime married would be accepted back as laymen. The rehabilitation of 3,000 priests and 300 monks was involved and Talleyrand, one-time Bishop of Autun, had himself married a divorced Englishwoman, Mrs Grant. Fouché grudged the confessing Church too easy a victory, and demanded the acceptance of a formula under which "constitutional" bishops would only be "advised" by the Pope to resign and in this way their episcopal office would belatedly be recognized as lawful. With the help of the police, he organized a

---

[1] The formula "state religion", which Bernier prudently inserted in paragraph 9, was, however, immediately included by Spina as the basis of the treaty in point 1, and this at once provoked Talleyrand's opposition. When he received the draft of the concordat from the nuncio he sprang up at the first sentences, took up a pen and for the expression "religion d'état", which would have created a right, immediately substituted a completely new formula, "religion de la très grande majorité des citoyens", which only stated a fact (cf. Leflon, op. cit., 185).

council of "constitutional bishops" in Notre-Dame, and this brought pressure to bear on Rome.[1]

Negotiations entered a second phase in Rome. The negotiatior, Cacault, was to bring things to a swift conclusion, since after his victories abroad Napoleon was now giving his attention to internal politics. However, the cardinals could not give up the concept of the "religion d'état", which for them was a matter of law. Pius VII, who was not accustomed to Napoleon's shock tactics, was quietly imperturbable. If only the French Government would at least declare itself Catholic! A counter-proposal to this effect went from Rome back to Paris. There, however, Napoleon had indulged in one of his scenes calculated to reduce the person to whom he was speaking to terror. He told Mgr Spina he would become a Calvinist, or else he would give recognition to the "consitutional" Church. The ambassador, Cacault, was ordered to leave Rome in five days and make room for Murat's troops if final agreement was not reached within that time.[2]

It was the action of the French ambassador which averted a final breach and paved the way for the third stage of negotiation. As he was leaving on the fifth day, he got the Vatican Secretary of State, Consalvi, to accompany him on his journey and set him off to act as negotiator in Paris.[3] He succeeded in reaching a compromise on the basis of Catholic recognition being given to the consuls. "Mme Grant's Clause", although left out of the Concordat, was to be incorporated in a brief. But when the time came to sign the document a wrong text was substituted,[4] and when Consalvi refused Napoleon threatened an ultimatum. The agreement, which was eventually signed on 15th July 1801—to become a model for the numerous concordats of the nineteenth century—regulated relations between the state and the Catholic Church in France right up to the time of their

[1] Ibid., 174.

[2] Against this, Leflon (ibid., 188f.) states that Cacault, theologically not very well informed, was partly responsible for the "Ultimatum of May 19th" because the report he conveyed to Paris was not strictly accurate.

[3] Ibid., 189. Consalvi was ordered to go to a reception in the Tuileries in "costume le plus cardinal possible". Unabashed, he thus made contact with Napoleon and "Autun" (the name always used by Talleyrand in correspondence with the Vatican). At Consalvi's audience on the first day of his stay in Paris, on the occasion of the parade which took place at the Tuileries every fortnight, Napoleon at once told him: "I give you five days. If the negotiations are not completed by the fifth day, you can go straight back to Rome. For as far as I am concerned, I have made my decision in this matter." There is an important point here. He would have been amazed if an alliance had been formed between the Pope and a non-Catholic power like Russia in connection with the restoration of the Jesuit Order which Paul I was asking for.

[4] Consalvi in his memoirs blames Bernier for dishonestly substituting the wrong text. Leflon destroys this interpretation by reference to a note from Bernier which reached Consalvi shortly before: "Lisez-le bien; examinez tout; ne désespérez de rien."

separation on 9th December 1905, and indeed, in the "système concordataire" of Alsace, is still valid.[1]

In accordance with the papal brief, "Tam multa", forty-eight French bishops handed in the required demission from office, but thirty-seven refused, and Pius VII declared their sees vacant.[2] In London an opposition group was formed with Mgr Dillon at its centre and they put it about that the Pope's decision had been given under duress. Out of the resistance which individual bishops were able to organize in France through the priests installed in their dioceses, there grew the schism of the "petite église" of Lyons, which attracted groups of Jansenist adherents.[3]

The "constitutional" bishops, who were accustomed to doing what they were told by the government, demitted office without creating difficulties. The form of resignation which they signed indeed referred to the irreproachable manner of their former episcopate,[4] since Napoleon wanted to include the "constitutional" cult in his religious settlement. When the Roman Legate expressed dissatisfaction with the bishops' formula it was agreed, by way of compensation, that they should make confession in secret before Bernier.[5] The new episcopate, as from 29th July 1802, had at its head Napoleon's uncle, Cardinal Fesch, as Primate of Gaul, and included ten "constitutional" bishops.

The situation was now favourable for Christians to make a new start. On 2nd February 1801, in Paris, six law and medical students joined together under the leadership of the ex-Jesuit Delpuitz to form the so-called Congrégation. When Pius VII came to Paris for the Emperor's coronation at the end of 1804 the group had increased its membership to 180. It got authority to organize other groups in the country. In 1809 the Congrégation disseminated the papal bull of excommunication against the plunderers of the Papal States, and this naturally led to its suppression by the Emperor. But at the Restoration the Congrégation again appeared on the scene—the matrix from which all the Catholic "oeuvres" of the nineteenth century were to grow.[6]

---

[1] Leflon, op. cit., 190ff. The first concordat to follow was that agreed in 1802 for the Cisalpine Republic. It granted the state religion, and was a setback to the anti-clerical minority in Italy. But the dispensation of Melzi's decree, the result of Josephinist influences, rendered it ineffective. Leflon, op. cit., 195f.

[2] Ibid., 203f.

[3] Daniel-Rops, op. cit., 147 (E.T., 72). The opposition replied to the Pope that they could not give back into his hands the episcopal office which they had received from the hands of the king (Lit. on the Petite Église, Leflon, 199).

[4] Leflon, op. cit., 304.

[5] The "rétractation" of the former constitutional bishops was reported by Bernier as complete, but this was contested by the bishops, who claimed it never took place.

[6] The Congrégation had the reputation of being a secret organization, influencing politics by the occupation of key positions and covering the country with a network of informers. This view stemmed from the ultra-royalist period, 1822–5, when

Opposition to the Concordat in the tribunes and in the legislature gave Napoleon considerable trouble. The old Jacobins, who kept their places there, were uneasy. The legislature made a point of electing as president the author of an anti-religious work. In order to win their support for a real "cohabitation" of Catholicism with the Revolution in France, Napoleon presented the Concordat along with the seventy-seven Articles Organiques in a single document. The Articles added to the provisions of the Concordat the prescription that worship should be subject to police regulation, but they had never been the subject of negotiation with the Curia and appeared to Rome to be a falsification of the terms of the Concordat. The Pope protested and declared twenty-one of the Articles to be uncanonical; these included the provision for a state "placet" of papal decrees, the subjecting of seminary teachers to the Gallican Articles, the prohibition of synods and of the residence of papal legates without government permission, differentiation between the paid parish clergy in the cantons and the clergy to the poor who were removable without further provision being made for them, also the acceptance of a new Cathechism approved by the government alone.

---

government measures were indeed influenced by religious factors. After Count Montlosier's polemic, "Mémoires à consulter sur un système religieux et politique tendant renverser le trône", this view became the basis of anti-clerical propaganda. Historians like Voulavelle, Lacretelle, and Dulauré embodied it in their works written after the fall of Charles X. It is also reflected in the works of Balzac, *Le curé de Tours* and *Les Employés*, and in Stendahl's *Le Rouge et le Noir*. Geoffroy de Grandmaison was the first to expose the legend with his work in 1889 (based on documentary research), which was accompanied by vigorous polemics. G. de Bertier explains the mystique attaching to the Congrégation by the fact that the Chevaliers de la Foi were in fact a secret society, some of whose members, like Montmorency, Polignac and Ferdinand de Bertier, were also members of the Congrégation. On the Congrégation's role as initiators of the "oeuvres" of French Catholicism in the nineteenth century, cf. I. B. Duroselle, "Les filiales de la congrégation", in *R.H.E.*, 4, 1955, 867ff. D. describes five "filiales". 1. The "Société des Bonnes Oeuvres" of the Abbé Legris Duval (1812–60) co-ordinated the three forms of charitable work: hospital visitation, prison visitation and the catechizing of the young "ramoneurs" (Savoyards and Auvergnats who came to Paris and often worked as chimney-sweeps). 2. The "Société St Joseph", founded belatedly in 1822 for the protection of young workers in Paris. 3. The "Société des Bonnes Etudes" was founded at the end of 1822 to encourage doctors and lawyers to undertake specialist studies for the education of a Catholic and royalist élite. 4. The "Société Catholique des Bons Livres". 5. The "Association pour la Défense de la Regligion Catholique". The "filiales" were not mentioned in any statute of the Congrégation. On the whole, only their leaders were members of the Congrégation. The Congrégation itself recruited only from the upper classes. They were responsive to all Ultramontane influences. It never became a mass movement. The "Société St Joseph" began with 200 patrons and eventually reached 1,000, caring for up to 7,000 workers. Up to 1830 the Société des Bonnes Oeuvres had 464 members, mainly laity, the Société des Bonnes Etudes 600, the Société des Bons Livres 8,000. Because it was too closely connected with the throne, the influence of the Congrégation and its "filiales" disappeared in the year 1830, but the impulses it had aroused did not come to an end.

5. NAPOLEON AND A DOMESTICATED CHURCH

Napoleon wanted a legate who would be "Pape à domicile", and he found in Cardinal Caprara a collaborator who was willing to conform to his wishes.[1] To act as a corresponding civic authority, Napoleon set up on 7th October 1801 the "Direction des Cultes". This post was entrusted to Portalis, a man who had the confidence of the clergy, but who, as a Gallican, could also be trusted by Napoleon.[2] His first task was to produce the Organic Articles.

Collaboration between Caprara and Portalis resulted in the "catechisme impérial" of 1806. The requirement, included in the Organic Articles, of a uniform system of religious instruction had previously been raised in the Church, in particular in the Assemblée of the clergy in 1785. The uniformity provided by the Trent Catechism had long been lost following developments introduced by Berulle, Olier, the Lazarists and Bossuet. In every diocese a variety of catechisms were used. The new production followed Bossuet, but it was really a mixture of official state teaching and Christian doctrine.[3] Napoleon's personal influence was responsible for the drafting of additional questions to follow the Fourth Commandment. There it was said that the Emperor was "the Lord's anointed", "raised up by God in a time of trouble".

Question: "What are a Christian's duties toward Napoleon, our Emperor?"

Answer: "Christians owe to Napoleon our Emperor love, respect, obedience, loyalty, military service, payment of prescribed levies for the preservation and defence of the Empire and of his throne. We owe him also fervent prayer for his salvation and for the spiritual and temporal welfare of the state."

Question: "What is to be thought of those who neglect their duties to our Emperor?"

Answer: "According to the Holy Apostle Paul, they are as those who

[1] Leflon, op. cit., 199f.

[2] Ibid., 200f. Until the creation of the Direction des Cultes, questions of politics and religion were dealt with by Fouché (Police) and Talleyrand (Foreign Affairs).

[3] On the basis of the sources, Latreille has clarified the previously strongly divergent theories on the composition of the Imperial Catechism. The text was composed from start to finish by Portalis, the Minister of Culture, who tried to bring together the interests of both parties. Abbé Jauffret took part in it. Mgr Emery, the oracle of the Paris clergy, checked the text. Publication was postponed because the proclamation of the Empire was about to be made. The Pope, forced by the French government to take up the question of the catechism, referred the matter to the Congrégation. On 12th August 1806 the "Moniteur" revealed the order for the new Catechism and the "Indult" of the Cardinal Legate Caprara, who had only become involved at the end. The defeat of Prussia was a favourable date for publication. The opposition of local printers had to be overcome.

oppose the order decreed by God and deserve eternal damnation."[1]
Ecclesiastical servility is no less evident in the prescription that the 15th
August was to be celebrated as the "Feast of St Napoleon". On the
question of who was the patron of the Emperor's name, Caprara declared
that it was a martyr of the fourth century from the prisons of Alexandria.[2]

After the Emperor's coronation on 2nd December 1804, which Pius
VII conducted in Notre-Dame, the Pope was no longer an abstract idea
in the minds of the French people.[3] Now the masses began to venerate
him, and their veneration increased when they learned of the Pope's
sufferings in the conflict which developed after 1805. On 2nd December
1805 the Bourbon dynasty of Naples was dethroned by Napoleon, without any regard to the fact that the feudal superiority belonged to the
Roman See.[4] Portions of the Papal States were handed over to Talleyrand
and Marshal Bernadotte as French fiefs. On 2nd February 1808 the whole
of the Papal States was occupied by General Miollis and a French government was set up. On 17th May 1809 the Emperor sent an edict from
Schönbrunn revoking the donation of Charles the Great to the Bishop of
Rome.[5] Pius VII replied by publishing the bull of excommunication
against the "plunderers of the inheritance of Peter". In defiance of the
French Government, bristling with arms and respected by none, the
Pope's government held on.[6] Then, on the night of 6th July, General
Miollis abducted the Pope from the Quirinale Palace and had him
confined in the fortress at Savona, his Secretary of State, Pacca, being held
at Fenestrella.[7] The cardinals were summoned to Paris. Thirteen of them,
foremost among whom was Consalvi, who had refused to attend the
Emperor's wedding on the ground that his divorce had been pronounced
not by the Pope but merely by the archiepiscopal court in Paris, were

[1] Napoleon himself wanted this section, which was given its first form by Bernier,
the Bishop of Orleans, who was disgraced on this account. This was the source of the
idea of formulating the politically important sentences as an appendix to the Fourth
Commandment. Of this Commandment it is said: Il regard aussi les devoirs des
inférieurs envers les supérieurs. Demande: Qu'entend-on par ce mot supérieurs?
Réponse: On entend ceux qui ont l'autorité dans l'Eglise et dans l'Etat. Demande:
De qui les chefs des Etats tiennent-ils leur autorité? Réponse: De Dieu. This text was
not acceptable to Napoleon. The Emperor then rewrote it himself.

[2] Leflon, op. cit., 235f.

[3] Ibid., 223ff. (Lit. on the imperial coronation).

[4] From Sicily, which was protected by the British, the Bourbons set in motion the
revolt in Calabria, in particular by making use of priests, who came over from the island.

[5] On 17th February 1810 Rome was declared by decree of the Senate to be the
second city of the Empire, and the crown prince was given the title of King of Rome.
The Pope was granted an income of two million francs per annum. Every future Pope
was to declare at his accession his adherence to the Four Gallican Articles of 1682.

[6] Leflon, op. cit., 241f. (Lit. on the conflict between "Sacerdoce" and "Empire").

[7] Ibid., 250. The details are disputed because of the unreliable and contradictory
reports of General Radet.

"decardinalized" and forfeited their revenues.[1] Isolated from his advisers, whom he needed so badly, and oppressed in spirit, Pius steadfastly refused to give canonical institution to the bishops the Emperor had appointed, and allowed the number of vacant bishoprics to grow to alarming proportions.[2]

Napoleon used the fact that the Pope was a prisoner in his hands to try to blackmail Pius into supporting his conception of a united Europe, with the Pope as its grand religious functionary, residing in Paris "in gold, silver and gobelins". With the aid of an initial credit of 1,450,000 francs, a Pope's palace was to be fitted out on the Island of the Seine. Since, following the Paris "Council" of 1811,[3] Napoleon was unable to carry out his scheme to have canonical institution of his bishops given "by the Metropolitan", he found himself after all having to apply to the Pope. When they met face to face at Fontainebleau[4] on 18th January 1813 the Emperor forced the Pope to give recognition to the method of "Institutio by the Metropolitan" which the Council had devised. Nevertheless, the Pope was racked by conscience and repudiated the agreement (as he was entitled to do, since the publication of this so-called "Concordat" was in violation of the agreed terms).

6. THE IDEA OF A "REICHSKONKORDAT" AND THE REORGANIZATION
   OF THE CATHOLIC CHURCH IN GERMANY

The reorganization in France had its effect upon the situation in Germany. The French occupation of the left bank of the Rhine in 1794 put an end to

[1] On 9th January 1810 the Paris diocesan authorities had annulled Napoleon's first marriage. The Metropolitan endorsed this on 17th February. Between Mgr Emery and Cardinal Della Somaglia there arose a controversy as to competence, and whether this was not a matter for the Holy See. Thirteen cardinals absented themselves from Napoleon's second marriage. Napoleon forbade them to wear their cardinals' robes, stopped their pensions and eventually banished them from Paris (Leflon, op. cit., 258, 254).

[2] On the seriousness of this position, cf. Leflon, op. cit., 254.

[3] At the "Council" of 17th June 1811, called by Napoleon so that the Metropolitan could carry out the "institutio canonica" of his bishops which had been refused by Pius VII, the French hierarchy affirmed more strongly their loyalty to the Pope. In particular Cardinal Fesch, Napoleon's uncle, influenced by Emery, wanted to appear to be independent of the Emperor. Napoleon dissolved the Council and arrested three of the opposing bishops. On the advice of Cardinal Cambacérès, Napoleon got eighty individual bishops to give their assent and reopened the Council so that the desired decree could be pronounced. Yet the stipulation, that this should be referred to the Pope for approval, disappointed Napoleon's expectations once again. The Italian bishops had some influence on the "Council" (Leflon, op. cit., 265f.).

[4] On the rigours of the Pope's journey to Fontainebleau, cf. the report of the Savoyard doctor, Dr Claraz, of 15th September 1814, Brit. Mus. Nr. 8.389. Alfred de Vigney's poetic potrayal of the Dialogue at Fontainebleau suggests that Pius was disgusted by Napoleon's melodramatic entry. Pius and Pacca deny this (Leflon, op. cit., 270).

the rule of the ecclesiastical Electors of Cologne, Trier and Mainz, and of the Prince Bishops of Speyer and Worms. Following on the French Concordat of 1801, Trier and Mainz lost their status as metropolitan sees. The appropriation of Church property by the state (already tried out in France) seemed also to be a possibility in Germany when, at the Peace of Lunéville in 1801, after losing the War of the Coalition, the German Emperor had to sign away in the name of the Empire the left bank of the Rhine. Article VII provided that the hereditary German princes should receive compensation from within the Empire, and this had the ecclesiastical territories in view. A commission of eight members of the College of Imperial Princes was set up as a special imperial delegation (Reichsdeputation) to give effect to the decision. In the event the plan of division was settled in separate negotiations in Paris between the various governments and the First Consul. The conclusions reached by the imperial delegation at Regensburg on 25th February 1803 (Reichsdeputations hauptschluss) went far beyond what was envisaged in the Treaty of Lunéville in the matter of secularization, a subject debated in the journals ever since the time of Frederick the Great and Joseph II. Under Clause 34, episcopal domains and the properties of cathedral chapters and their dignitaries and, under Clause 35, "all properties of endowed institutions, abbeys and monasteries" were to be handed over to be "at the disposal of the respective sovereigns for the purpose both of meeting the costs of worship and of improving their finances". The overall loss to the Church worked out at 1,719 square miles. In addition, eighteen Catholic-endowed universities were lost. It was the greatest blow ever suffered by the external organization of the Catholic Church in Germany, a "monstrous infringement of the law" (Treitschke). The fact that the Church was financially dependent on government support to carry out its work emphasized still further the state church system. Nevertheless, at one stroke certain abuses which had been steadily mounting were done away with (e.g. accumulation of offices, incorporation of parishes). The way was clear for new organizations to come from the faithful themselves, with new ideas being propounded first in little groups, and later in societies and mass movements.

As long as the Empire lasted, that is, until 1806, ideas of the Catholic reorganization that would have to take place centred round the notion of a concordat for the Empire ("Reichskonkordat"). The Prince Primate, Freiherr von Dalberg, Archbishop of Mainz and Bishop of Constance, who was in favour with Napoleon and in a position to influence the course of events, advocated such a concordat. But when negotiations began in Vienna and Regensburg irreconcilable opposition emerged. Later concordat discussions which the nuncio, della Genga, was conducting with individual South German states were thwarted by the pressures Napoleon was exerting for a separate concordat (after the French model) for the Confederation of the Rhine, which had been founded in 1806. When the Congress of Vienna brought about a political and ecclesiastical settlement in central Europe by means of a Restoration, Consalvi, the Cardinal Secretary of State, did indeed manage to achieve the restitution of the Papal States, but, although he had the backing of the "Orators" of the former ecclesiastical princes, Dean von Wambold of Worms and Canon Helfferich of Speyer, worked in vain for the restoration of the empire and the return of confiscated Church property.

Advocating a national Church, the Vicar General of the Bishopric of Constance, Ignaz Freiherr von Wessenberg, suggested that the German Church question might be solved by the creation of an ecclesiastical head who would hold the office of German Primate. By a concordat with the German Federation, a "German Church" would be legally set up and would have only a loose connection with Rome. But the diplomats of the Curia were opposed to Febronian elements in Wessenberg's scheme. Thus Catholic reorganization took the form of separate concordats with various territories.

7. TERRITORIAL CONCORDATS

The first such concordat to be concluded was that with *Bavaria*, on 5th June 1817. This was made possible by the dismissal of the anti-Catholic Minister, Count Montgelas, and was negotiated by the Bavarian envoy to the Holy See, Kasimir von Haeffelin. It secured for the Catholic Church retention throughout the kingdom of all rights and prerogatives which were based "on divine ordinance and on canonical regulations" (Art. 1.) The bishops of the two Bavarian ecclesiastical provinces, Münich-Freising and Bamberg, being themselves nominated by the Catholic King and receiving canonical institution from the Pope, were to have unlimited power of administration in their dioceses, spiritual jurisdiction, superintendence of schools, direction of diocesan seminaries (in accordance with Trent) and free access to Rome. The King promised to allow the suppression of books offensive to the Catholic faith. The Bavarian Concordat was an attempt to act yet once again as though a purely Catholic state was a possibility. No account was taken of the fact that Protestant areas such as Ansbach-Bayreuth were included, nor of the fact that internal movement of industrial labour was bound to lead to more mixing of the confessions. Although the Bavarian Concordat remained in force until 1918, it was not, in fact, workable, because it failed to accord with the real situation with regard either to the state or to schools. With the conclusion of the Concordat there was an outcry among Protestants

and liberal Catholics, and the Bavarian Government reacted by publishing too late the terms of the agreement as an appendix to an Edict
on Religion, which itself was bound up with the new constitution of
26 May 1818. In this, the royal "Placet" and the "recursus ab abusu"
were retained, the old state church situation revived and civic and
political equality guaranteed to the major confessions. In the eyes of
Rome this was deviation from the terms of the agreement; Bavarian
priests refused to take the constitutional oath unconditionally. The
royal declaration of Tegernsee of 15th September 1821, which followed
discussions with the Curia, was an attempt to iron out the contradictions.
At the height of the Catholic Restoration in Bavaria under the ministry
of Abel (1837–47), the clauses of the Edict of Religion which related
to the state church ceased in practice to be applied.

Prussia had in fifty-three years acquired so many Catholic areas that
two-fifths of the population under its Protestant crown were Catholic.
Various factors had contributed to this: the War of the Austrian Succession.
the partition of Poland, the act of secularization and the Congress of
Vienna. The General Law (Allgemeines Landrecht) of 1794 allowed every
citizen "complete freedom of faith and conscience". But now a discreet
manipulation of the royal prerogative was giving rise to a situation in the
new Catholic territories which threatened the disintegration of the Church.
Negotiations of eight months' duration, conducted in Rome by the
historian Niebuhr, as Prussian envoy, and Consalvi,[1] produced an arrangement which was set out in Pius VII's Bull of Circumscription of
16th July 1821, "De salute animarum", and was published by Frederick
William III, "without prejudice to his rights of majesty", as the law of the
land. The Prussian national newspaper commented thus: "The form
of a bull which has been subject to negotiation is to be preferred to a
concordat, because the King would not wish to make the exercise of his
rights of majesty dependent on foreign recognition."[2] Prussia avoided
getting involved in the machinations of the state church system and gave
cathedral chapters the right to elect bishops. Nevertheless, the papal brief,
"Quod de fidelium", directed chapters only to elect persons who they

[1] There was a great deal of discussion at the consultation in Berlin on the instructions to be given to the envoy concerning negotiations with the Curia. At this,
Werkmeister's observations on the Bavarian concordat were made use of. Niebuhr
himself was critical of church policy in south-west Germany and dissociated himself
from it. The newly founded See of Cologne was the most important in the kingdom;
the Bishop was Count Spiegel.

[2] The mode of election of the bishop was the most difficult point of the negotiations. Consalvi proposed the "Irish veto" (reduction to three candidates). Prussia did
not wish to relinquish the royal veto on an unacceptable election. The real extent of
government influence on the cathedral chapter is given in detail in the memorandum
sent by the Minister of Culture, V. Mühler, to Bismarck on 31st August 1865.

were satisfied would not be "minus gratae" with the King. Niebuhr's point of view is expressed in the closing sentences of his "Memorial": "It is not the Government's intention to create a dozen popes in their own territories but rather to let the Roman court keep them in order. To be concerned about independence is understandable among Catholics, among Protestants it is absurd."

In Schleswig-Holstein, under the national laws of Denmark, the Catholic faith was not permitted and the Bishop of Osnabrück (1858) and, indeed, even Pius IX himself (1860) had appealed in vain for relaxation of this prohibition. But here, the tolerant attitude of Prussia opened the way for unrestricted Catholic development, by virtue of a joint ordinance of the Austrian and Prussian commissioners on 23rd April 1864. When Schleswig-Holstein was annexed on 1st October 1867 the provisions of the Prussian constitution came into effect.

The *south-west German territories* held out longest against the standard development of Catholic life which took place in the nineteenth century. From Constance, Wessenberg poured out a stream of ideas. In 1809 he had introduced a German order of service, in 1812 a book of hymns and devotions which even included poems by Gellert. He had enjoined preaching. In his view, "form without spirit is an abhorrence to Christianity". In the seminary for priests at Meersburg, Wessenberg occasionally took classes himself in order to produce "spirituality to be respected for its scientific proficiency and moral worth". His pastoral conferences served the same end. He sent young priests to schools founded by his friend Pestalozzi, and put their knowledge to work in new boys' seminaries. Founding on the early Fathers, he got the laity to study the Bible and also had a Catholic translation distributed. He manipulated canon law so as to allow a gradual relaxation of the law of celibacy and even consecration of mixed marriages.

Yet because Wessenberg's reforms were embedded in a state church system they incurred the hostility of Ultramontane Catholicism which was on the increase,[1] and sowed the seeds of death into the life of the Church. Döllinger was to witness the result of this development in the course of his journey to Baden after the Revolution of 1848. "In no part of Germany has religion been so persistently undermined and the Catholic Church so

---

[1] When Irish emancipation, the self-determination of Belgium, and de Lamennais's Ultramontane propaganda were setting the tone in Europe, the ecclesiastical policies of the governments forming the church province of the Upper Rhine were looked on with suspicion. There was talk of subjugation of the Catholic Church in Germany. An article on this by Moy appeared in the "Memorial". Pius VII, in an encyclical of 30th June 1830, reproved the pusillanimous attitude of the bishops of the Provence of the Upper Rhine. The reproached bishops attributed the Brief to French and Belgian zealots.

systematically disrupted as in Baden. This has been brought about by total regimentation, over even the most specific and trivial matters, or rather by the complete subjugation of the Church by state officials, high and low, which is so abundantly evident."[1]

Also to be considered along with Wessenberg's kind of Catholicism is the fact that in 1818 representatives of the states of Würtemberg, Baden, the two Hesses and Nassau met in Frankfurt and made a joint "Declaration" intended for the Curia, passing an "Organic Statute" which had been tentatively discussed in secret.

The Febronian spirit pervading these documents made negotiations with Rome difficult. In 1821 with the Bull of Circumscription, "Provida solersque", Pius VII constituted the ecclesiastical province of the Upper Rhine with Freiburg as the archiepiscopal seat and with separate suffragan bishoprics for each of the small states. Difficulties with the Curia ensued over the selection of episcopal candidates, upon whom the government, on their side, wanted to impose an oath relating to the Organic Statute, now rewritten as the "Pragmatics of the Church". Wessenberg had been appointed episcopal administrator for Constance in 1817, and, although his appointment was quashed by the papal brief, "Ob gravissimas causas", he was retained in office by Archduke Charles of Baden. But Rome withheld ratification when he was elected Archbishop of Freiburg and later Bishop of Rottenburg. It was not until 1827 that the see of Freiburg could be filled—by Bernhard Boll—and the bishopric of Constance dissolved.

In *Switzerland,* during the period 1803–1816, the nuncio's office under Testa Ferrata had constantly served as a convenient depository for complaints against Wessenberg.

Sharing the desire to check Wessenberg's influence even in Catholic Switzerland, Pius VII dissolved the Swiss parts of the diocese of Constance and made new circumscriptions. But the ideas of Josephinism and of a state church were by no means dead. In 1844, when Lucerne let the Jesuits take over the teaching of theology there, the Liberals organized an expedition of volunteers against that canton. The seven Catholic cantons thereupon formed a defence alliance, but this simply led to the War of the Separate Alliance, which ended in 1847 with their defeat. After the adoption of the Federal Constitution in 1848, the Jesuits and kindred orders were forbidden to maintain settlements in Switzerland.

---

[1] Döllinger discussed the topic at the third Katholikentag in Regensburg. He saw two reasons for the death of the state church in Baden, the corruption of public education by the teachers at seminary schools, who destroyed the faith of those entrusted to their care. Hence a decline in vocations. Hundreds of parsonages had been empty for years. The second reason was the introduction of a "church council" alongside the bishop, which appropriated episcopal powers and left the bishop with little more than a shadow of episcopal authority. Hence the alienation of the clergy from the bishop.

In pre-revolutionary *Austria* late Josephinism remained normative, but more because of the reformed Catholics' concern for inner renewal than because of the omnipotence of the state church. Coming at the end of the wave of concordats in the first half of the nineteenth century, Austria got its Concordat on 18th August 1855, when anti-liberal forces under Pius IX and reaction to the events of '48 were at their strongest.

Negotiations were conducted on the Austrian side by the Archbishop of Vienna, Cardinal von Rauscher, who was one of Clemens Maria Hofbauer's circle and who enjoyed great influence as the one-time teacher of the Emperor, Franz Joseph. It was he who carried through the liquidation of Josephinism. Political circles hoped that the Concordat would enable Catholic unity to serve as cement for the multi-nation state of Austria and that in foreign affairs it would set the Empire on the road to becoming the leading Catholic world power. In repitition of Article I of the Bavarian Concordat, the Catholic Church was given all the rights "in toto Austriae Imperio" which belonged to it by God's ordinance and by canonical regulations, and following on this the concluding articles revoked such laws of the state as contravened the "teaching of the Church or its present practice as approved by the Holy See". The extent of Protestant and liberal Catholic rebellion against the Concordat is indicated by the words of Franz Grillparzer: "Catholicism is responsible for it all. Give us two hundred years of Protestant education and we would be the first nation on earth. But as things are, our only aptitude now is for music and the Concordat." The 77-year-old warrior had himself carried into the Upper House for the session on 21st March 1868, so that, leaning on the arm of Count Auersperg (the poet Anastasius Grun) he could vote against the Concordat. Auersperg said at that time that the Concordat was a "Canossa in print", in which nineteenth-century Austria had to "do penance in sackcloth and ashes for the Josephinism of the eighteenth century". The state was forced to substitute for the Concordat a unilateral piece of legislation which let it be understood that its intention was to follow the path of a liberal constitutional state. After the proclamation of infallibility, the government revoked the Concordat.

CHAPTER VI

ROMANTICISM, RESTORATION AND CATHOLIC RENEWAL

The fascinating thing about the change in spiritual outlook which occurred in the Catholic Church and gave it new strength is that it was free of any conscious confessional assertion, taking place in the open atmosphere of the literary world and not as a result of bishops' orders or theologians' arguments: it was the outcome of the spiritual destiny that was Europe's.

The new sensitivity which sprang up after 1770 all over Germany had its effect in brightening the spiritual life of a number of Catholics at Münster. Reaction to the guillotine, the English statesman Burke's analysis of the Revolution, which became influential in Germany through Gentz's translation, the discovery of the "harmony" of the Middle Ages, the approach to mystery from the side of aesthetics—all these factors contributed to the creation of a typical "generation" which found its identity in critical debate with the Enlightenment and with a common vision of the society of the future. The Catholic Church did not create this generation, but this generation created for itself a renewed Catholic Church.

I. THE ROMANTIC GENERATION

In 1799 the first discoveries were made from which the change in the spiritual climate and the unforeseen renewal of the Catholic Church were to stem. A Frenchman living as an émigré in London, the Vicomte de Chateaubriand, put pen to paper on his influential work, *Génie du Christianisme*. Two years previously, a paper he had published on revolutions, ancient and modern, had caused a scandal in émigré circles in London because of its anti-Christian and politically sceptical emphases. But in 1798 the torture taking place in prisons and the execution of his relatives in revolutionary France made such an impression on him that he was converted, and Chateaubriand's present work was to be by way of reparation. As in a vision, he saw: "The last and highest stage of atheism is when one wants faith but can no longer grasp it." For Chateaubriand, religion is awe in the face of the mysterious. Here, from a Frenchman, for the first time, the anti-rationalist accents of Romanticism are to be heard. He returned to Napoleonic France in 1800 and published, as a sample, a chapter of his book (*Atala*) which brought him fame overnight. The complete work appeared in 1802, and at this time fitted in well with Napoleon's Concordat policy. With his *Génie du Christianisme*, Chateaubriand did not indeed bring about any Catholic renewal, but he did regain for Christianity the interest and sympathy of the élite. His method was not that of logical argument, but rather to commend the Christian religion by means of human criteria. It was, "the most poetic, the most human, the one most favourable to freedom, art and the literary life". From there, however, he went on definitely to justify Catholic dogma. "O enchanting dogma", said Chateaubriand of the Virgin Birth, "which tempers the terrors of God by interposing beauty between true majesty and our nothingness."

In the same crucial year, 1799, Wackenroder, a north German Protestant, was on a journey to Bamberg when he wandered into a Catholic church and there witnessed a Lady Day celebration. Out of this experience there grew a new Protestant openness to things Catholic, which is reflected in the Romantic first work of Wackenroder and Tieck, *Herzensergiessungen eines kunstliebenden Klosterbruders* (*Meditations of an art-loving Friar*). With Novalis, brought up as he had been in the pious atmosphere of Herrnhut, the aesthetic appeal of the Catholic Church was equally strong, the Middle Ages, which had been so despised by the Enlightenment, were elevated to a place of honour, and the attempt was made to justify Catholic teaching. The Popes' rejection of the Copernican system was to be excused on the ground that they were only trying to safeguard respect for man's heavenly home. Novalis also had criticisms to make of Luther: "He misunderstood the spirit of Christianity and introduced another emphasis, namely, the sacred authority of the Bible, and this had the unfortunate result that another, quite alien, earthly science became confused with matters religious, namely, philology, the decadent influence of which has since been unmistakable." Nevertheless, it appeared to Novalis that historical Catholicism could be superseded by a new and universal Catholicity.[1]

Romanticism in Germany led more quickly than that in France to important decisions being taken in favour of the Catholic Church. Under the influence of the Redemptorist, Clemens Maria Hofbauer, various Protestant Romantics in Vienna were converted: Freidrich Schlegel, Zacharias Werner, Adam Müller.[2]

[1] K. Barth, *Die protestantische Theologie im 19. Jht* [2]303–42 (E.T. *From Rousseau to Ritschl*, London, 1959, 225–67).

[2] The fact that Leibnitz's *Systema Theologicum* had been published in 1819 in terms of the literary bequest of Emery (the MS. having been sent to him in Saint Sulpice from Hanover), and that this work was thought to be "Catholic at heart" strengthened the impression that the Protestant world was moving towards Catholicism and underlined the importance of the Romantics' conversion. Goethe was disgusted at Schlegel's conversion: "Sonst buhlt er mit Lucindchen, Jetzt möcht er mit Marien sund'gen" ("Little Lucinda he used to court, now with Mary he'd resort"). It is incorrect to link the conversions of these Romantics with Stolberg's conversion in 1800. The Count

2. THE SOCIAL CIRCLES

Intimate circles—social creations of the time—were particularly well suited to the new Catholic life.[1] The first, and exemplary, group was that which formed the "familia sacra" of Münster.

In the summer of 1779 Princess Amalie Gallitzin, the daughter of Schmettau, settled in Münster. In 1774 she had withdrawn from society, in which she had shared the station occupied by her husband, the Tsarist ambassador in the Hague, and in her concern for the proper education of her two children took up afresh investigations into matters spiritual. When she had exhausted the resources of Hemsterhuis, her Dutch spiritual confidant, she chose as her new adviser the Freiherr von Fürstenberg, who was the administrator of the chapter at Münster, and whose educational reforms had drawn her attention.

When Fürstenberg's reforming activities in politics came to a sudden end in 1780 with his enforced demission from office, he retired and devoted himself entirely to the work of educational reform and to acting as spiritual confidant to the Princess.

Amalie Gallitzin's forcefulness is apparent from the influence she exerted on her friends—having played Diotima to Hemsterhuis she now played Egeria to Fürstenberg. She was later to strive after a relationship of a similar sort with Sprickmann. Her "divine amitié" gave the Münster circle and its symposia a compelling power. As spiritual director, the Princess picked a country vicar, Overberg, whose skill as a teacher Fürstenberg had discovered in 1784 when he had secretly attended his catechism class in the village church of Everswinkel, and whom he forced to come to Münster so that he could make him a "teacher of teachers".[2] It was in the Princess's library that Hamann got to know the writings of Sailer and began to use his prayer-book for his daily devotions. When he died in 1788 the Princess arranged that he should be buried in her garden.

---

from Holstein left the state church with its "neological" perversions because in its narrowness it did not correspond to his ideas of a Lutheran Catholicity. Within the Catholic Church, Stolberg followed neither the way of Hofbauer nor that of the Tübingen School. He remained an individualist. Very different was Friedrich Schlegel. He abandoned his idealist point of departure.

[1] Apart from the groups referred to there were similar "Romantic" circles in Kassel (round Radowitz) and in Mainz, Coblenz, Aachen, Düsseldorf, Bonn, Cologne and Breslau.

[2] Anna Gallitzin felt herself drawn by the course in religious instruction which Overberg gave every Sunday afternoon in the Convent of the Lotheringian Ladies. In 1786 she went to him for confession. In 1789 she asked him for spiritual direction and induced him to move into her house in the Grüne Gasse.

When the Holstein poet, Count Stolberg, who had hitherto lived as a pietist, visited the Münster circle for the third time in 1800, he was received into the Catholic Church by Overberg in the Princess's oratory in the Grüne Gasse, then demitted office at Eutin under the Grand Duke of Oldenburg and settled permanently in Münster. In this conversion did the Princess play the part of the serpent (Voss)? Was this a case of "fishing for souls" (Sauer)? Did Stolberg in truth not really know the Catholic Church (Grand Duke of Oldenburg to the Tsarina)?[1] In any event, with the help of the ecclesiastical historians at the University of Münster (which Fürstenberg had founded) Count Stolberg went on to complete his *History of the Religion of Jesus Christ*.[2]

Princess Gallitzin also took into her care the four Counts Droste-Vischering, who, with Katerkamp as their tutor, were studying in Münster. Thereafter she combined the education of her own children with that of the young counts from Westphalia.

The specifically Catholic nature of the light that shone from the Münster circle increased about 1790. This is not to say that, if Stolberg's conversion is left out of account, anyone underwent a dateable, dramatic change. To Jacobi the Princess acknowledged that she had come to the faith by following the teaching of Christ: "Try it, and you will discover if this teaching of mine is of God." This kind of Catholic piety was influenced by the Enlightenment inasmuch as disputes over details of dogma were alien to it. No attempt at interim solutions of problems was ever made: they accepted the traditional facts and strove for religious perfection in the realm of the personal. Christian community was for them realized

[1] Stolberg's conversion was in Goethe's words an unbelievable sensation: Voss rejected Stolberg's farewell visit to Eutin, Jacobi saw in this an act of madness, Goethe's analysis was that Stolberg had never had any confidence in himself. Freiherr vom Stein tried to be fair in his assessment, Claudius and Lavater claimed that his decision was a personal solution.

[2] The *History of the Religion of Jesus Christ* (New German edition, 1952) was basically a joint project of the "familia sacra". The object was to oppose rationalism ("as if the depths of the divine wisdom could be sounded with the lead of human reason"), but also Spinozism, which "endows every stone and every drop with divinity". This book introduced the French theologians to the spiritual movement of German Romanticism. Stolberg brought important elements directly from his background of Lutheran piety to his understanding of Catholicism, especially the concept of revelation, as a possibility resting solely on the mercies of God and being mediated through the "Divine Charter" of scripture. "Divine charter and holy tradition (unite in the Church) in the topmost curve of the arch"—Stolberg's literary work was thus of interest to the Protestant reader as well. It was by design that a Lutheran, Perthes, Claudius's son-in-law, was chosen as publisher. By 1826, 8,000 copies had been produced. But in 1829 Perthes was to discover that times had changed. The *History of Religion* was now regarded with suspicion by Catholics. The archiepiscopal Vicariate-General in Vienna opposed its distribution. "Good priests tell me that they dare not recommend it in public. The time in which faithful Protesants and faithful Catholics feel at one in their faith is coming to an end."

in their symposia, for they were convinced that with the meeting of ideas new light would emerge.

While the Enlightenment prevailed in the electorate of Cologne and in its university at Bonn, Fürstenberg kept the academy at Münster, which was also administered politically from Bonn, in an unwavering Catholicism fortified by the resources of the "familia sacra".

What would *Paris* have been at the time of the Restoration without the salon of Mme Svetchine? This little Russian convert had been won over in 1815 by Jesuits working among the nobility in St Petersburg, and when her Jesuit fathers confessor were expelled on the Tsar's command she took the road to Paris with them, de Maistre having previously written recommending her to de Bonald! Mme Svetchine's salon became a focal point for the life of society in the capital. To it went the gifted young priests who were to renew Catholic France, de Lamennais, Lacordaire and Prosper Guéranger. Despite her conversion, elements of Eastern piety continued in Sophia Svetchine and through her made their way into Catholic France. Following the Russian custom, Mme Svetchine set up a private chapel, and how pleased the most important priests of the capital were to act as celebrants there![1]

The theologian Johann Michael Sailer became the focal centre of the circle at *Landshut*. After the demise of the Jesuits, it is with him that the first re-encounter of the Catholic Church with German culture takes place. His moral teaching owed much to Kant, his philosophy of religion to Jacobi and his educational theory to Pestalozzi, but in his work this is not obvious, since he avoids quotation from non-Catholic authors. His friendship with Protestants like Matthias Claudius, Lavater, Savigny, Anna Schlatter and the princely family of Stolberg-Wernigerode made for increased mutual understanding and respect. Sailer must be regarded as much more than a typical Enlightenment figure, as modern research admits. It was precisely for this reason that he was able to transcend the Enlightenment in Catholic Germany. Through his connection with Ludwig I, he influenced the Catholic restoration in Bavaria, for which the Concordat had merely provided a legal framework. "The Bavarian clergy", wrote Sailer in his biography of Zimmer, his Dillinger friend, "is now particularly before my eyes and in my mind, because in these very days there is taking place the restoration of the Catholic Church in the kingdom of Bavaria, for which we have to thank the wise generosity of our King and the inexhaustible fervour of the Holy Father. . . The archiepiscopal and episcopal sees are occupied, the senate of the higher clergy in the Cathedral chapters is filled. The Catholic peoples are watching

---

[1] S. Bolshakov, *Russian Nonconformists*, 1954. Döllinger did not neglect to visit the salon of Mme Svetchine during his visit to Paris in 1839.

Bavaria and waiting with laudable impatience to see if the spirit of the Great Apostle moves among the Bavarian clergy with new power . . . The fulfilment of this expectation depends on whether the priests now emerging have the ability to combine knowledge *and* faith,—faith *and* divine love, love *and* active obedience . . . Yes, my beloved, be spiritual men in a spiritual manner."

At the University of *Munich* (which had been transferred in 1826 from Landshut to the Bavarian capital), Ringreis had been installed as Rector by Ludwig I, and managed in the appointments he made to build up a circle whose strength lay in being a real community. It was Görres who gave the lead.[1] He opened the eyes of Ignaz von Döllinger[2] to the possibilities of development which were open to the Church in the modern world. The converts, Jarcke and Phillips, became influential in Görres's circle, and under their anti-Protestant inspiration, Döllinger attempted to provide a reply to Ranke's history of the Reformation. He was highly skilled in the analysis of doctrinal systems and would have been attracted to dogmatics if he had not been so conscious of the inferiority of Catholic as against Protestant scholarship in the historical field. But Döllinger's method was not to write history so as to present a disinterested, historical picture, but always to extract from history arguments to support current theses—and during the first thirty years of his academic life these arguments were always favourable to the Catholic Church.

[1] On 2nd July 1828 the periodical *Eos* was taken over. The influence of Görres' article "Mirror of the Times" was, according to Diepenbrock, indescribable. "One of the first divine warnings, which interrupt the revels. It is as though one were reading an ancient, oiled, handwritten parchment scroll of Isaiah and saw the present time through the transparent skin." It appeared that the influence of *Eos* would increase. Yet, in September 1828, when a member of this circle, von Schenk, became Minister for Internal Affairs, King Ludwig gave the instruction, "Let Edward von Schenk take counsel with God and be independent; let him pay no heed to congregationalist insinuations."

[2] The "Historisch-politische Blätter" in particular show an anti-Protestant emphasis, due to the influence of converts. On 19th January 1842 Jarcke wrote to Döllinger: "Protestantism is going through a strange crisis." The "Blätter" were to form a dam against the flood of Protestant pietism. Döllinger's *Die Eucharistie in den drei ersten Jahrhunderten*, 1826, was a reply to Protestant history of dogma, especially to its aim of demonstrating a constant change in dogma. Döllinger's object was "to demonstrate the perfect consistency of the Catholic conception of doctrine with the faith of the Early Church". A reprint of *Die Reformation* (1846-8) is in preparation (1962). The "Eichstädt confederates", a group opposed to Wessenberg, joined up with Görres's circle. The Münich circle was given the nickname of "Congregation", after its French counterparts. Döllinger's controversy with Heine, who "has neither religion nor country", was characteristic of the Münich group. Heine took revenge on the Congregation ("The Romantic School"); cf. his poem "Einem Abtrünnigen" ("To an Apostate"), 1848.

3. GERMAN UNIVERSITY THEOLOGY: HERMES, GÜNTHER, "THE TÜBINGEN SCHOOL"

While theological studies and the education of priests were at a low ebb in France and Italy,[1] Catholic theology in the German universities was entering its period of great achievement. The new theology inherited the rationalists' contempt for scholasticism.[2] The systematic reconstruction of Catholic dogmatics, using the tools of thought of German idealism, was attempted by Hermes at the University of Bonn and Günther at the Vienna Censorship Office—in the latter's case only by his writings, since the Josephinist bureaucracy would not admit him as a professor at the University.

Georg Hermes had been introduced to psychological, critical methods by his teacher, Ferdinand Überwasser, S.J. Truth, according to the traditional Catholic conception, consisted in the conformity of knowledge with that which is known. In truth of this kind, all men are interested. It is this appeal to human "interest" which gives Hermes' system its specific character. In its entirety, it is characterized by psychologism, radical and decisive. All way of knowing in which philosophers and theologians have tried to find the certainty of objective truth are, on critical reflection, shown to be unreliable and open to question. The way thus becomes open for a "cogito ergo sum", radically psychologized. "What I hold to be true may, in itself, be true or false: when I find that I *must* hold it to be true and that I have no alternative, then for me it is and remains true. What I cannot doubt, I *can not* doubt. Any guarantee of its truth is superfluous for me, and any evidence against its truth is as far as I am concerned ineffective." The basic principle of Hermes' thought is, then, the notion of reality as "what we are directly convinced of in ourselves". There can therefore be no theoretical proof of the truth of revelation. Its content can only consist

---

[1] Lamennais bitterly criticized the state of education in French seminaries. The French bishops hoped that the state would set up a centre for higher ecclesiastical studies. When all hope of this was destroyed by the Revolution of 1830, Mgr Affre founded on his own initiative a study centre in the Carmelite monastery. This development did not escape the sagacious Newman, even though it began modestly in 1845 with only six students. Lavigerie in 1850 was the first doctoral candidate. Cf. Leflon, *La Crise révolutionnaire*, 482f. Lord Acton testified that Döllinger had little love for the French clergy, but more for the laity. "There we perceive what is lacking in Italy, a powerful body of laymen." But in France there was no school of scholars. As a result, the clergy were being shut up in isolation. In Rome, theological studies were in a state of stagnation. Meignan, the future cardinal, complained in 1846 that Roman theology had no interest in what was going on round about it. There was little acquaintance with rationalism. The Austrian, Flir, was, in 1854, astonished at the total absence of what in Germany was called scientific method.

[2] With the exception of Gerbert of St Blasien, the theological world was insufficiently acquainted with scholasticism, and that mainly the late variety of Suarez.

in an extension of reason's knowledge of God. Revelation is a short-cut, by-passing the normal and natural way of understanding. In Hermes' system, faith in revealed truth is an act of understanding in which Kantian ideas are reflected in a manner which is almost comic: as "practical reason" comes to the aid of "pure reason" when the latter is incapable of discovering what is moral, so in the Bonn theologian's system the heart's faith comes to the aid of the mind's faith when the latter is incapable of perceiving its object.[1]

Günther was a man imbued with German idealism who had, however, been brought to a knowledge of redemption by Clemens Maria Hofbauer. He understood man in a dualistic sense, as a being with two souls, one rational, the other perceptive. This led to a double theory of knowledge, which enabled Günther to include even the mysteries of the Trinity and the Incarnation within his system. His concept of God was also dualistic. "God-Subject" is to be distinguished from "God-Object". The consciousness that God-Subject has of Himself represents the First Person of the Trinity. The consciousness that God-Object has of His equality with God-Subject forms the Second Person. The consciousness which the Second Person has of this equality with the First Person forms the Third Person. In this way the human mind can demonstrate scientifically the truth of the mysteries, and, as science advances, can penetrate them more and more. While the Tübingen School were transforming Catholic theology into a philosophy of history, Vienna's attempt at reconstruction took the form of speculation in the manner of German philosophy.

Günther saved a whole generation of young Catholics from Hegel's understanding of religion. In the eighteen-forties he was much in favour with Cardinal Schwarzenberg, who had been a student of his, and with not a few members of the episcopate. His students took over teaching posts, even in Prussia where it suited the government to appoint them rather than Hermesians, which would have led to trouble with the Catholic authorities, or men connected with Archbishop Geissel, which would have strengthened the opposition. The part the Güntherians were in a position to play in the Catholic movement of 1848 led them to start publishing their own journal, Lydia.

The achievement of the Tübingen School (Drey and Möhler) was that they brought to reflection on Catholic dogma a highly developed sense of its historical dimension.[2]

<hr />

[1] J. Leflon, op. cit., 473f.
[2] Ibid., 472. Since apologetic motives were involved—the unbroken chain of discoveries of patristic texts and the critical investigation of tradition which this made possible had to be rescued from rationalist and Protestant interpretation—the Tübingen

In his examination of the history of dogma, Drey introduced the idea of organic development. "The Father, the Councils and the decisions of the Popes manifest the collective intelligence of the infallible Church, which is brought to bear on revelation and which lets the divine seed ripen without ever letting it become parched."

4. THE BEGINNING OF THE AGE OF ECCLESIOLOGY

The nineteenth century as the age of ecclesiology really began when Sailer and Benedikt Stattler parted company. Initially, Sailer had followed his teacher, Stattler, in defining the Church in sociological categories. It was to be understood according to the laws of nature, as a construct of human society, and so its juridical and hierarchical elements were to be stressed. The Enlightenment's individualistic understanding of man had brought things to the point that the collective was always thought of in the first instance as simply the outcome of agreement between individual believers.[1]

Influenced also by the mysticism of men like Lavater and Claudius, Sailer went on to become the first to take up the Pauline idea of the Church as the Body of Christ, whose members form a community filled with grace and compassing heaven and earth.[2]

Johann Adam Möhler's early work, *Unity in the Church from the Mind of the Early Fathers* (1825)[3] was really the first infusion of patristic thought into the Catholicisim of the Romantic period and was stimulated by the work of Neander, the Protestant Church historian in Berlin. This affected

---

school directed itself more towards history than to systematic speculation. This very development produced a crisis in the school when the wave of neo-scholasticism poured over from Rome. The sphere of Tübingen's influence spread when Hirscher and Staudenmaier went to Freiburg. Staudenmaier opposed the Hegelian philosophy of history with a Christian theology of history, which demonstrated in history the living and free activity of God progressively proceeding from revelation. The Catholic verdict on Hirscher: "A priest of glowing piety, but with a quixotic brand of intelligence."

[1] Thus Stattler and Sailer.

[2] The new understanding of the Church did not at the same time influence Sailer's theology and overcome his individualism and moralism. Yet in the second edition of his *Pastoraltheologie* of 1794 the parish is viewed in a new way derived from his concept of the Church. A further advance was made in the third edition of 1812.

[3] J. A. Möhler, *Werke: First new critical edition by J. R. Geiselmann*, Cologne, 1957ff. (impeded by the loss of two-thirds of the sources in the Second World War). Leflon, op. cit., 472 (Lit.). Leflon's verdict on Möhler is uneasy: There were tendencies here which led to modernism. In the German school we are dealing with scholars rather than doctors of the Church. Möhler had himself written about his first book that this work of his enthusiastic youth contained many propositions which needed correction (Leflon, op. cit., 474f.).

the concept of the Church. For a whole generation of Catholics,[1] Möhler rediscovered the mystical Church behind the structures of the juridical Church. It was at this moment that the limitation of the concept of the Church to what was purely juridical (a limitation introduced to Catholic ecclesiology by Bellarmine in the Counter-reformation struggle) was once more broken through—and this was to have important consequences. Through his influence on Vilmar, Möhler affected Lutheran ecclesiology as well.[2] The first three centuries were understood, as they had been in classical theology, as the period of history in which the concept, "Church", had emerged into fullness. To this was added the Romantic idea of a community, determined by the Spirit and forming its organs as it develops. If the Church is the creation of the Spirit, then it can accommodate individuality and yet achieve perfect community. So Möhler's inexhaustible structure had been understood as organs of that organism, divine-human and developing visibly, "the Church".

Cyprian's formula, "the church in the bishop", was taken up again and the hierarchical forms of Church government once more became susceptible of a mystical interpretation. Thus an episcopalianism was presented which, as yet untroubled by Ultramontane questions, could look on the papal primate in the Febronian manner as "centrum unitatis", while avoiding the illegitimate use to which this theory had been put by the Josephinists with their notions of state absolutism.

Möhler's *Unity in the Church* already developed a concept of "heresy" which brought together Catholic absolutist claims and an idealist philosophy of history. From Drey, his teacher at Tübingen, Möhler had learned to think of history in terms of Schelling's concept of antithesis. He now turned to Hegel's understanding of history as advance from thesis (i.e. Catholic dogma) through antithesis (i.e. heresy) to a synthesis in which Catholic dogma is recovered after heresy has performed its function on it. Catholic claims to absolute truth prevent a thorough Hegelian relativization of the (Catholic) thesis and the (heretical) antithesis: in heresy, evil is at work. "Heresy, as something outside the Kingdom of God, has no proper

---

[1] Ignaz Döllinger still testified to this in 1879: "The warmth and sincerity which emanated from this book enchanted all of us young men. We considered that Möhler had recovered out of the debris and overgrowth of later times a fresh and living Christianity. There was held before us the goal of a Church freed from defects and abuses, as close as possible to the ideal of the Early Church.' Möhler influenced Döllinger's work (in 1826) on the Eucharist in the first three centuries. Sebastian Merkle understood Möhler's early writing as being in opposition to de Maistre's book *Du Pape*. He claimed that on his return from his student travels, Möhler followed the initiative of an older friend, G. Herbst, who had published (in the *Th.Q.* for 1822) a sharp review of de Maistre. Geiselmann rejects this theory.

[2] Vilmar was encouraged to plan his *Theology of Events* through reading Möhlers' Symbolics.

being. Like evil, it is mere negation, merely there to bring to clearer and clearer consciousness that which really is."

This concept of heresy, a mixed theological and philosophical construct, is also dominant in his "Symbolics" of 1832, the crown of his creative achievement. Here, for the first time in Catholic theology, differences in Catholic and Protestant doctrine were compared in systematic fashion.[1] A salutary objectivity could be claimed for it in that Möhler excluded all "subjective" expressions of doctrine and confined himself to consideration only of "public statements" of the two confessions.

As a student of Drey, for whom a fact could only be understood scientifically when it was presented in its necessity, Möhler in his Symbolics insisted on expounding individual points of doctrine only within their total context of interdependence. The reason why, for example, the Protestant Church *had* to understand justification in the way that it did understand it could never be grasped merely by setting out actual differences of doctrine. Möhler's constant concern was to understand Protestantism and Catholicism in their basic principles.[2] He stood in the line of systematic thinkers of German philosophy whose claim was to comprehend everything in an inviolable system.[3] His intention was to show how a basic

[1] Behind Möhler's attitude stands the moving (at the instigation of Württemberg government in 1817) of the Catholic faculty of Ellwangen to Protestant Tübingen with the hope of amalgamating the two confessions. Instead of a merger the changed atmosphere gave rise to a conscious controversy with Lutheranism. As a theological student in the Catholic Wilhelmsstift, Möhler was well acquainted with the confessional problem. Kling, "Repetent" of the Protestant "Stift", knew him well enough at that period to report: "Even then he began to steep himself in the source material of the Reformation." Möhler's technique was to serve the cause of unity by the most vivid presentation of opposing elements. In his preface Möhler emphasizes "that for years at all German Lutheran and Reformed universities" lectures on confessional problems had been given. Thinking this to be a highly useful practice, he had decided to introduce it into the Catholic area as well. Möhler's critical discussion of G. B. Winer's *Comparative Presentation of the Doctrinal Teaching of the Various Church Parties* (1824) hinted that he would not be content with a mere recital of the detailed doctrinal differences, but tried to show their "necessity" in terms of the basic principle of the different confessions. In his discussion of the Anglican Bishop Milner's "Aim and End of Theological Controversy" (*Th.Q.*, 1828, 346) Möhler emphasizes that the matters of controversy had been handled more deeply by German theologians in detail, but that there was no German work which outlined the controversy as a whole. Hence, Möhler was interested in the entire picture. Up to 1900 his Symbolics went through twenty-five editions, including fourteen translations. Here relations between European Catholicism and the Protestant world were fixed for the nineteenth century. With the foundation of the Johann-Adam-Möhler Institute in Paderborn in 1957 Möhler's approach was realized again. Greek Orthodoxy's understanding of the place of confessions in Protestant Christianity was also influenced by Möhler.

[2] J. A. Möhler, *Symbolik*, ed. J. R. Geiselmann, Cologne 1958 (E.T. *Symbolism*, London 1843).

[3] By contrast, the Reformation century differentiated points of doctrine which were controversial from those which belonged to the general consensus. Möhler's systematic thinking now had the effect of bringing to light antitheses in areas of teaching which had not been previously thought of in terms of controversy.

idea "was reflected in every detail and permeated the whole as well as its parts". In his "Symbolics", Möhler traced a line from the anthropology of Lutheranism to its ecclesiology, and throughout, the same basic Lutheran error is to be seen. It had to do with doctrine concerning Adam's original state: his state of favour before God was understood not as something supernatural but as something essential;[1] to deny freedom to fallen man was to remove all responsibility from him,[2] and the doctrine of original sin was so sharpened that man's very nature seemed corrupted and "the capacity for God with which he was created and which was proper to his nature" was deemed to be lost.[3] According to the Lutherans, the true image that was begotten in man was that of the devil.[4] Accordingly, even re-birth could not wipe out original sin from mankind.[5] Whereas Catholics could account for the transition, even in fallen man, from original sin to actual sin by man's exercise of freedom, in Lutheranism all personal sins consciously committed were seen only as manifestations of original sin, like the boughs, branches, blossom and fruit of a bad tree.[6] With the Lutheran view of the obliteration of the image of God in man's nature, God could only act in a mechanical way towards man. From the time of Adam to Christ there could really be no discussion of sin, and all moral evil became changed into something physical.[7]

While Möhler saw the process of rebirth as being accomplished by divine and human activity ("The holy power of God comes first and inspires, but man must follow freely"), he reproached Lutheranism for conceiving man as "utterly passive". In terms of timing, man must first be brought by the preaching of the law to the point of despair, then God would declare him righteous, even though, in fact, the sinner was not, Then, in an unconnected way, sanctification began.[8] The moral difference existing between the old man and the new man was presented as something gradual, not an actual difference at all.[9] Lutheran polemics were "incoherent" in that on the one hand the real and therefore effective presence of Christ in the Church was maintained, on the other hand it was maintained that this Church had fallen away from Him.[10] With

[1] Ibid., 64.
[2] Ibid., 56f., 75.
[3] Ibid., 100f.
[4] Ibid., 107.
[5] Ibid., 110.
[6] Ibid., 111f.
[7] Möhler broke new ground in that he demonstrated, on the basis of material on the history of religion then available, the different attitudes of the confessions vis-à-vis paganism.
[8] Ibid., 138ff.
[9] Ibid. The eschatological aspect of consummation present in Lutheranism was quite unknown to Möhler.
[10] Ibid., 320.

Romanticism, Möhler interpreted the Reformation as being the forerunner of the French Revolution.[1] His "Symbolics" also included Reformed and Anabaptist teaching so as to show that everything was to be laid to Luther's charge. "Only when his own ideas came back at him from the mouths of others did he discover how untrue and dangerous they were".[2]

Möhler's "Symbolics" had an irenic purpose. But his philosophical-theological concept of heresy forced him to work out as sharply as possible the differences between Protestant and Catholic thought. Only when it was recognized how great these differences were could a fresh start towards unity be made.

5. THE RESTORATION AND POLITICAL PHILOSOPHY IN FRANCE

The émigrés returning to France brought back a new vision. In 1797 the Comte de Provence, the Pretender to the throne who up till then had been a philosophical sceptic, wrote in a message to the bishops: "I want the priests to foster in my subjects the royalist spirit and at the same time the religious spirit, that they may be convinced of the inner connection that exists between altar and throne and of the necessity of the mutual support of the one by the other." The formula, "Throne and Altar", was to become decisive for Europe.[3] The men of the Restoration were to display an exemplary faith. Even if secretly they were admirers of Voltaire, they would still solemly follow the most intricate ceremonial. There thus developed a "clericalisme sans Dieu". When political power fell exclusively into the hands of the émigré nobility, this had its parallel in the Church.[4] Of the ninety bishops installed in fifteen years, seventy came from

---

[1] E. Burke was the first to suggest this. "The present revolution in France is a revolution of doctrines. The last revolution of doctrine which has happened in Europe is the Reformation." Cf. "Thoughts on French Affairs, 1791", W.W., IV, 1899, 318. J. A. Möhler, op. cit., 27 (Geiselmann's Introduction), gives citations for the interpretation of the Reformation as revolution: Novalis, Baumgardt, Franz von Baader, Adam Müller, Friedrich Schlegel, Görres. Möhler could say that Luther would have seen no hindrance to uniting his dogma with the Catholic Church: "It seemed to him to be more honourable as father to command than as son to obey" (ibid., 384).

[2] Ibid., 321f.

[3] When Pacca visited the army of occupation in Coblenz he could state how dechristianized the French emigré nobility had become. But some were beginning to return to the Church, the most sensational conversion being that of the Count of Artois. This indicates how the rechristianization of this level of society is already intermingled with class interests. Cf. Leflon, op. cit., 328.

[4] Della Genga's failure to prevent the agreement between state and Church in 1814 provoked such a rebuff from Consalvi that when Della Genga later became Pope, Consalvi was at once disgraced (Leflon, op. cit., 282). Louis XVIII replaced Napoleon's Ministry of Culture with a Church Committee with new members led by Bishop Talleyrand-Perigord, who had supported him during the emigration. Emissaries were sent to the individual bishoprics. The desire was simply to reinstate the pre-concordat

the nobility. Mgr de Quelen, the Archbishop of Paris, was typical: effemi-
nate looks, graceful movements, good company. A sermon he preached in
Notre-Dame revealed the importance he attached to a good background:
"Jesus Christ was not only God's Son, he was also of very good family on
his mother's side, and there are good reasons to think that he was the heir
to the prince of the throne of Judaea." The fact that Joseph was a carpenter
was an embarrassment to be glossed over. Mgr de Quelen drew up a programme to "thin out" the episcopate. He made the Duc de Rohan Vicar
General of Paris the very day after his ordination as a priest, purely because
he was the bearer of one of the great names of France. (Six years later, the
Duc de Rohan became Archbishop of Besançon and a cardinal, with an
oratory hung with silken tapestries).

The parish clergy produced by the Restoration had little connection with
the spiritual life. This made it easy to fill the seminaries again. The Napoleonic era had not brought enough new blood into the French clergy, which
had previously been drained dry. Between 1802 and 1814 there were only
6,000 ordinations. Under the "ancien régime" that had been the number of
ordinations every year.[1] Renan, however, described the spiritual climate of
Saint-Sulpice when he was a seminarist as "like being compassed about by
three thousand miles of silence". Lamennais gave a fierce account of his
experience: "Never was the clergy, taken as a whole, so uneducated as it is
today, and yet never was true knowledge more necessary." This was the
origin of the great gap between the Catholic Church and modern culture,
the bridging of which was later to require such strenuous efforts.

The French Restoration provided the theoretical basis for the Ultramontanist movement of the nineteenth century. Inspiration came from
two political philosophers, Count Joseph de Maistre and Count Louis de
Bonald. The concept of "Tradition", which had hitherto been understood
in Catholic theology as a source of divine revelation alongside scripture,

---

bishops. Della Genga was working in the same direction. But Rome observed that
this group of nobles was not to be shaken from its Gallicanism, and accordingly
slowed down the Restoration in France. The settlement of 1816 signified only that the
Concordat had ceased to be effective. Since political circles feared a restitution of the
property in mortmain, the King made the proviso at the time of subscription that the
agreement would not affect the Gallican freedoms. Because of this the Pope refused to
ratify it. In the compromise text of Count Blanca, the Organic Articles were revoked
only in so far as they were at variance with canon law. New opposition to the agreement between Rome and Paris came from the jurists of the state council, who claimed
that a vote in the chamber was constitutionally necessary. Crown rights in the Gallican
sense were validated. The prospects for the future appeared to be entirely unsettled.
Count Portalis, therefore, brought the Concordat of 1801 into operation again
(Leflon, op. cit., 329ff.).

[1] In 1821 the French educational system was brought under clerical control, in
the first instance the universities, higher and secondary education. Primary education
followed in 1824.

was secularized and reinterpreted politically. A contrast was drawn between ("legitimist") tradition and (revolutionary) reason, between the community and the individual (as understood by the Enlightenment). In the new plan for society political organization required authority, in a pyramid-like structure, and the authority at the head of this structure was to be secured by the authority of the Pope. De Maistre, who was Sardinian ambassador in St Petersburg from 1802 to 1817, was the author of the manifesto of Ultramontanism ("Du Pape"). In view of the worldwide spread of the Church, it had to have a monarchical form of government. The Pope's decisions must not be open to question and must therefore be thought of as infallible. The fact that historically the papacy had undergone changes was no proof against its divine origin. "Everything that is lawful and is to exist for hundreds of years exists first as seed and then develops." Secular sovereignty and papal infallibility were to be thought of as parallels. "No human community without government, no government without sovereignty, no sovereignty without infallibility".[1] The dogma of papal infallibility is here postulated on the basis of political psychology.

De Bonald, whose assessment of the Revolution was to the effect that it had been the realization in society of the abstract philosophy of the Enlightenment, intended his counter-revolutionary ideas and his political collaboration with the Restoration to be used to help overcome what amounted to metaphysical distintegration.[2] He therefore himself took the philosophical concepts of the Enlightenment and gave them an inner dialectic. Reason is reduced to the ability to give things linguistic expression, its truths are equated with the truths of Christian revelation, which in their turn are equated with a monarchical and Catholic ordering of society. The "volonté générale" is identified with the will of God, and is seen represented in the possession of power which is given in history. It was this adaptation of the idea of God to express a social function that made it possible later to replace the word "God" altogether. The complete system with the political, religious and family organization given it by history forms a whole from which nothing might be removed. Throughout, de Bonald exhibited the short-circuit methods which are typical of Restoration thinkers.

There is a characteristic difference between philosophers of the French Restoration and the Catholic social philosophy of German Romanticism:

---

[1] Vigener makes this judgment on de Maistre, that he knew how to take just as much out of theology and the Church as could be systematized with romantic-absolutist ideas. How little the Roman Church associated itself in the long run with the Restoration philosophers was shown by Cardinal Rauscher's warning at the time of the Vatican Council against the "argument of a laymen (like de Maistre) whose talent is more seductive than reliable".

[2] M. H. Quinlens, *The Historical thought of the Vicomte de Bonald*, Washington 1953.

the French supply the theory for a new political system, on which they have decided. Because of this, they are accused by Schlegel (in *Signs of the Times*, 1820) of "partisanship". German Romanticism, aiming at something more exalted, evaded any political decision and became "the servile accomplice of alien decisions".

6. RESTORATION CATHOLICISM IN GERMANY

Mainz was prepared for the special role it was to play in German Catholicism by the fact that it had shared in the fate of the French Church. Bishop Colmar and Liebermann, the theologian, had been "réfractaires". At Mainz, a "colony of confessors" was formed and their experiences in France were communicated first-hand to their German students.[1] They were convinced that it was the dissolution of the Jesuit Order that had been responsible for the Revolution. Hence the openness of Mainz to the order when it was re-established.[2] Like the whole of Napoleonic France, Mainz immediately conformed to the Restoration. The seminary at Mainz had been founded in 1805 as a seminary for French priests and as such had been pledged by Napoleon to the Gallican Articles. When Napoleon fell, it was released from this dogmatic shackle. The Grand Duchy of Hesse now had jurisdiction over it, but it had no experience in the field of ecclesiastical politics and found itself for the first time having to cater for areas with a Catholic population. After 1814, Liebermann who was the director of the seminary, could preach the reverse of what he had originally been pledged to in 1805. Two of the products of his seminary were Weis and Räss, the founders of the Mainz *Katholic* (1821).

In Mainz, Catholic reaction to the Lutheran tercentenary celebrations of 1817 was even more vigorous than it was in München. Liebermann launched a literary attack and Bishop Colmar ordered the reprinting of Bishop Zirkel's work, *The German Catholic Church, Germania, 1817*.

That de Maistre himself had a direct influence in Germany cannot be maintained. It was Schlegel who first called for a German translation of his works. After his newspaper *Konkordia* had ceased publication and the "Literary Annuals" of Vienna had become the organ of the converted Romantics, Schlegel tried to use it to draw attention to de Maistre. Similarly, the *Katholik* of Mainz gave de Maistre publicity. In 1822, the first translation—by Moritz Lieber—came out. Immediately, however, the new system of thought was opposed by the *Tübingen Theological Quarterly*: it contained only "the foolish declamations of a dilettante".

---

[1] Later on, Liebermann, too, built up contacts with his native Strasbourg.
[2] Mainz enlarged its stock of theologians by receiving the first students to finish at the Germanicum in Rome.

Baron Eckstein challenged Schlegel's high estimate of de Maistre; "the Church is not an absolute monarchy à la Louis XIV". When agreement was lacking, tradition ought not to be imposed upon by any absolute will.

The ideology of the Restoration only penetrated Germany with the enthronement of Gregory XVI and the publication in 1833 of new Italian and German editions of his early work, *Il Trionfo della Santa Sede*, which he had written in 1799. The *Katholik* immediately commended the Pope's book and the Bavarian bishops called for its distribution. This created a breach in the anti-curialism of the Germans. The Viennese edition which Perrone published in 1842–3, with its emphasis on the infallibility of the Pope, superseded the Manual of Doctrine written by Liebermann, who, like Overberg, Stolberg and Diepenbrook, had represented infallibility as belonging only to the Church and not to the Pope. It was the Münich canonist, Philipps, who provided the theoretical basis for the emerging restatement of relations between Church and state.[1]

7. DE LAMENNAIS, A VISIONARY

With the July Revolution of 1830, the Catholic Church discovered the extent of the chasm that had opened up between itself and the bourgeois world of culture in France with its scientific and technological developments. Heinrich Heine wrote at that time from Paris that religion was dead and already decomposing. Most Frenchmen spoke of it as if it were a corpse and, when the conversation turned to the Church, politely held their handkerchiefs to their noses. Casimir Périer, the Prime Minister in 1831, told a priest: "The time is coming when you will be left with only a tiny number of grey-haired old men." Victor Cousin, the official philosopher of the bourgeoisie, taught that philosophy was patient. Happy to see almost all mankind in the arms of Christendom, it would be content gently to offer it its hand and help it to lift itself even higher. Everything pointed to a tedious period content to leave unanswered questions alone. The French Government and the Curia treated each other with respect.

[1] De Maistre, too, was now more acceptable in Germany. Klee's *Dogmatik* (1835) referred to him under the section on "Infallibility of the Primate" as expressing a view "very well worth attention" which was "not to be condemned so frivolously and scornfully." Gregory XVI's *Triumph of the Holy See* was published in a third German edition in 1841. The Jesuits attacked in 1841 with Weninger's book *The Apostolic Authority of the Pope in Matters of Faith*, which, though classified in the Münich *Archiv für theologische Litteratur* as worthless, appeared in a second edition in 1842. At the same time Kaiser launched the controversy on infallibility in the Münich theological faculty. In 1846 infallibility was firmly established in Vol. II of Philipps's *Canon Law*. But Döllinger in his lectures of the same year was teaching: no personal infallibility. As a private person the Pope can err. The view that the Pope was infallible when taking decisions on his own had tradition against it. This thesis was directly opposed to Philipps's *Canon Law*.

It was at this time that one man took it upon himself to root out the problems: Abbé Félicité de Lamennais, the visionary of the nineteenth century. He drove a sharp plough through the soil of Catholicism in France, and the result was that the next generation was able to reap an unexpected harvest. In de Lammenais's house at La Chênaie, a new generation of Catholics came together, held by the logic of his arguments: Lacordaire, Guéranger, Count Montalembert, Gerbet. In 1828 this élite band of pupils formed themselves into the "Congrégation St Pierre".[1]

Completely new ideas now sprang up, ideas which were Ultramontane and liberal at the same time. It was the Pope who had the right to nominate bishops. Contemporary bishops who did not consider themselves dependant on the Pope were "tonsured lackeys". For de Maistre, an infallible papacy had been the final point guaranteeing the entire legitimist system. For de Lamennais it was the starting-point for the renewal of society: "Without the Pope, no Church, without the Church, no Christianity, without Christianity, no religion and no society; so true is this that the life of the nations of Europe has its sole source in the power of the Pope." The monarchy, with its compromising actions, paying the Church from the same coffer as the theatre, was attacked. In trying to use the Church for its own ends, it committed treason against it. So Lamennais demanded freedom for the Catholic Church. The monarchy was also oppressing the people. Now, when two parties are subject to the same oppressor, an alliance is created. The theocratic ideal of Romanticism remained, but the instrument which was to bring it about changed: Lamennais said that the parties which must unite were no longer papacy and monarchy, but papacy and people.

This new teaching brought repercussions both in the episcopate and in political circles. Nevertheless, it was justified by the revolution of 1830. De Lamennais now went further. "Break for ever with these people who, if they had the upper hand, would debase your altars until they became nothing more than a throne."

Three months after the July revolution the first number of *L'Avenir* appeared. The starting of this paper was the hour in which liberal Catholicism was born. Its sub-title was "Dieu et la Liberté". Lacordaire, who had been in the liberal opposition during the Restoration, was on the editorial staff. Of himself he said: "I have arrived at my Catholic convictions by way of my social convictions. Since the Christian religion is the only means

---

[1] Leflon, op. cit., 478ff., also considers Lamennais's Christian concepts to be "essentiellement sociologique". L. believed in the imminent transformation of society. In this radical change it would be valuable to preserve a "consentement universel". Through their belief in the same things, existing humanity involved in the change should preserve its Christian unity. In French research there is still radical disagreement on the view to be taken of the Liberal Catholics.

of bringing society to fulfilment, it must be divine." As a priest who was both a liberal and a controversialist, Lacordaire had been shelved by Mgr de Quelen. He was on the point of emigrating to the United States when he met de Lamennais and came to realize the new task that lay before him.

The young Romantic, Montalembert, read the first number of *L'Avenir* while he was on a journey to Ireland. He immediately offered his services to the editors and took over the reporting of foreign affairs. The young editors called for freedom in every form: freedom of religion by the separation of Church and state, freedom in education, freedom of the press, freedom of association (even for congregations), electoral freedom and regional freedom.

In a Catholic programme such as this, the claim for freedom of religion was truly revolutionary. De Lamennais knew that Catholic doctrine could never allow freedom for evil; but in a situation in which the religious unity of the nations was broken anyway and the powers of state were in a position to impose an ideology, he considered freedom to be the best guarantee of independence for the Church. In an open conflict, truth could be relied on to conquer. There were many opponents for whom the proposal that the Church should abandon the financial budget provided for it by the state was intolerable. But which was the greater sacrifice, money or freedom?

The editors of the *L'Avenir* had such a strong sense of mission that they not only wrote, they took action. They got together the paper's friends to form the "Agence générale de la liberté religieuse", as a group prepared to act and contest arbitrary measures in court.

As a protest against the state's monopoly in education, in May 1831, despite the existence of a ban, they opened up a school, in the Rue des Beaux-Arts. On the opening day Count Montalembert gave a lesson in grammar to fourteen children and Lacordaire taught religious instruction. In the afternoon the Commissioner of Police served notice, and the next day the school was closed. At the trial in the Criminal Court which followed, Montalembert took the opportunity of making a great speech and Lacordaire attacked the educational policy of the University as being intolerable as far as the Catholic Church was concerned. It was only many years later that French Catholicism realized that it had to engage in a crucial struggle over the question of schools.

For the Catholic élite, nothing was more stimulating than debating the *L'Avenir's* proposals. The episcopate, however, with its legitimist outlook, was already worried by the fact that there was a "Usurper" on the throne, and could not countenance the idea that a priest should be working for an alliance with those who, in their opinion, wanted to destroy the Church. Cardinal Rohan began by banning the paper. Seminarists who read *L'Avenir* were refused ordination. By the autumn of 1831 the editors had reached the end of their financial resources, and the only way out of their predicament that they could see was to appeal to the Pope.

It was probably the three young editors' lack of experience that made them think that the Holy See would support them against the solid ranks of the French episcopate. But Gregory XVI was too thirled to the Restoration to have been able to take up the concern of the editors of *L'Avenir* with their proposal for an alliance between Church and people. He was the Pope, in fact, who had denounced the Polish rising of 1831, even though it had the support of Catholic forces, on the ground that it was revolt against a prince. He was the Pope who, when Belgium rebelled in 1830 because it was Catholic and broke away from Protestant Holland, refused it a Vatican chargé d'affaires until 1842. On 28th February 1832 Cardinal Pacca conveyed to Lacordaire the reply to the memorial he had submitted, and this was to the effect that the Holy Father permitted him to return to France, there to await the examination of his teaching. De Lamennais and Montalembert insisted upon a papal audience. This took place on 1st March, but it was in the presence of Cardinal Rohan, their declared enemy, and their reception was far from cordial.[1] De Lamennais should not have been treated with such coldness. He set off back via München, and it was while he was attending a soirée there that de Lamennais received the encyclical of condemnation, "Mirari vos". On 10th September the editors of *L'Avenir* officially announced their submission. This was a blow which went to the heart of Catholic Romanticism in France. Though de Lamennais died an apostate, he is nevertheless one of those who by their unseen, intellectual influence, have served to inspire Catholicism up to the present day. The power which forced his condemnation, legitimist Catholicism, finally struck again when the "action française" was condemned by the Pope in 1927.

8. MONASTIC AND LITURGICAL RENEWAL

The monastic and liturgical movement which began in France in 1833 provided a refuge within the Church for a disillusioned generation of Romantics. To understand the new situation, one must bear in mind the destruction of monastic life which Josephinism and the French Revolution had brought about. On 13th February 1789 the Assemblée Nationale had passed a resolution dissolving all the Orders. The number of Benedictine monasteries alone which were destroyed in France

---

[1] At that time, because of the revolutionary situation in the Papal States, the Pope needed the support of the great powers, who were disturbed by de Lamennais.

amounted to 691. The Concordat had avoided discussion of the future of the Orders, but in 1807 Napoleon had permitted the Sisters of Charity to resume activities. Because of the uniformity they observed and which could be controlled and because of their social utility, they were encouraged by the Emperor and were soon to spread all over the world, becoming numerically the strongest congregation of nuns.[1]

The Jesuit Order was reinstated in Russia in 1801, in the Kingdom of the Two Sicilies in 1804, and finally, in line with the Restoration, it was reinstated throughout the Church in 1814 by the bull, "Solicitudo omnium ecclesiarum". It began to acquire a new importance under the generalship of Roothaan (1829–53). Its influence vastly increased under General Beckx, who got on better with Pius IX than Roothaan had done.[2]

The new beginnings of monastic life as the life of meditation actually date from 11th July 1833, when Prosper Guéranger and three companions took up residence in the Benedictine Abbey of Solesmes, the buildings of which had been deserted for forty-three years. Solesmes was not far from the city of Sablé, where Guéranger was born. Opponents of the new settlement spoke of "apocryphal Benedictines". Nevertheless, when Guéranger went to Rome in 1837 he managed to get Gregory XVI to give official recognition to the new community—no mean achievement considering that he was thought to be a pupil of de Lamennais. In 1862 Dom Maurus Wolter incorporated the Benedictines of Solesmes in Beuron, which had been reconstituted.

The recommencement of monastic life at Solesmes also saw the beginning of a Catholic liturgical movement. The community of monks restored a liturgical pattern of life. For this, the abbot demanded "complete understanding of the mysteries". He was not content with a kind of fulfilment that was merely formal. This liturgical life was to radiate

---

[1] At the accession of Ludwig I there were still twenty-seven monasteries in Bavaria. Under von Schenk the number rose by sixteen, under Wallenstein by forty-one. It had previously been said that Bavaria was a refuge for darkness. Under Abel the number of monasteries increased in ten years by another seventy-seven. By the time of King Maximilian's death in 1864, 441 monasteries had been founded. Under the ministry of Lutz, who was hostile to the Church, the female orders undertook the education of girls. Three hundred and fifty-one more new monastic houses were started.

[2] Ludwig I had a positive attitude to the admission of Jesuits into Bavaria. First, Bavarian nobles sent their children to the Jesuit college at Freiburg. In 1840 the first proposal to lift the ban on Jesuits in Bavaria was made. In 1841 the Bishop of Passau proposed to permit Jesuits to come to Alt-Ötting as preachers to the pilgrims, but even this was still refused by Ludwig. In a letter of 14th March 1843 the King commented on the exaggerated claims made by Jarcke as to the value of the Jesuits as educators ". . . as if young men could be handled like dough". In 1839 an application was made by the Jesuit party in Switzerland for permission to teach at the Theological Institute at Lucerne. The text of Möhler's anti-Jesuit lectures of 1831 was published by Leu in Lucerne in 1840, with the anti-Jesuit passages omitted.

through the society of the nineteenth century, effecting its renewal.[1]

At Solesmes, Dom Guéranger completed two works which were to serve as programmes for the liturgical movement: "Les institutions liturgiques" appeared in 1840, "L'année liturgique" in 1841.

The Jansenists had tended to regard religious ceremonies as external matters of form. If they lacked a biblical basis, they were changed. For this reason, the "Salve Sancta Parens" and the "Gaudeamus in Domino" had been removed in the Archbishop of Paris's missal. Responses and antiphons were discontinued. Also, a rationalizing trend had prevailed. Thus, because at a private mass only one person is present, the plural "Dominus vobiscum" was altered to the singular "Domine, Exaudi orationem meam". Traditional hymns were replaced by compositions in contemporary style. According to Gallican episcopalianism, it was the individual bishops who had authority over the liturgy, and bishops had put their own personal ideas into practice in their own dioceses.[2] But for Guéranger the ceremonies were what expressed the continuity of tradition.[3]

The principle of liturgical unity corresponded to the visible unity of the Church.[4] Guéranger therefore insisted upon adhering to the Roman

[1] Whoever was received as a guest into the community of Solesmes carried thenceforth through life a nostalgia for this liturgical paradise. Remarks in a letter from the young Montalembert convey some indication of this. "Especially in November and during Advent I find my love for you increasing; for during these two beautiful months of the year you introduced me into the beauties of the liturgical year." Priests who gained their experience at Solesmes took the liturgical life to other places. Abbé Pie, the future Bishop of Poitiers, wrote to Guéranger in 1841: "For some time I have been so convinced that our century must be led to the liturgy to become Catholic, that I have exerted myself greatly in my little environment, and I am thinking of preaching all winter on the saints, angels, reliquaries, feasts, services, churches and the bells."

[2] As a result of the new division of bishoprics after the Revolution, the existence of most diverse luturgical notions side by side in the amalgamated dioceses had become highly disturbing. In the diocese of Langres five different liturgies were in use; in the dioceses of Versailles and Beauvais there were respectively four and nine breviaries and missals.

[3] O. Rousseau, *The Progress of the Liturgy*, Paris, 1945, (E.T. Westminster, Md., 1951). In 1830, when the *Memorial Catholique* gave Guéranger his first opportunity of publishing, he commented ironically on the Abbé le Boeuf's notation of the Paris antiphon and gradual, that le Boeuf, after he had spent ten years putting notes on the lines and lines under the notes, had made the clergy of the capital the gift of a dreadful composition. God wanted to make men feel that there were things that were not to be imitated because they could never be changed. For Guéranger there was an inspiration in liturgical forms, which the historicity of the liturgy did not, however, remove. The Church, like the father of a family, drew from its store treasures old and new and fitted them judiciously to the needs of every age. It was a dangerous error to believe that the discipline of the first four centuries must have been so complete that it would be impossible in the future to touch it without destroying it (*Considération sur la liturgie catholique*, 1830).

[4] Guéranger attributed the schisms of the ancient and medieval Church to the fact

order of mass, which he had got his superior's permission to use in 1828. In France, Gallican-Jansenist trends had disrupted the liturgical unity which Trent had introduced, and as a result only twelve out of more than a hundred dioceses had retained the Roman liturgy. But by 1851 Jules Morel could write in *L'Univers*: "In ten years, Guéranger has seen ten dioceses bring back the Roman liturgy." A year before Guéranger's death, the last diocese to do so, Orléans, accepted the liturgy of Rome.[1] Guéranger's "L'année liturgique" was responsible for awakening spiritual appreciation of the cycle of the Christian Year. The French abbot looked upon the circular course of the astronomical year as the means which God had chosen to weld the eternal mysteries into time. Through the liturgical cycle "the Church renews her youth, because she is visited by her Bridegroom". In his meditation on St Gertrude he declares: "There are some souls who are so affected by the divine succession unfolded in the Catholic cycle that they manage to experience its progress physically, whereupon the supernatural life absorbs the other, and the Church's calendar absorbs that of the astronomers." It was as a result of French inspiration that Maurus Wolter, at Beuron in 1864, compiled his Book of Gertrude (a translation of the exercises of St Gertrude), which made possible daily devotion following the rhythm of the Church's year and the introductory passages of which led to a new kind of practice of piety in Germany.[2] The Brussels musicologist, Fétis, had discovered that Gregorian music had in the course of history undergone a change in its notation, and this started a controversy over the original form. This gave rise to anarchy in the field of liturgical notation. In 1856 Guéranger got one of his monks, Dom Paul Jausions, to make a special study of the question, and the outcome of this was to confirm that the manuscripts testified to an integral tradition existing up to the sixteenth century. Solesmes and Beuron, which for the

---

that "Rome was unable at the proper time to bind these distant provinces to those of European Christendom with the twin bond of a common speech and a universal liturgy". Guéranger viewed Church history from the angle of the struggle with the "anti-liturgical heresy", expressing itself in iconoclasm, the Reformation, and Jansenism (the Protestantism of France). By destroying the forms, the anti-liturgical heretics rejected the contents of faith. Guéranger engaged in a controversy on this with Lacordaire, who wanted to maintain that only "failure to agree with the Church makes heresy" (O. Rousseau, op. cit.).

[1] The suppression of the Gallican liturgies removed at the same time elements of the ancient Gallic liturgical tradition. The present-day French liturgical movement has a nostalgia for material from the old tradition.

[2] *L'année liturgique* was translated into German after 1875, and later into Italian and English (*The Liturgical Year*, Worcester, 1895–1903). The Paris *Freemasons' Journal* commented on this work: "Voila un oeuvrage qui fera autant de mal, que les contes de Voltaire ont fait de bien".

time being had been at odds, arrived at unanimity once more on the basis of the old notation.[1]

9. THE PRIESTHOOD AND NEW INTEREST IN RELIGION

One of the consequences of the terror at the time of the Revolution was that it was the Catholics of Lyons, who had to endure special suffering, who emerged as leaders in spiritual renewal. The men of the "clandestinité" came to the fore.[2] The Seminary of St Irenée produced a new generation of priests, of whom Jean-Baptiste Vianney,[3] the pastor of Ars, and Louis Querbes,[4] the founder of the Clercs de Saint Viateur, were typical in that to them striving for holiness was an essential part of the pastor's task. The mortification which they practised was of such rigour that the Widow Bibost, who had gone with Vianney to Ars in February 1818, eventually fled from his rectory. The Revolution and the trials of war had left Ars without a priest. Vianney, who got to know his parish as a peasant knows his field, had good reason to declare: Leave a parish without a priest for twenty years and they will be worshipping the blessed cattle. The spiritual feats by which the pastor of Ars wrenched the people from the power of his adversary, the "grappin" (grapnel), were accomplished in the confessional. From 1840 on, Ars was besieged by pilgrims. They had to provide special transport to give access to this remote village, and diocesan missionaries had to be installed. Vianney himself attributed the grace that was being received to a hitherto unknown Neapolitan martyr, St Philomena, whose relics he had been given.

Ars demonstrated for the first time that the backwardness which for the nineteenth century was typical of village life in contrast to the progress of urban life could bring credit to the Church.

In Italy the priests of Piedmont showed special apostolic zeal in resisting the strident anti-clericalism of the nationalist movement. Don Bosco is witness to the arrival of the age of specialization in the Church. He concentrated on a single problem, the plight of the neglected youth of

[1] A gradual, published by Pustet of Regensburg, seemed, especially after Pius IX declared it to be authentic in 1873, to be determinative for future musical development in the Catholic Church. Yet at a congress of church musicians at Arezzo in 1882, Solesmes proved strong enough to enter into open conflict with Pustet. The brief of 17th May 1901 finally brought recognition to the Benedictine line.

[2] Linsolas, Ruivet, Ricorbet.

[3] F. Trochu, *The Curé d'Ars*, Colmar 1944 (E.T. London 1955); W. Nigg, *Great Saints*, London 1948. In 1862, as an extension of the poor little church of Ars, which was the focal point of Vianney's life, the church of St Philomène was built. From there Thédenat inspired the "national pilgrimages" in 1871.

[4] To the same group belong Champagnat, Colin and the future Marists, also L. Furmion, the founder of the "adoration perpetuelle du Sacré-Coeur". Querbes's achievement was to mobilize support from the laity for the Christian attitude to education.

Turin. But he pressed this problem home so forcibly on his contemporaries that they gave him their assistance in what was truly a magnificent achievement. In effect, Don Bosco was a clerical version of the typical figure of the age of the entrepreneur, reckless but shrewd. In 1856 he started the Valdocco educational institute, which was to exert a worldwide influence on education and which became the model of more than five hundred similar institutes. In 1855 he started the first "holiday home". It then became clear to him that he would have to found a congregation to form a body of teachers for the young people who were being neglected. The obvious name to give this congregation was "Salesians",[1] since François de Sales was the national saint of all the subjects of the House of Savoy. Don Bosco's educational method was characterized by creating the closest possible relationship of trust between teacher and pupil, a helper system to secure a family atmosphere, drawing out of the young people a cheerful sense of joint responsibility and letting them understand the reasons for any punishment they might incur.

The nineteenth century's loss of uniformity and the concurrent working of opposing trends can be seen in the realm of Catholic spirituality. On the one hand, the Bollandists resumed publication of works of criticism and ecclesiastical history was rewritten by the Catholic Church historians of Germany, using the standard critical method of the universities; on the other hand, there emerged an uncritical openness towards all things mystical. (For example, in Germany, Görres's work on mysticism, Brentano's edition of the Visions of Katharina Emmerich and its distribution by the Redemptorist, Schmöder.)[2] Liguori's Mysticism of the Cross was recommended by the Roman congregations and circulated far and wide, being introduced to England by Faber of the London Oratory.[3]

---

[1] A. Auffray, Un grand Éducateur, St. Jean Bosco, Lyon/Paris (6), 1947 (E.T. Blessed John Bosco, London 1930).

[2] Katharina Emmerich, visionary and bearer of the stigmata, was received into the convent of Agnetenberg in 1802, and after its suspension in 1811 remained as an invalid in private lodgings for a long time. She had suffered haemorrhages from 1798, and after 1812, in the course of ecstasies, two small crosses appeared on her chest and a larger stigma, corresponding to the forked cross at her birthplace of Coesfeld, which also featured in the visions, also the marks of the nails. Since 1899 the process of her beatification has made little progress, because of doubts cast on the reliability of Brentano's report. Since Chapman in 1928 the Catholic Church has been veering back towards a supernatural interpretation (H. Thurston, The Physical Phenomena of Mysticism; and Surprising Mystics, ed. J. E. Crehan, 1955, 38ff.; Leflon, op. cit., 472).

[3] Frederick William Faber, an Oxford man, joined Newman in 1836, discussed Tractarianism with the poet Wordsworth, became a convert soon after Newman and was sent by him to London in 1849 to found an Oratory. His entire literary output appeared in the seven years after 1853. It alternated in intention between the theological and the devotional, and represented a Roman type mystical piety. Cf. R. Chapman, Father Faber, London 1961; also his edition, F. W. Faber, Growth in Holiness. London 1960.

Authors like the Abbé Gaume defended the legendary on the principle that anything that had been traditionally believed was to be accepted if it helped to foster piety.[1]

From Romantic sources came a passion for anything associated with the Middle Ages: pilgrimages, processions, veneration of saints and the relics of saints, Marian devotion. At Solesmes, Guéranger tried to train monks who would resemble as closely as possible the monks produced by the Middle Ages. To Count Montalembert he wrote: "Do join me in working to re-create without any fuss a miniature version of our beloved Middle Ages." Montalembert set about compiling a collection of Lives of the Saints. Ozanam and Faber did the same. Pius IX took a personal interest in the fast-growing practice of veneration of St Joseph and eventually, in 1870, proclaimed him patron of the worldwide Church. Former popes had indulged in canonizations only sparingly, but now they were carried out with great show.

From the middle of the century priests became more conscious of the need, through disciplined prayer, to make the supernatural world their dwelling. The laity began to take part in retreats organized by the Jesuits, which followed the pattern laid down by General Roothaan ("De ratione meditandi"). They did not, however, manage to go back to using the original exercises of Loyola.

10. THE ULTRAMONTANE EXPERIMENT IN GERMANY: THE COLOGNE CHURCH CONFLICT AND GERMAN CATHOLICISM (DEUTSCHKATHOLIZISMUS)

The Ultramontane movement also flourished in Germany, where the more the bishops' influence declined in individual states the more they tried by way of compensation to establish a closer connection with the universal episcopate of the Pope. Two situations show Catholicism in Germany achieving self-consciousness and gaining its political orientation. These were the Cologne Church Conflict in 1837 and the dispute with "German Catholicism" (Deutschkatholizismus) in 1844—a challenge from two directions at the same time, from above and from below, as against absolutist sovereignty and as against liberal, bourgeois society.

In the western territories, which had been united with Prussia in 1815, matters came to a head over the question of mixed marriages between parties of different confessions. Protestant officials and officers stationed in these Catholic territories frequently married into local families. In the

---

[1] Gaume argued in support of the most incredible legends, which Mabillon and and the Maurists had explained a century earlier.

Rhine Province, the Code Napoléon was still in operation and this gave the father, by virtue of his parental authority, a free hand in determining the religious upbringing of his children. The self-conscious Catholicism of the west succeeded not infrequently in forcing Protestant fathers to promise to bring their children up as Catholics. In Westphalia, the "General Law" had been introduced, also in 1815, and this provided that in the case of mixed marriages sons should follow the religion of their father and daughters that of their mother. The situation became critical when, on 17th August 1825, Friedrich Wilhelm III issued a cabinet instruction extending to the Rhine Province and Westphalia the application of a royal declaration of 1803 designed originally for the situation in Silesia. Under this, children born in wedlock were always to be brought up in their father's religion. Suspicions were aroused among the Catholics, and not entirely without reason. In fact, the text of the order had been submitted to the King by the ministry with the comment that it would provide "an effective measure against the proselytising methods of the Catholics." Cases of Protestant men marrying Catholic women would certainly be more frequent than the reverse. Protection of their religion had been promised to the Catholics of the west in the Letters of Occupation of 1815. The question now was whether this cabinet instruction was in breach of the royal promise. In the Catholic opposition sociological motives were also at work: the leading families wanted to protect themselves and their property from the consequences of marriages with Prussians, and they exploited religious difficulties for social and political ends. The resulting confusion appears from what a priest named Reinerz wrote on 7th December 1825 from Krefeld to his Archbishop, Count Spiegel of Cologne: "Whatever is going to happen to Catholicism in our country, with Protestant officials swarming over like bees from the old provinces to the new, marrying their way into the most distinguished and wealthiest Catholic families, devouring the Catholics' religion, thanks to the cabinet instruction, and with it their property as well, and gradually setting themselves up as our country's protectors?"[1]

This was the beginning of Catholic severity in the matter of mixed marriages, which even today makes it so difficult for the confessions to live together. Priests refused to consecrate mixed marriages if the promise to bring up all children as Catholics was not forthcoming. They refused Catholic women absolution if they entered a civil marriage without fulfilling the Catholic conditions or if they had had a Protestant wedding.

[1] Even in the diocese of the otherwise very moderate Sailer, there were in 1830/1 cases of priests refusing to participate in the consecration of mixed marriages. The periodical *Das konstitutionelle Bayern* carried a violent article on the subject in February 1831.

Now Catholic brides were reluctant to have a wedding at all. It was on this point that conflict broke out.

The efforts of the Prussian envoy in Rome, Josias Ritter von Bunsen, succeeded in getting something of a concession from the Pope with his brief "Litteris altero adhinc anno" of 25th March 1830, to the effect that, in the absence of a declaration concerning the upbringing of children, the priest should confine himself to attendance at the wedding. The government, proceeding on the basis of the text of this brief, entered into new negotiations with Archbishop Spiegel and these led to the secret Convention of 19th June 1834, which was more favourable and even allowed a priest to take part. The government's policy could succeed because it was impossible for the bishops inside Prussia to communicate directly with Rome. All correspondence had to pass through the Ministry in Berlin, which only forwarded to Rome or to the Prussian sees communications advantageous to their Church policy. The Suffragan Bishops of Trier, Münster and Paderborn acquiesced in the arrangement and issued identical pastoral instructions.

Matters came to a head again in 1835 with the enthronement—at Prussia's request!—of the new Archbishop, Clemens August Freiherr Droste zu Vischering. As a result of the death-bed recantation of Bishop Hommer of Trier, the Curia had now been informed of the deviation from the terms of the papal brief which the Convention had effected. The Archbishop decided in September 1837 that from then on the arrangement was to be ignored to the extent that it was at variance with the brief. This led to the "Event of Cologne", which lit up the situation of the Catholic Church in Prussia like a flash of lightning: on 20th November 1837 Archbishop Clemens August was arrested in his archiepiscopal palace at Cologne without trial or judgment, but solely on the royal command, and was committed to the fortress of Minden.[1] This was an act of violence on the part of the absolutist bureaucracy, an act which the envoy in Rome, Josias Ritter von Bunsen, had persuaded the anti-Catholic King to take. The conflict spread to the archdiocese of Gnesen-Posen, where the Archbishop, Martin von Dunin, was deprived of ecclesiastical

[1] Bunsen described the mood of the Rhine province thus: Most of the parish priests who are now seen as ignorant or heretical, modelled on Belgian fanatics educated or led by Jesuits, have been trained by Hermes. One feels that behind the ardour against the so-called Hermesians stand Belgian, Austrian and Italian Jesuits. Döllinger found it ridiculous that the state should compel "assistentia activa", which according to Canon Law at the time was not at all necessary to constitute marriage. Weis, soon to be Bishop of Speyer, said in a letter to Döllinger: "God has let this event take place, that pernicious indifference should come to an end and that the Catholic Church might be seen in her unique truth. There is now a great religious ferment all along the Rhine which is leading men to reflect on the higher truths. Catholics are becoming Catholic again."

office by a judgment of the Posen Court of Appeal on 23rd February 1839, and sentenced to six months' imprisonment.[1]

When Frederick William IV came to the throne, bringing with him a Romantic appreciation of the Catholic Church, ecclesiastical peace was soon restored in Prussia. The Archbishop of Gnesen-Posen was allowed to return to his diocese; Klemens August of Cologne received a personal apology, but Johann von Geissel was appointed administrator of his diocese, and given right of succession. The "Placet" was done away with and bishops were permitted to communicate directly with the Holy See. In 1841 the Ministry of Culture set up a Catholic department (the closure of which was to be one of the issues of the later "Kulturkampf"). In coming to an arrangement with the Curia, the government left the question of mixed marriages entirely to the decision of the bishops. The revolutionary constitution of 1848 secured for the Roman Church the right to make independent ordinances and to administer its own affairs.

Yet the vitality which had emerged in Catholic reaction to the Cologne arrest remained a feature of German Catholicism. A vast flood of Catholic newspapers had appeared, especially in Bavaria, where censorship did not make for printing difficulties. This was the beginning of the Catholic press. Josef Görres had started his *Rhenish Mercury* in 1814, with an attack on Napoleon, and Prussia found this publication so disturbing an influence in its newly-won Western Provinces that it was prohibited by a Cabinet order dated 3rd January 1816. In his *Athanasius*, Görres showed that he had lost none of his touch. Besides him, there were Moritz Lieber and Hermann Müller. The Görres circle in Münich began the *Historical and Political Papers*, which in its very first number set forth a programme of Church policy, taking up the old demand for parity which the *Rhenish Mercury* had made. What is more important is the fact that the papers which were to give German Catholicism its political education managed to avoid reactionary preoccupations, which would have been all too easy at that time in view of the close associations that existed with Metternich's Austria. The editors had the vision to see (as Pfeilschifter with his Church newspaper failed to see) that there could be no dependable freedom for the Catholic Church unless freedom prevailed throughout the political system.

[1] When on 19th Nov. 1841 the government of Hesse deposed K. Riffel, the Catholic church historian of the University of Giessen, the Catholic public was roused as it had been at the time of the arrest of Droste-Vischering five years earlier. Contemporary Catholics explained the government's action in the light of views expressed by the Professor on Luther. Then the prevalent explanation was that there had been personal issues involved. The Bishop of Mainz had been consulted. Johannes Kraus has recently brought to light new documents which show that it was only Riffel's pages on Luther which prompted the Protestant state authorities to depose him. The Acts themselves were destroyed in the burning of the Hessian Archives in the Second World War.

The change in the state of Catholic feeling at the time of the Cologne troubles did not, however, go unobserved. It was at this point that Franz von Baader took up his polemics against the new papalism ("Concerning the separability or inseparability of the papacy from Catholicism" (1838) and "On the feasibility or infeasibility of emancipating Catholicism from the Roman dictatorship" (1839)). Man could never be the ultimate authority over man. "Spiritual bondage" was no less evil than bondage of the flesh. The autocratic appetite for infallibility was an expression of inner secularization. The only form of organization capable of producing a deeper Catholicity was a free, spiritual "world corporation". "Punctualization" or the visible concentration of power in the papacy made the Church "comprehensible to world power because similar to it".

In these years of transition from the Catholicism of late Josephinist reforms, which could no longer provide solutions to the problems of the nineteenth century, to the Ultramontane outlook which was fast gaining ground the atmosphere among German Catholics was extremely tense and the slightest thing could cause an explosion. This became clear when, in the autumn of 1844, an article in a newspaper started a movement which for a short time put the whole of Germany in turmoil: "German Catholicism" (Deutsch-Katholizismus). The author, a Silesian curate, Johannes Ronge, had resented the pressure from Rome which forced his bishop, Count Sedlnitzky of Breslau, to resign because at the time of the Cologne Church struggle he had not shown as much severity as Rome would have wished in the matter of mixed marriages and, as a late Josephinist, not enough solidarity with the German bishops who had been arrested. This young curate, indeed, was not the only one to be scandalized by the struggle which ultimately arose between the Ultramontane and the Josephinist-Reform Church parties on the question of who was to occupy the episcopal See of Silesia; but only he dared to voice his displeasure in public, in the leftish newspaper, *Sächsische Vaterländische Blätter*. Ritter, who was a curate of the Chapter in Breslau, felt particularly challenged by the article. He had formerly been a Hermesian himself, but was now in the process of becoming a Curialist and accordingly took the opportunity of demonstrating his new affiliation to Rome. It was he who had been responsible for having the refractory chaplain suspended. Ronge's months of activity from the spring of 1843 to the autumn of 1844 as director of a private school in Laurahütte were for him a time of preparation for the future public appearance he was so feverishly anticipating. Now, having renounced the Catholic priesthood, he wanted to summon the public to a great effort of Church reform. The Germans were to find God in their own way without clerical or hierarchical mediation. All that Ronge lacked was the right opportunity and this was provided in the summer of 1844 by the pilgrimage to the Sacred Robe. In a few months more than a million pilgrims from Germany, Luxemburg and Belgium came to Trier to see the Seamless Robe. To the German representatives of early Liberalism, which was gaining ground in the forties, this seemed to constitute a veritable challenge to the spirit of the century. As one who shared this view, Ronge wrote his open letter to Bishop Arnoldi of Trier, and it was published on 18th October 1844, again in the *Sächsische Vaterländische Blätter*. The climax of the letter was the high-sounding sentence: "Already the historian is reaching for his pen and is holding up your name, Arnoldi, to the scorn of generations, present and future, calling you the Tetzel of the nineteenth century." Despite its banality, the open letter worked like a fanfare and thousands of copies went from hand to hand, meeting with passionate approval or violent opposition. The leader of the Silesian Restoration and future Prince Bishop of Breslau, the preacher Förster, spoke out against Ronge; but it was just such Catholic attacks which provoked Ronge now to take the final step. He was excommunicated on 4th December 1844, and on 12th January 1845 he called for the setting up of a new church independent of Rome, which, after an initial Council in Leipzig at the end of March, assumed the name of "German Catholic Church" (Deutschkatholische Kirche). From the very start, Ronge was disappointed that only a few priests answered his call, even although he knew better than anyone the mood of discontent that prevailed among the younger clergy.

For the first time and indeed on Catholic soil (later to be repeated in Orthodox and Protestant areas—the Autocephalists of the Ukraine, Obnovlency; the early history of the Evangelical Federation, "German Christians") the attempt was made to form a church from non-ecclesiastical motives, and it was proved that such an attempt must, of necessity, fail. Early Liberal writers like Blum of the Rhineland and Schusselka of Sudeten Germany helped to organize the new church. The criteria by which they judged the Roman Church were largely political: with men like Metternich and Gregory XVI, it could only be described as a centre of reaction. The political significance of the weakening of the Roman Church, so they thought, would be the weakening of state absolutism. The new "German Catholic Church" would provide most important backing for the liberal, democratic movement. Men like the historian Gervinus expected that in such a church the divisions between the confessions in Germany would be overcome. Political factors had produced an initial wave of interest in the "German Catholic" movement, but its creed as composed by Robert Blum was purely negative, consisting of objections to the papal primate and hierarchy, auricular confession, Latin as the language of liturgy, and celibacy of priests—and this was not enough for anyone to live by. Certainly, even in 1847 it succeeded in holding a council in Berlin at which no fewer than 259 congregations were represented; and the number of adherents won over from the Catholic Church mounted to 80,000. But the application of the principle of freedom soon led to divisions, and the pre-revolutionary governments, especially in Vienna, refused to tolerate the new movement.

"German Catholicism", however, was by no means dead. Despite the fact that the Praesidium informed the heads of the Austrian states that the "so-called German Catholics" were illegal associations, their appearance raised new hopes in the hearts of late Josephinists. Even Bolzano, in Prague, expected great things. Ronge's writings were translated into Czech and were published at Hirschberg in 1845. The March Revolution of 1848 prepared the way for great celebrations in the Prater in Vienna. Drexler wrote demanding nothing less than the "liberation of the Austrian Church from the supremacy of the Roman See", and "an independent national Church with its own patriarch in Vienna". In August, 8,000 people assembled in the Odeon, the largest hall in Vienna, for a "German Catholic" rally.

The effect of "German Catholicism" was to force the Catholic faithful in Germany to face up to the dilemma of the century, and by resisting it they increased the strength of the Ultramontane movement. The voice of Görres was again to be heard, with his *Pilgrimage to Trier*. August Reichensperger, who at that time was a judge of the District Court at Trier and who was later to become a Centre Party Member of Parliament, was urged by Bishop Arnoldi to come out in defence of his bishop's position, and this he did in the *Luxemburg Newspaper*, since he did not have access to any paper in Prussia.

CHAPTER VII

PIUS IX AND TRIUMPH OF ULTRAMONTANISM

The transformation of Catholicism by the Ultramontane movement: that is the content of the history of the Catholic Church in the nineteenth century. During the period of absolutism the Catholic sovereigns had obviated centralization in Rome by virtue of their state-church policy, either Josephinist or Gallican in character. But there was an abrupt change in the situation when the French Revolution created a truly national state in which the clergy was deprived of all support. Support from Rome provided the substitute they needed. In the history of the Church, the first event that can really be called Ultramontane was Mgr Boisgelin's appeal to Pius VI in October 1790, asking for guidance at the time when the Church in France was being threatened with the introduction of the "constitution civile du clergé". At that time the Pope refused. Under the Gallican system, care had been taken to exclude the Pope, but Napoleon gave him back his place in the life of the French Church, since he needed the Pope's authority to remove the émigré bishops and the "constitutional" bishops of the Revolution from office and thus restore peace to the ecclesiastical life of the nation.

New types of associations and Catholic assemblies, political parties and a Catholic press all contributed to the formation of Ultramontane group-ings in the European nations after their internal liberalization. In addition, by setting Roman standards of piety and theology and by giving instruc-tion on the social question, Rome took over the role of leadership, and the First Vatican Council finally settled the structure of the Catholic Church in accordance with Rome's understanding of it.

As this development took place there was a change in the kind of criticisms made by Protestants, and judgments which were based partly on the old ways of thinking in terms of state churches gave way forthwith to criteria of a nationalistic kind. This can be discerned, for example, in the speech Bismarck made to the Prussian Landtag on 16th March 1875: "At the head of this state within the state . . . stands the Pope, with his autocratic powers. This monarch is in our midst at the head of a closed party which elects and votes according to his will. Through (his) semi-official press in Prussia, the Pope has the power to have his decrees publicly proclaimed and to declare the laws of our country null and void! Furthermore, he keeps on our soil an army of priests, he collects taxes, he has cast about us a net of associations and congregations which have a great deal of influence—in short, since we have had our constitution, there has scarcely been anyone so powerful in Prussia as this lofty Italian prelate, surrounded by his Council of Italian clerics. In itself, such a position would be highly dangerous and would scarcely be tolerated by the state, even if it were held by and restricted to a subject. But here it belongs to a foreigner."

Now that the Protestant Churches are overcoming their latent nationalism and are beginning to live with their analogous structures within ecumenical associations, it is necessary to understand the Ultramontane movement rather differently.

I. THE RISORGIMENTO

In 1821 the Great Powers sent the Curia proposals for political reforms in the Papal States, and these were repeated in a Memorandum of 1831. But neither Gregory XVI nor his Secretaries of State, Bernetti and Lambruschini, could bring themselves to concede that laymen might hold office in the state or that communities might be given responsibility for their own administration. Throughout Europe modernization was taking place through the introduction of railways and gas lighting, but this did not apply to the Papal States.[1] The fateful encounter with the Risorgimento, which was embodied in La Giovane Italia, the radical party led by the advocate from Genoa, Giuseppe Mazzini, began with the risings of 1831–2 in various parts of the Papal States (e.g. Garibaldi in Ravenna). The authorities' refusal to countenance political change only drove the Italian national movement to adopt a thoroughly anti-clerical ideology, which was reflected in its moment of triumph in the enactments of the Parliament in Florence in 1867, aimed at the destruction of the Church.[2]

During the reign of Gregory XVI, there were, of course, also moderate liberal patriots (the New Guelphs, such as the romantic poet Alessandro Manzoni, the philosopher-priests Gioberti and Rosmini, and the statesmen Cesare Balbo and Massimo d'Azeglio). These men thought in terms of a reconciliation between the papacy and political liberalism, and wanted to solve the Italian question by creating a confederation of states with the Pope as president and under the protection of the Piedmontese army.[3] Could this group play any real part in the development?

[1] Leflon, op. cit., 435f.
[2] Mazzini understood God as the sanction of the unwritten moral laws. But this did not help the theory of the relation between Church and state.
[3] The Turin pastor Gioberti introduced the Risorgimento with his work *Il Primato*. In his principal work, *Del rinnovamento civile d'Italia*, the Catholic Church and the state were seen as the two aspects of Italian greatness, which were to be purified of their accidental faults, the Church especially from the "confusione dello spirituale col

The Liberal movement's main concerns were the expulsion of Austria, national unity in Italy and constitutional guarantees, and when the new Pope, Pius IX, declared an amnesty for the state prisoners languishing in the Engelsburg, the Liberals were convinced that Pius was ready to place himself at the head of their movement. They had their first disappointment when the internal reforms undertaken in the Papal States turned out to be no more than half measures. Apparently the Pope thought that papal independence, which he held to be necessary for his spiritual task, might be infringed if he were to hand over constitutional rights to the laity. He preferred to concede freedom of the press and freedom of assembly. The Pope summoned a Consultà of twenty-four counsellors in October 1847, but he limited its role to a purely consultative one. It was, however, just this trickle of concessions which fostered revolution.

The new Pope hoped to use the Risorgimento to bind the Italian states more closely together. He accordingly took an interest in the customs union between Tuscany and Piedmont and in the all-Italian defensive alliance which Florence had been pressing for. But the Pope's policy was soon overtaken by events. Sicily rose up against the absolutist Bourbons, the north against Austria and agitators had convinced the Pope's subjects that joint military action would be the best defence against an Austrian attack. In this situation, Pius made a speech on 10th February 1848, in which he began by recalling that up till then disaster had been averted not by military power but by the spiritual prestige of Rome, and finished with the words, "Bless Italy, Great God, and preserve her with Thy most precious gift of faith." His audience noted only that the Pope had implored the blessing of heaven on their new idol, the concept of Italy, and began to think that if he could pray for the faith of Italy he would soon come round to praying for a successful war. Farini, the patriot, wrote to a friend: "This blessing upon Italy comes to the same thing as a curse upon Austria, a crusade." Thus the ambiguity of the situation increased. While Italian arms were flashing in Lombardy, the Archbishop of Florence called for the exhibition of the Holy Sacrament, and in Milan the bishop authorized his seminarians to enlist in a battalion of volunteers.[1]

---

temporale". Ecclesiastical Rome still refused to recognize the national and civil principle. Yet the "credenze italiane" should not for this reason be changed. That would rupture concord in Italy. See Leflon, op. cit., 438.

[1] Liberal pressure was expressed in the "Address" to Gregory's successor, in the loyal petition to Gizzi, the Secretary of State, and in Mazzini's open letter. Preachers like Ventura added fuel to the fire, e.g. in the funeral sermon on O'Connell, which praised the alliance of religion with freedom and recommended the Church to address itself to democracy as against the aristocracy and, untamed and heathen as democracy was, to baptize it as once she had baptized the Germans.

The Pope, therefore, was faced with a difficult decision. He could not become so committed politically that the result would be an Austrian schism. But still less could he remain indifferent to the way in which the Italian problem was to be solved. If Piedmont had at least taken prompt action on the idea of a defensive alliance, then mobilization of troops in the Papal States would have had the appearance of being the consequence of a treaty and not the deliberate decision of the Pope. As early as 25th April the Pope had confessed to one of the diplomats: "My authority gets less every day, and the temporal power I can exert is now purely nominal. Do these men, whose excessive nationalism nothing can halt, want to force me to declare war, me, the head of a community of believers, who want only peace and concord? Well, I shall protest." In the course of his decisive public oration before the Consistory on 29th April, in which he rejected the idea of declaring war on a nation whose children were Catholic, he said: "Faithful to the obligations of our supreme apostolate, we embrace all countries, all peoples, all nations in the same sentiment of paternal love." Now the mists were scattered. The nationalists recoiled in profound dismay and scented treason; reactionary circles interpreted the Pope's speech as being favourable to them. For the first time voices were heard to declare that if the duties of an Italian sovereign were not compatible with those of spiritual leader of the Church, then the Pope must relinquish his portion of temporal rule in the Papal States, since this was proving harmful to the whole Italian nation. The "Roman Question" had been put.

As head of his Ministry, Pius had appointed a moderate, Count Pelegrino Rossi. On 15th November, as he was entering Parliament, Rossi was murdered. The next day, the Pope came to the conclusion that he was completely surrounded by revolutionaries, and fled, in disguise, to Naples. He summoned Cardinal Antonelli to Gaeta to be his Secretary of State, and it is Antonelli who must bear responsibility for reactionary policies which unfailingly sanctified the existing order and were able to solve no problems, at best rather cleverly keeping them under the surface. In carrying out the restoration of the Papal States, Antonelli resorted to the employment of foreign troops. The result was that when the Pope returned to Rome in April 1850 he was branded as a reactionary.[1] In fact, Pius IX's pontificate, lasting as it did for thirty-two years, did serve to block the path of liberalism, which seemed to be striding out so optimistically. This Pope represented a contradiction of the nineteenth century. In our assessment of the nineteenth century we can at least learn as much from Pius IX as in our criticisms of this Pope we can learn from the liberal assessment of that century.

[1] H. Acton, *The Last Bourbons of Naples*, London 1962, 283ff. (Pius IX in Gaeta).

During his sojourn in Gaeta, Pius IX developed an interest in the *Civiltà Cattolica*, the Jesuits' new enterprise in the field of journalism. The idea that the Order might produce a periodical had been in the air since 1847, but Roothaan, the General of the Order, inclined more to the idea of a learned journal in Latin. In the storms of 1848, however, a young Neapolitan, Father Carlo Curci, had been taken with the idea of starting something of more general cultural interest which the laity could read and which would act as an antidote to revolutionary ideas. While the General hesitated, concerned as to the difficulties of government censorship, Curci pressed on and gained an audience with Pius IX. The Pope had recently issued a "motu proprio" encouraging bishops throughout the world to make use of the new medium of the press in defence of Catholic truth. He therefore agreed to the new plan, paid for the costs of the first number and informed the General of the Order that if need be he would alter the Order's rule as laid down by St Ignatius prohibiting the Jesuits' involvement in political problems. Since everyone knew that the *Civiltà Cattolica* was the quasi-official voice of the Pope, the number of subscribers quickly rose to 12,000, not a few of whom were abroad.

While the Papal States continued to be ruled with the methods of the "ancien régime", Piedmont, which had had a liberal constitution since 1848, was flourishing as a state, under d'Azeglio and Cavour, and it was on Piedmont that the supporters of national unity set their hopes. Here, secularization took a sudden stride forward when Cavour was forced to enter a coalition with the anti-clerical left. On 22nd May 1855, under pressure from this party group, the notorious Monastery Law was passed, dissolving all monastic institutions not engaged in the care of the sick or in education. Some 604 settlements were involved, and the Pope excommunicated all who had had any part in the passing of this law. Despite the irreconcilable nature of official pronouncements, it might still have been possible to restore peace to the Church in Piedmont. That was what the King was aiming at, and Cavour, who had family ties with the Protestant "Eglise Libre" in French Switzerland and was in contact with liberal Catholics in France, stuck to the formula, "chiesa libera in libero stato". Although opposed to concordats, which in his view only shackled the Church's freedom and treated the Church as a source of law like a temporal state, he still considered it possible to arrive at a *modus vivendi* with Rome. But on 21st July 1858, at a secret meeting at Plombiéres,[1] Napoleon guaranteed the Piedmontese statesman military aid to drive the Austrians out of North Italy and to annex a large part of the Papal States. In this, Napoleon exploited French public indignation over the Mortara case, involving the activities of agents of the Papal States in Bologna and which

[1] L. M. Case, *Franco-Italian Relations*, 1860–5, Philadelphia 1932.

had been reported as a sensation. (A Jewish child who had been baptized "in periculo mortis" by a Christian servant girl was removed from his parents and sent to a Catholic school.) In April 1859 the war which had been agreed to broke out with Austria. Victory at Magenta and Solferino followed swiftly, and this sparked off revolts in the central states of Italy. The Pope lost control of Romagna and in 1860 Garibaldi landed in Sicily with a thousand Redshirts and outflanked the Kingdom of Naples. The papal army was reorganized with the help of volunteers from the Catholic nations of Europe, and when this appeared to threaten overland communications between Piedmont and southern Italy, Piedmont marched on Umbria and the marches and defeated the papal General Lamoricière at Castelfidardo on 18th September. The Papal States were now reduced in size by two-thirds, but still bearing responsibility for the whole, virtually ceased to be a viable entity. On the outbreak of the Franco-Prussian War, the French garrison was recalled from the Cività Vecchia, and the Piedmontese saw this as their opportunity to occupy the Eternal City. This they did on 20th September 1870, thus preparing the end of the Papal States.

In their anxiety to mollify the Catholic powers for this action, the Italian politicians hastened to settle by law the two open and closely connected questions: the future legal position of the Pope and relations between Church and state in Italy. The "Law of Guarantees", passed on 13th May 1871, granted the Pope "the independence, freedom and outward marks of respect due to a spiritual sovereign", but nevertheless, though the law lacked international recognition and was not irrevocable, handed over the Holy See to the Italian state. On 15th May 1871, in his encyclical "Ubi vos", Pius IX rejected the law along with the compensation he had been offered of $3\frac{1}{4}$ million lire per annum (at least as regards the second and future payments).[1] He would prefer to live off the "Peter's Pence", a first appeal for which was made in Belgium.

The intervention of Don Bosco made it possible for specific cases of dispute arising between Church and state to be settled in an amicable atmosphere. But anti-clerical activities did not stop: for instance, the Collegium Romanum was confiscated, to which the Pope reacted by turning the Collegium into the Pontificia Università Gregoriana. Still hoping for a miracle, Pius remained "the prisoner in the Vatican", accepting the homage of international bands of pilgrims, who came to Rome to celebrate his twenty-five years as Pope and the 800th anniversary of Gregory VII.

Insistence on the continuation of the Papal States did the Catholic Church great harm. In face of the secularization that had taken place all over Europe, which had prevailed in the German bishoprics, in Liège

[1] R. A. Graham, *The Rise of the Double Diplomatic Corps in Rome,* The Hague, 1952.

and in Avignon, the Papal States were an anachronism. The desire to preserve complete independence for the Holy See was laudable enough but there was no attempt to think this out at the right time on a new basis. The result was that Catholic energies were absorbed in a question which was pre-eminently political. Important new developments which might have taken place were hampered. As an example of this, in 1869 a group of Catholics in Florence came forward with the idea of setting up groups of associations and Catholic assemblies on a national basis. "The Society for the Advancement of Catholic Interests", founded by Curci and Prince Chigi in December 1870, provided a suitable organization to give effect to this idea. But when the first Catholic assembly met in Venice in June 1874 it failed to attract the intellectuals, simply because they were weary of "the Roman Question", which dominated everything.

2. THE CATHOLIC PARTIES

In Ireland[1] and Belgium the Catholics had had considerable success in organizing themselves politically. Their example was not without influence in France during the "July Monarchy". Count Montalembert, one of the founders of the "Agence générale pour la liberté religieuse", raised the question of Catholic political organization afresh in his pamphlet, "Du devoir des catholiques dans la question de la liberté d'enseignement" (1843). "We offer no systematic opposition," he wrote, "but at the same time we cannot accept the degraded position given to us in Cousin's philosophy: the clergy reduced to the role of moral policemen and the Church reduced to the level of a burial institution. Let us organize ourselves in the same way as the Belgian and Irish Catholics, let us get to work, with petitions, through the press, and in elections. Even if we do not carry the majority, let us at least provide the support necessary for their education." The fundamental ideas of L'Avenir were further developed here:

---

[1] O'Hegarty, History of Ireland under the Union, 1801–1922, London 1952. The Irish example was discussed in Germany, too, notably when the Bavarian second chamber was debating union in 1848. Here attention was drawn to O'Connell. "Let no one expect to be able to do what he did. To this man alone was it given not only to set the masses in motion, but also to hold them back again." Döllinger: "I can scarcely think of anything more misleading than to compare one union, the Irish one, with the kind of union which has developed here . . . I ask, Why has the Irish type of union found such great sympathy throughout the entire continent? Because a highly unnatural situation prevailed there, which everyone knew could not continue, because what was involved there was nothing less than the political, indeed almost the physical existence of a whole nation. What was the result of this union and O'Connell's agitation? It was that O'Connell really became master of a great country and that in the British parliament it was openly declared to be in opposition to the Ministry, that the government of the British Empire no longer had any power in Ireland."

it was not the King but public opinion which was sovereign. The Church must make a place for herself in it. Hence the need to organize a Catholic party.

Up to this point the bishops had been accustomed to look after the affairs of the Church on their own. In this connection, the Archbishop of Rouen, with Montalembert in mind, declared: "It is not the job of the laity to trouble themselves with the laws of the Church." Mgr Parisis, however, came out in support of the new ideas. ("Sur la part que doivent prendre aujourd'hui les laïcs dans les questions relatives aux libertés de l'église.")

Montalembert started up everywhere local branches of a Committee for the Defence of Religious Freedom. Too weak to put up their own candidates at an election, these Catholic committees got involved in existing political organizations and promised to rally Catholic votes for candidates who were prepared to give firm undertakings to support a specific Catholic programme. In this way, in 1846, 146 candidates, pledged to support measures of the Catholic programme, were elected. Montalembert's methods had proved successful. In the Chamber an immediate change in atmosphere was noted. Early in 1847 Guizot made a speech in which he acknowledged that in the question of education rights of families and of churches had priority over those of the state.

By the time the July Monarchy came to an end the political unity of French Catholicism was still intact. Yet along with Montalembert there had appeared the figure of the journalist, Louis Veuillot, the editor of *L'Univers*. He became the voice of the clergy. A difference of opinion had already arisen over effective methods of political action. The education law of 1850, the Loi Falloux, was the outcome of Montalembert's educational policy, and it divided political Catholicism in France into two camps, right and left. Under Veuillot's influence, the majority of bishops were hostile to the law, and it was only as a result of Mgr Dupanloup's advocacy of the law with the Pope that Pius IX instructed the bishops to give effect to it. When Napoleon III acceded to the throne (1852) the split between the "liberals" and the "intransigents" widened. Under Napoleon, the Catholic Church certainly received undeniable benefits: the state budget for the Church rose from 39 to 48 millions; the number of priests, which had reached 47,000 in 1848, quickly mounted to 56,000. But while Veuillot and the intransigent Catholics wanted to fight against the trends of the century by reinstating authority, Montalembert advocated freedom for all as of right and wanted the Church to adapt to the secularization of the century. The view of the intransigents was ironically represented by Montalembert thus: "If I am the weaker, I claim freedom—that is your principle: but if I am the stronger, then I do away with the principle of freedom—that is my principle."[1]

The growth of Catholic parties in *Germany* spread from the Landtags of southern Germany, in which parliamentary Catholic groups had formed. In *Contemporary Discussions on State and Church*, which "the Catholic Prussian", Radowitz, composed in 1845 when he was taking the waters at Wildbad, representatives of the various religious and political forces struggling for power in the middle of the century are portrayed debating the questions of the day in conversations which appear haphazard, but which are actually worked out systematically. Orthodox and liberal Protestants, atheist materialists of a socialist kind, Hegelian advocates of an all-powerful state, and faithful Catholics are all there, confronting each other. Radowitz himself proposes the following formula: "Conserving, preserving is not of itself good, neither is abandoning, progressing of itself bad. Preserving the good is a duty; preserving what just happens to be there is unjust and unwise. Progressing towards that which is better in a legitimate way is praiseworthy; progressing towards that which is bad or towards that which is good but by illegitimate means is reprehensible. The tasks of the present cannot be conceived in such cheap formulations." This is the first elaboration of the future line of the centre.

At the National Assembly of 1848 at Frankfurt (at the instigation of Diepenbrock), Radowitz, Döllinger and Ketteler organized into a Catholic alliance twenty-three representatives who had previously either belonged to the various clubs or remained isolated. At the same time, Catholicism in Germany, with its Ultramontane orientation, was endeavouring to find the kind of organization which would be capable of action, and settled for the typical nineteenth-century form of association, the Union, and in it brought together its militant laity. This new sociological structure first developed with a Catholic group whose focus was the *Mainz Journal*, and behind this new periodical were a number of theologians who had been educated in Rome at the Jesuit Collegium Germanicum, after it had been reopened in 1819. A "'Pius' Union for Religious Liberty" was started. Religious freedom had been granted in 1848 and on the basis of this new found freedom, representatives of all the forces in Germany with the same outlook were invited in October to the first German Katholikentag (Catholic Assembly), at Mainz. Catholic members of the National Assembly of Frankfurt took part. The bishops, who had previously, under the absolutist police state, been kept in isolation, could now meet to discuss joint policy and action, and the first German episcopal

[1] Now the Provincial Council of Paris pulled the clergy out of the front line of politics. In accordance with Gregory XVI's Constitution, "Sollicitudo ecclesiarum", in which it was stressed that the Holy See, free of all concerns of party, had before its eyes as its only goal that which redounded to the eternal salvation of the peoples, the clergy were warned, "Let no one include any political matter in preaching."

conference was held in October and November 1848, at Würzburg, under the chairmanship of Archbishop Geissel of Cologne. The memorandum the Bishops drew up demanded from the governments complete freedom for the Church to order its own affairs. The episcopate thereby gave notice that it did not intend to leave the management of its affairs entirely in the hands of the unions.

It was, unfortunately, impossible for a lay element to develop in synods. After the second General Assembly of the Catholic Unions (in May 1849 at Breslau), Hirscher wrote *The Present State of the Church*, making a plea for diocesan synods. Because there were no legally constituted bodies of this kind in the Church, the lay unions concentrated on bringing pressure to bear in support of their own special positions, which indeed they could not avoid, as they had no authority in the Church and everywhere were representative only of specialist interests, which gave them not so much a Catholic character as a particularist one. Particularist movements, however, had the effect of bringing into existence counter-movements, and prevented the Church winning those of her children who were not of the same mind. The bishops were not happy with this situation, but neither were the unions. So the attempt was made to discredit Hirscher's reputation as a scholar. Döllinger was approached for this purpose. Bishop Blum of Limburg wrote to him on 29th July 1849: "What Wessenberg wrote on the diocesan synod will, on the whole, make little impact; but if 'the celebrated Hirscher' comes out as champion of the so-called contemporary church reforms, this can certainly have serious consequences. I therefore think it of great importance that this booklet should be discredited at the earliest possible moment, both by the authority of the Church and by scholarship". By contrast, Bolzano's circle in Bohemia let it be known that they agreed with Hirscher. But the theologians Dieringer and Heinrich, the journal *Historich—politische Blätter* and H. v. Andlav, representing the Catholicism of the unions, were more than enough to outweigh Hirscher's proposals for reform.

In Prussia, considerable stimulus was given to political Catholicism by "von Raumer's Decrees". Since 1850 missions run by the Jesuits and Redemptorists had been bringing about far-reaching revival in the dioceses.[1] In May 1852 the Minister of Culture, von Raumer, had instructed the authorities to keep these missions under police surveillance; in the Catholic diaspora their activities were to be prohibited altogether.

---

[1] The wave of missions originated at the Episcopal Conference at Würzburg in 1848, which recommended missions as the "most influential medium", and were held in the dioceses of Limburg, Constance and the city of Cologne. Addresses were given three times a day to audiences of up to 15,000 people. Here was the Church "just like the youthful David with the rod of faith" confronting "the Goliath of the unbelieving spirit of the age".

In July he issued a second decree, in terms of which the study of theology at the Germanicum was restricted to Prussian subjects, and then only if they received special permission from the state, non-Prussian Jesuits being excluded altogether. In future, the bishoprics would have to submit their accounts for approval. In November 1852 the "Catholic Fraction" (Catholic party) was formed in the second chamber (Reichensperger, Malinckrodt) and they now went into battle in parliament to support the constitutional protest of the episcopate and the press for the rescission of the decree. Because they sat in the middle of the house, this group was given the name of "the Centre".

The armed exchange in 1866 between Protestant Prussia and Catholic Austria and the break-up of the Deutscher Bund (German Alliance) weighed heavily on the political consciousness of the Catholic section of the German people. Catholicism tended to think in terms of Gross-deutschland (greater Germany), and as long as Austria remained united to Germany the Catholics were in the majority and enjoyed the backing of the Court in Vienna. "Consummatum est," wrote Reichensperger, who was a representative, on 9th August, "Austria is now cast out of Germany! Only the far-sighted leadership of Bishop Ketteler enabled German Catholics to recover from the internal wound which the disaster of König-grätz inflicted. Ketteler attracted those who felt as he did to follow him "out of the rocky wilderness of unfruitful hatred of Prussia". The fact that his diocese of Mainz was a small one (he had become bishop in 1850) allowed him to concentrate on political developments, his Vicar General, Lenning, being able to act for him in the diocese. He put pen to paper on every issue that arose. In *Germany after the War of 1866*, which appeared at the beginning of 1867, though he lashed out fiercely at Prussia's warlike actions, he nevertheless forced Catholics to take a realistic view of the situation. His pamphlet, "Catholics in the German Empire", written after the Proclamation of Versailles in 1871, completed the new way of looking at things, and the Centre Party entered the new German Reichstag with sixty-three members (16.5 per cent of the total).

In *Belgium* the Congress of Catholic Activities at Malines, modelling itself on the Mainz Catholic Assembly, swiftly resolved, in face of the anti-clerical radicalism of the Liberals, to organize a political party with the object of ensuring that the liberal constitution would be applied to the full in the Church's favour. If society was to be renewed by Catholic forces, then the Church would have to be prepared to attack on the political level. Individual, local "cercles catholiques" were quickly set up, later becoming registered unions and finally electoral associations, united in a Fédération Nationale. The leader of the new Catholic party was Adolphe Dechamps, a brother of the Archbishop of Malines, and he exercised his leadership in an authoritative manner, thus saving the party from the appearance of being too dependent on the episcopate and the clergy. As the "parti conservateur", political Catholicism gained a great victory in the election of 1870, and one of its leaders, Jules Malou, agreed to form a government. Here the process of secularization which the Liberals had been advancing for fifteen years was actually halted.[1]

The continued attacks of Veuillot's supporters on the Belgian constitution could not be stopped, even by letters which Archbishop Sterckx wrote in support of the constitution, and these were responsible for putting the political position of the Catholic party in question. After 1870, the newspaper, La Croix, with its thrusts, and Charles Périn, the national economist from Louvain, managed to revive the controversy as to whether the constitutional freedoms were, in fact, to be regarded as "libertés de perversion".[2]

The victory in the 1870 Belgian election was the first time in the history of the Catholic parties that they had won a majority and been able to form a government. From then on reference was always made in Catholic discussion to "the Belgian model".

Since in various European countries Catholicism had adopted the structure of political parties, led by liberal Catholics, the moment had to come when the Pope would lay down principles to regulate the political activity of Catholics. The encyclical "Quanta cura" was published on 8th December 1864, with an appendix listing eighty modern errors. The background to this was the political antagonism that existed between the Papal States and Young Italy, but it was also directed at the liberal Catholics in Belgium, Lord Acton's circle in England, Count Montalembert in France and Döllinger's activities in München. As early as 1849 Bishop Pecci of Perugia, the future Pope, had proposed that the errors of modernity should be listed and condemned. In fact, the Curia started work on a Syllabus, and planned to publish it in conjunction with the declaration of the Marian Dogma in 1854. But this work, in which Perrone took a leading part, was delayed. When the Bishop of Perpignan sent Rome an "Instruction sur les erreurs du temps présent", designating eighty-five propositions as erroneous, this work was used as a basis for the Syllabus. It was now expected that the Pope would make his anti-liberal declaration at the same time as the canonization of the Japanese martyrs. However, a sizeable group, led by Mgr Dupanloup and also supported this time by Antonelli (who wanted to avoid annoying France and losing her military

---

[1] H. Haag, Les Origines du Catholicisme Libéral en Belgique, 1789–1839, London 1950.

[2] Périn was a native of Mons, a pupil of Lamennais, and collaborated in l'Avenir.

protection of Rome), succeeded in delaying it further, and Pius IX confined himself to an oration, "Maxima quidem", in which he had bitter criticisms to make of the modern trend towards freeing philosophy, morality and politics from the control of religion. The text of the Syllabus was conveyed, as confidential, to the bishops present, with the request that they should send in their comments within two months. But the text fell into the hands of the French ambassador and of a weekly journal in Turin, and such a storm broke out in the anti-clerical press that the Pope was compelled to find another form for his proposed intervention.

The Pope's mind was finally made up for him by the events of the first Catholic Congress at Malines in 1863. Count Montalembert was there as a guest and he had been welcomed by Adolphe Dechamps thus: "You must use the audience you have here to advance our common cause. It is of the utmost importance that the results should be liberal and that the programme issuing from here should be your programme: Catholicism and Freedom." The four thousand participants at the Congress had been completely won over to his ideas. If democracy were already sovereign in half of Europe, it would be sovereign in the other half tomorrow. The mere impression of too close an alliance between Church and Throne would be enough to compromise the Church. The Church had no alternative but to take its stand on the basis of the common law, under which the Church's freedom would be guaranteed by the general freedom for citizens. Civic toleration of error was preferable to what had happened before. Italy, Spain and Portugal, the countries of the Inquisition, demonstrated how impracticable a system of repression after the pattern of the old alliance between Altar and Throne was to serve as a defence of Catholicism.

Montalembert's speech was published under the provocative title, "L'église libre dans l'état libre", and anti-liberal opponents were soon moved to act.

A Belgian friend of Veuillot's, Count Duvas de Beaulieu, attacked Montalembert's address in a pamphlet entitled "L'erreur libre dans l'état libre". Mgr Pie, who, in a recent criticism of Renan's Vie de Jésus, had declared it a scandal that such a book was allowed to circulate without the intervention of authority, appealed to the Pope to take some official action against Montalembert. Pius IX had not even read the Malines speech, but he considered that it represented a dangerous trend. He told a visitor: "The Church will never concede it as a principle that error and heresy may be preached to Catholic peoples. The Pope certainly desires freedom of conscience in Sweden and Russia: but he does not desire it as a principle." Pius IX was afraid that an independence of thought, over against the magisterium of Rome, might develop in Malines as it had developed in the Döllinger circle. Yet all that winter in Rome Mgr Dupanloup was constantly reminding them of Montalembert's merits, attempting to protect his friend from papal rebuke. After much agonizing, the Pope instructed Cardinal Antonelli at the beginning of March 1864, to dispatch letters to Montalembert and the Archbishop of Malines, conveying the Pope's disapproval.

Cardinal Sterckx held up further action by the Curia again when in the same month of March he published his justification of the Belgian constitution. In a memorandum to the Pope, Dechamps listed the dangers that would be involved in any condemnation of the principles on which modern constitutions were based. On his instructions Count Liedekerke attended personally in Rome to explain prevailing attitudes in Catholic circles in Belgium on the eve of a crucial election. King Leopold I sent a letter to Pius supporting these moves. At the same time, the French ambassador made representations to Antonelli. Once more, the condemnation of modernity was deferred.

However, the Ultramontane bishops in France demanded that the Pope should speak, and the Holy Office pressed on. By September it had become obvious that by holding back the Pope was not going to gain any benefits from Napoleon III, and thus the main reason for Antonelli's caution was removed.

The encyclical "Quanta cura" condemned all modern "isms": "Rationalism", which denied the divinity of Christ; "Gallicanism", which wanted the exercise of ecclesiastical authority to be subject to the sanction of a secular power; "Etatism", which wanted a monopoly of education and the suppression of the Orders; "Socialism", which integrated the family in the life of the state; "Economism", which saw material gain as the sole aim of the organization of society; "Nationalism", which advocated giving power to the laity, separation of Church and state, freedom of the press, equality before the law of all forms of worship, and freedom from punishment for those who committed offences against the Catholic religion. The Syllabus, which was appended to the encyclical, extended the condemnation so as to include "Indifferentism", Freemasonry and Liberalism. Evangelical Christians found their Bible Societies referred to as "illa pestis", and this was something that burned itself into their memories, persisting right up to the present day. The extracts from papal pronouncements which were collected together in the Syllabus had been easier to understand in their original contexts, especially the concluding condemnation of Opinion No. 80: "The Roman Pope can and must reconcile himself and come to an understanding with progress, liberalism and modern civilization."

The comments of the intransigent party enabled the anti-clerical press, which the Syllabus was bound to enrage, to inflate the scandal. In Naples and Palermo, Freemasons burned the papal documents in public. Döllinger wrote a pamphlet in reply, but let it lie unpublished. Austria would have prohibited the publication of the text if that had not amounted to a breach of the Concordat. The Deutscher Katholikentag (German Catholic Assembly), meeting at Trier in September 1865, avoided trouble by interpreting the papal pronouncement as being directed against anti-Christian liberalism and not against ideas of freedom within the Catholic camp. A great deal was salvaged for the Catholic Church by Mgr Dupanloup. This tireless champion of liberal Catholicism among the French episcopate worked day and night with Cochin on a pamphlet in which the papal citations in the Syllabus were interpreted out of their original context, use being made of the device of distinguishing "thesis" from "hypothesis". Dupanloup even managed to make the dangerous proposition No. 80 acceptable by declaring its meaning thus: The Pope does not indeed need to reconcile himself with what is good in modern civilization—for he has never ceased promoting it—nor with what is bad in it. Faguet remarked with some exaggeration that Dupanloup had brought out a commentary on the Syllabus which was really a respectful condemnation of it. Albert de Broglie wrote that never in his life had he seen a piece of writing produce such an effect as Dupanloup's pamphlet did. "Society, which hardly dared to breathe, felt relieved, like a man being throttled when someone cuts the cord round his throat." The first edition of Dupanloup's pamphlet was exhausted in two hours, and in three weeks 100,000 copies were in circulation, as well as innumerable translations. Six hundred and thirty bishops from all countries, but particularly America where the situation of constitutional freedom made the Syllabus utterly impracticable, wrote messages of gratitude. It is to be noted that the Pope himself was able to admit to a friend of the Bishop of Orleans: "He has made it possible to understand the encyclical as it is meant to be understood."

The intransigents did everything they could to show up Dupanloup's harmonizing interpretation as a "liberal illusion" (the title of a pamphlet by Veuillot). In Germany, the Jesuit, Schrader, interpreted the Syllabus as strictly as possible and was opposed by Scheeben. Bishop Ketteler was forced to defend his liberal position. The Pope's action accordingly proved incapable of healing the deep divisions which existed among Catholics in the sphere of politics.

3. THE BEGINNINGS OF SOCIAL CATHOLICISM

The first traces of social Catholicism are to be found among leading figures of the "constitutional" cult at the time of the Revolution, Bishop Fauchet of Calvados and Jacques Roux (who later became an apostate), the head of "the Enragés".[1] The Restoration's contribution took the form of literary discussions. Ballanche had warned, in 1818, in his essay, "Sur les Institutions sociales dans leurs rapports avec les idées nouvelles", and later in his "Palingénésie sociale", that new powers were emerging from the people. Industry, "which cannot support those whom it has begotten", was criticized by de Bonald. For him, the remedy lay in an organization in which man is nothing and society is all. French Catholics had been conscious of the social question since 1822, due to the fall in industrial wages. De Lammenais, to whom everyone paid attention, spoke bluntly in two articles in the Drapeau Blanc: "Modern politics treats the poor only as a working machine, from which the greatest possible benefit is to be drawn in a given time. But you will soon see the excesses to which contempt for man can lead. Are these men free? Compulsion makes them your slaves!" Eckstein, the Danish Jewish convert, repeated these warnings in Le Catholique.

From these beginnings, social criticism developed in two entirely different political camps. First, there were the legitimists. The Congrégation, through one of its almoners, the Abbé Lowenbruck, got employers to support the "Société de Saint-Joseph", which both exercised some concern for young workers and at the same time provided manufacturers with a supply of reliable workers. In Paris, a house was opened for the young men who were streaming into the capital from the country in search of work, and jobs were found for them.[2] A network of "Country Lads' Hostels" was built up in the provinces. Vicomte Alban de Villeneuve-Bargemont, struck by the social consequences of industrialization in the northern departements, was active in the Ministry of the Interior, and when he was dismissed by Louis Philippe, he had time to collect his thoughts in his "Traité d'économie politique chrétienne" (1834). "A choice has to be made between an outbreak of violence by the suffering proletarian classes against property-owners and industrialists and the practical general application of basic principles of justice, morality, humanity and love". He wanted to avoid class warfare by means of thorough-going reforms.[3] In 1847 the "Societé d'économie charitable" came into existence, with Armand de Melun as president, and its aims were to study social

---

[1] Daniel-Rops, L'Eglise des révolutions, Paris 1960, 645ff. (E.T., 326ff.).

[2] The founder was Lowenbruck, who said: "I had first to recruit, from every part of Paris, all masters and foremen of craftmen's businesses and merchant houses who were practising Christians and who employed one or more young men as apprentices, workers or clerks. I succeeded in persuading them that they would have to support me." Mlle de Lucinière persuaded her friend Lamennais to put his pen to the service of this work. Thus an article of his appeared in the Drapeau blanc of 20th November 1822, the first document of Catholic socialism. The groups of Paris workers who belonged to the Société de Saint François-Xavier complete the picture.

[3] Daniel-Rops, op. cit., 647f. (E.T., 329f.).

questions and make representations in the Chamber, albeit with a somewhat paternalistic attitude.

A second Catholic movement, which had no connection with these legitimist circles, grew up under the liberal Catholics of *L'Avenir*. After the closure of *L'Avenir*, Charles de Coux and the Abbé Gerbet took to publishing their views in books. "Cut the exorbitant profits of capitalism so that the worker can have bread!" Thus wrote Coux. Fifteen years before Marx, he maintained that "all capital is simply accumulated labour". The Abbé Gerbet observed that "the classes that overthrew feudalism are now themselves creating another kind of feudalism, a feudalism of wealth, in relation to the lower classes".[1] Practical solutions were at this stage still lacking, but the strength of the criticisms is remarkable.

The two men who did get down to practical solutions were both products of the controversy with the Saint-Simonians: Buchez and Ozanam. Buchez, self-taught and thinking of himself as a man of the people, was originally a Saint-Simonian himself. After a spiritual crisis, he adapted his early socialist views to his faith in God as creator. He was the first "Christian socialist". He spread his ideas abroad not only in books but in a newspaper, the *Européen*, and when he was elected as a Representative in 1848 he tried to promote his views from the tribune of the Palais Bourbon. "Christianity and revolution are one and the same thing, and the Church's only fault is in not being revolutionary". In his eyes, charity was only a sedative. Christians must take the lead in initiating structural reforms. "The last stage of Christianity must be the realization of that equality, the principle of which the first stages have converted into a dogma" (1832). Buchez constantly identified "individualist" with "egotistic", likewise "association" with "unselfishness". Social questions would be solved not by class warfare against the employers but by workers' associations taking possession themselves of the means of production.[2]

Among Buchez's followers were three of the first Dominicans recruited by Lacordaire. Under Buchez's influence, Olivaint, who later became a Jesuit, found his faith. The supporters of Buchez succeeded in publishing for ten whole years (1840–1850) a Christian socialist periodical *L'Atelier*, written exclusively by Christian workers for the working-class world.[3]

Frédéric Ozanam was induced to make his literary début in connection with the debate with the Saint-Simonians of Lyon.

[1] Ibid., 648 (E.T., 330).
[2] F. A. Isambert, *Christianisme et classe ouvrière*, Paris 1961, seeks to interpret Buchez and *l'Atelier* as extra-Catholic phenomena.
[3] Between 1835 and 1848 there was no lack of Catholics who came under the influence of Fourier, such as La Morvonnais, or of Fourier's converts, such as Abel Trauson, Louis Rousseau, Gilliot, Calland.

Some aspects of Saint-Simon's thought he never disagreed with: "To each according to his ability, to every ability according to its exercise—that is a fine, Christian maxim, a comforting promise when it comes from God, but in the mouth of a man how easily it can become a terrible threat." Ozanam, however, criticized the demand to do away with private property. Property is a necessity for men, "an extension of my ego". "A man who owns nothing becomes a hireling." Saint-Simon had accepted many Christian principles, such as the hierarchy, the commandment to love, the idea of a universal association. "But when Saint-Simon tries to be original and leaves off using Christ as his model, his teaching immediately becomes either retrograde or an absurd exaggeration."

When the elderly Chateaubriand, writing in the *Revue Européene* of December 1833, drew attention to the fact that a few individuals possessing fabulous wealth existed alongside and unreconciled with the nameless, starving multitudes, student circles which had formed round Ozanam began to ask what was now to be done. Could one be diverted any longer by dispassionate discussion of aesthetic subjects? Ozanam indicated the direction that was to be taken: "La bénédiction des pauvres est celle de Dieu. Allons aux pauvres!" The celebrated Sister Rosalie of the Quartier Mouffetard helped the students by providing them with a list of addresses. In May 1833 seven students founded the "Société de Saint Vincent de Paul", and began by visiting the hovels of the back courts. They did not want, like Buchez or Saint-Simon, to reconstruct society on a new basis, nor like the "Société d'économie charitable" to work out a new social theory; their aim was rather to bring about personal contacts between the fortunate and the unfortunate, the rich and the poor. House-to-house visiting was the only possible way they could do this. In 1839 there were as many as thirty-nine Vincentian conferences in France, and in 1848, 282. In 1845 the idea was taken up in western Germany, though not, it is true, in student circles.

The revival of "charity" after a gap of 200 years was also marked by the appearance of Vincentine nuns, whom Napoleon had authorized because of the shortage of staff in his hospitals. Strasbourg's ties with Mainz enabled the Order to gain a foothold in Germany, too. A licence was obtained from the authorities and the mother-house at Strasbourg was able to send over German-speaking Vincentines. Between 1807 and 1843 no fewer than five biographies of St Vincent appeared in German. After it had been introduced by Ozanam as a kind of socio-political action, "private" charity eventually came to be accepted by one school in France and Belgium as the proper solution of the social problem. This obviated the necessity of pressing on for reform of social structures within a society organized on liberal lines. The fact that this was not enough for German

Catholicism led to the dilemma in social and political affairs in which the Roman Church was later to find itself.

The violence and bloodshed of the Commune in the spring of 1848 affected French Catholicism so profoundly that for the next forty years social reaction triumphed. The only attempt to swim against the tide was the *Ere Nouvelle*, which the Abbé Maret edited. In October 1848 Ozanam attempted in this paper once again to set down and clarify the task of social Catholicism. "Do not be afraid if wicked men of wealth treat you as communists." Maret, the editor, was fighting for a constructive effort: "The Catholics' greatest fault is their indifference to economic and socialist projects which are, however, inspiring and exciting the classes of the people who are most numerous and who are suffering most. It should be imperative for us to develop a social school ourselves." Yet, with Veuillot calling it the *"Erreur Nouvelle"*, this courageous journal failed under the attack of reactionary forces, leaving a great vacuum in French Catholicism.[1]

The second phase of social Catholicism was staged in Germany. It was only when Albert de Mun and La Tour du Pin, as prisoners of war of the Prussians in 1871 (they were, in fact, in the office of the military attaché in Vienna), became acquainted with developments that were taking place in Germany, and brought them back to France with them, that French social Catholicism began to enjoy a new period of success.

German social Catholicism took over the picture of society which the German Catholics of the Romantic period had drawn. Among them the English statesman Burke's critique of the Revolution (*Reflections on the French Revolution*, 1790, and translated by Gentz (1793)) had exerted considerable influence. Adam Müller, a friend of Gentz, whom Novalis had awakened to the claims of religion and who was converted in 1805, saw that his role was to engage in debate at a deeper level with the Enlightenment's teaching on the state. It was by no means the case "that the freedom of each individual member of the state is an indispensable condition of political life". Rousseau's idea of a social contract was unhistorical. "Nothing contradicts freedom more than the concept of an external equality. If freedom is none other than the general striving of different kinds of nature after growth, then one can conceive of no greater contradiction than the introduction at the same time of freedom to do away with all individuality, that is, all variety in these natures." Adam Müller thought of the state as the overwhelming totality of the community, encompassing the individual. For him, the state was, therefore, not only an "insurance association or trading company" but an "inner union of the entire physical

---

[1] Daniel-Rops, op. cit., 670ff. (E.T., 338ff.). Exception: the Legitimist Armand de Melun.

and spiritual wealth of a nation". Müller applied to the state the concept of the "organic product of nature" which he had taken over from Schelling's philosophy of nature.[1]

In 1808-9 Adam Müller opened the Catholic campaign against the dogmatics of liberal capitalism with an attack on Professor Kraus of Königsberg, who had introduced Adam Smith's teaching on national economics to Prussia.[2] Whatever was to be learned from the concrete British situation could claim no general validity. Smith was concerned solely with goods, not at all with personal values. Smith's principle of division of labour would mechanize the whole of industrial life. Müller's later writings put it pointedly: Division of labour would mean that "the completely free man (would) be broken up into wheels, drills, rollers, spokes and spindles". In the so-called freedom of the contract of employment liberalism was betraying its own principles.

Franz von Baader was basically in agreement with Adam Müller and made his own criticism of the "shallow, mechanical social teaching" of the Enlightenment. Liberalism might indeed be able to release people from the bonds of society, but it did not understand how to re-integrate them into it again. Bogus freedom was the "bugbear of our time", really the freedom of the outlaw. Baader defended the benevolent paternalism of the Middle Ages and the kind of corporations that existed then. He wanted society to be constructed as a hierarchy of orders, but he nevertheless never forgot the fate of the wage-earners. "Christianity, which generally favours freedom in society, has always been particularly favourable to the creation of social orders and corporations. With the rejection of Christianity, we have seen these conciliatory organs too becoming weaker and degenerating." In its "indifference to Christianity as a principle of society" Liberalism was really being "anti-liberal, that is, heading back towards the despotism and servitude of old". In 1835 "the incongruity between those who have no wealth and the wealth of the property-owning classes" was fastened upon by Baader as the main reason why "society was everywhere ready for revolution and easily inflamed". The state should set up a compulsory association for the protection of workers "without status", for whom the priests should then speak.

When Friedrich Schlegel came under Adam Müller's influence he found a place for social philosophy in his ideas. In his article, "Signatur

[1] Because of its organic nature the state was internally divisible into various levels.

[2] In France, Villeneuve-Bargemont was the first to criticize Adam Smith from a Catholic point of view. In 1869 Ketteler was still speaking on these lines (in Offenbach): "Unconditional freedom in all areas of political economy in the first place reduced the working class to a desperate situation. The working class was dissolved into mere individual workers, totally lacking in power. Financial power, on the other hand, was organized into units of ever increasing size."

der Zeit", he agreed with those "who seek the real remedy for the political maladies of our generation in the maintenance and development of self-supporting corporations and of the corporate principle". Karl Ludwig von Haller of Switzerland, in his work *The Restoration of Political Science* (1816–34), transferred Schlegel's poetic picture of the community of corporations to the world of legal thought. He in turn was regarded as an oracle by the *Berliner Politischen Wochenblatt*, run by the Catholic von Radowitz. The school of Haller was not, however, to last long, since it was capable of thinking of corporations only in the narrow context of an antiquated feudalism. Here it was Görres who showed himself free of Restoration nostalgia.

Though the political ideas of the Romantic period faded into the background in the constitutional struggles of the middle of the century, yet the social theory of the Romantics continued to provide Catholics with ammunition against the social economics of the liberals right up to the 1880s. Natural law only began to be expounded as the basis of Catholic social teaching when Neo-Scholasticism became influential through Baron Georg von Hertling.

The attempt to arrive at a social philosophy was early accompanied by action: in 1822 a curate in Aachen protested against the "Truck" system, under which a proportion of men's wages was paid in goods, which the worker himself had to convert into money or provisions; in 1824 a pastor in the Mönchen-Gladbach district complained about children of school age working at night; in 1827 Bishop von Hommer of Trier warned that the unruliness of the younger generation was the direct result of their factory experience.

On 25th April 1837, in the Chamber at Baden, a representative, Professor Buss, made a speech on the bright side and the dark side of incessant industrialization, and demanded protective legislation. Though it did not achieve anything at the time, this speech was later hailed as the starting-point of the social politics of the Centre. In 1848 Radowitz considered that an alliance between the monarchy and the proletariat might be a possibility: "The proletariat is certainly not in itself republican. This is an error commonly made. A government which boldly and wisely takes up its interests, institutes progressive taxation, a general system of poor relief, control of the opposition between capital and labour, would have the support of the common man, and with him, an enormous source of power."[1]

The clergy in France were bound by the Concordat, which made them act cautiously, and produced no one who could be called an initiator in the realm of social politics. They had to leave the task of leadership to the laity. But it was otherwise in Germany.

[1] Radowitz to the King.

The most fruitful initiative came from an Elberfeld curate, Adolf Kolping. With a group of workers who were impressed by the example of unions of Protestant youth in Wuppertal, he founded the journeymen's unions. He was moved by priestly concern for the status of the worker, which was being threatened by industrialization, and for the rising generation of workers whose moral welfare was being endangered as a result of social despair. Paris and Switzerland were the main centres of attraction for the wandering journeymen, as well as the breeding-grounds of communism and atheism, and workers returning from these places introduced elements of subversion into German workshops. The pietistic narrowness of the Protestant youth unions taught Kolping what not to do. His aim was "social" life. "If the life of the people is to be church-going life, then the church must become 'popular'." On 6th May 1849 the Kolping "family", consisting of seven workers, started work in the Columba School in Cologne. The most important means of really making men good workers and fathers was seen to be an education which stressed family life and vocational training. Kolping therefore applied the old forms of family pastoral care, which Sailer had taught, to the growing area of the pastoral responsibility of the unions. There emerged from this the urgent need to offer members a home in a workers' hostel in which the atmosphere would be thoroughly religious. Though Kolping's thinking was as conservative as this, yet his teaching on the social classes of society was free from the hierarchical pre-suppositions of the Middle Ages. He saw that in the proletariat there was "a basic lack of status". This would have to be changed without trying to treat it in terms of status.

Lassalle was responsible for getting social Catholicism to take up the question of labour. The turning-point was the Catholic Assembly of 1863 at Frankfurt, the city in which Lassalle had just opened his victorious campaign against Schulze-Delitzsch, the leader of the Liberal workers' educational unions. Charity was still recommended to the Catholic Assembly of 1848 as the remedy for social need, and Ketteler in his Mainz sermons on "The great social and ethical questions of the present day and Christianity", had confined himself to discussing the use of private property for the common good within the framework of Aquinas's teaching. But Ketteler's work, *The Question of Labour and Christianity* (1864) took seriously the "Production Associations" which Lassalle had proposed. The bishop suggested that these should be financed, not indeed by state aid, but by Christian giving. "For this purpose I could make available some 50,000 guilders." The "law of wages" was acknowledged in Lassalle's analysis, and it was as a result of this that "with us work has become a pure commodity, which is therefore subject to all laws governing commodities".

As an heir of the social philosophy of the Catholic Romantics, Bishop

Ketteler now evaluated working-class associations from the standpoint of the corporation, which was to prevent the atomization of the individual and the accumulation of all power in the hands of the state. Of course, he continued to reject the idea that Catholic workers might be members of the Socialist Party. But the fact that here, for the first time, a bishop had managed to take a firm stand on the social question meant that Ketteler had helped social Catholicism to take an important step forward.[1]

While the German Catholic socialists were demanding state intervention for their structural reforms, the school of Périn at Louvain rejected the idea of state interference. The division in Catholic social teaching was now obvious and needed an authoritative opinion from Rome. When the first of the social encyclicals decided in favour of one school (originally the German school), Rome acquired a great reputation as the teacher of nations in social-political questions.

4. NEO-SCHOLASTICISM AND GERMAN UNIVERSITY THEOLOGY IN CONFLICT

While the theologians at the German universities were moving towards new and important achievements, a different development had for some time been taking place in the reconstruction of Roman theology: Neo-Thomism. From 1810 Buzetti had been teaching the ideas of Saint Thomas. He won over two young Jesuits to his position, Dominicus and Seraphim Sardi. The former was called to a chair of philosophy at Naples in 1831, and from then on devoted his life to Thomist researches. As Rector of the Collegium Romanum, he won Curci, the future publisher of Civiltà Cattolica for Thomism, and that journal now provided a platform for Neo-Thomism. Against Hegelian philosophy, the creator of revolutions, it was desired to present the balancing influence of Saint Thomas. It was through the Jesuit Kleutgen at the Gregorian University that Neo-Scholastic theology gained an entrance to Germany.[2]

---

[1] W. Hoyan, *The Development of Bishop von Ketteler's Interpretation of the Social Program*, Diss., Univ. of America, Washington 1946. While writing his work Ketteler carried on an anonymous literary exchange not only with Lassalle but with the Protestant social theorist, Victor Aimé Huber.

[2] G. F. Rossi, *Le origini del neotomismo nell'ambiente di studio del collegio Alberoni*, Piacenza 1957, shows that the Great Seminary in Piacenza, run by the Vincentians, had continually held to the teaching of St Thomas. It was there that Buzetti received his theological education. Ten years earlier his teacher, F. Grossi, was already exerting a "neo-Thomist" influence. The Romantic era had cleared away the bias against scholasticism. Even before the impact of Italian neo-scholasticism this was noticeable in the Tübingen school, especially in Staudenmaier, who in a brilliant passage in *Christliche Dogmatik*, 1844, 235, compares scholasticism with the Gothic cathedral of the Middle Ages.

A group of theologians in Mainz were beginning to represent Roman ideas in Germany. Lennig, Moufang and Heinrich had already collaborated with Döllinger in 1848 and followed with sympathy the progress Günther was making in Austrian Catholicism. The aims seemed to be identical: to free the Church from the Josephinist bureaucracy and to enable the laity to offer resistance in the midst of an anti-Catholic public. But soon differences appeared. For Günther and Döllinger it was a question of training the educated classes who needed to be relieved of their feelings of inferiority in face of the flourishing secular and Protestant cultural world. Mainz, on the other hand, had the Catholic masses in mind, not, at that time, the working classes, but the middle classes in the towns, and the farmers. The aim was to take them in hand by creating a new kind of union and a devoted clergy, conformed to Rome and designed to put the hierarchy's teaching into practice in every area of life. This was why special stress was laid in Mainz on creating a protected ecclesiastical atmosphere in which the education of the priests and the future leaders of the Catholic movement could take place. Hence, too, the refusal to allow open faculties affiliated to state universities, since conditions there were less favourable for the encapsulation of Catholics in diocesan seminars.[1] Hence, too, Mainz strove for a "free" (i.e. not state controlled) Catholic university for the education of the laity after the pattern of Louvain. As against this, Döllinger considered that to cut off young Catholics from the scientific pursuits of the state universities in this way, covering them up like a piece of cheese, would be dangerous—and all the more so since Mainz was the first centre in Germany to champion the return to scholasticism. This was the emphasis of the Mainz periodical, Der Katholik, after 1849, when Bishop Ketteler made the newly named professors of his diocesan seminar its editors.[2]

Reconciliation between the Catholic Church and the world of modern culture, which had been fostered with so much goodwill by the university theologians, was now declared to be an impossibility. The new trend was critical of the university theologians on the ground that they had left no place for the Magisterium Petri. Denunciations, mainly circulated by the nuncio in Munich, poisoned relations between Rome and the German scholars, and when the denunciations came to be considered by the Congregation of the Index, they were examined in a partisan way by Kleutgen, S.J., who was employed there as consultant.

In 1835 the bull "Dum acerbissimas" had condemned Hermesianism

---

[1] Reminiscences of student festivities played a role in Ketteler's rejection of the University faculty.

[2] The Mainz group soon had allies, with Clemens going to the University of Bonn, von Rauscher and von Reisach gaining influence in the episcopate, and the Jesuits taking over the theological faculty of Innsbruck.

and this had alarmed the academic world in Germany. Now the reactionary scholastic movement gained its first success in 1857 when Günther was condemned. The initiative came from the Rhineland, where the anti-Hermesian group attacked Günther's pupil, Knoodt, at the University of Bonn. In December 1853 Rome had requested a formal report on the activities of a Güntherian at the seminary at Trier, and Archbishop Geissel entrusted the preparation of this report to one Clemens, who was a private enemy of Knoodt attending Bonn. This opportunity was used to produce a virulent denunciation, and Günther's writings were placed before the Congregation of the Index. News of these proceedings had scarcely leaked out when Günther's opponents redoubled their attacks. In Vienna, Rauscher, a pupil of Hofbauer, had just become Archbishop, and with absolutist reaction in full sway, the campaign was intensified. Günther was now out of favour on account of his liberal sympathies, and the bitterness of the polemics in this affair soon surpassed that of the Hermesian controversy. Once again old friends were able to ward off his condemnation in Rome. But when Rauscher's position was strengthened by the Austrian Concordat he was able to compel Rome to let Günther fall. The Pope selected the mildest form of condemnation, and merely placed Günther's works on the Index.[1]

Encouraged by this success, the Neo-Scholastics pressed on with their offensive. The publication of Clemens's "De scolasticorum sententia philosophiam esse theologiea ancillam" was a sort of party manifesto, and when Kuhn tried to defend philosophy as a discipline in its own right, *Der Katholik*, which followed theological developments very closely, came out in support of Clemens's position. The Mainz group succeeded in creating a breach in the university front, when they got Denzinger, an alumnus of the Gregoriana, appointed to the chair of dogmatics at the University of Würzburg. His "Enchiridion Symbolorum definitionum et declarationum" was intended to make the university theologians aware of the definitive interpretation of the Magisterium Petri. Soon Denzinger brought in two other Romans, Hergenröther and Hettinger.

Ignaz von Döllinger was depressed by the progress of Ultramontanism, which contradicted his understanding of the national episcopate's status, and for the time being seemed to retire, as if to an island, and concentrated on research.[2] But he took the stage again in 1861 with his lectures at the Odeon which were unmistakably directed against the way the Romans were distorting the problems of Church and state. He wanted to enable the Catholic public to assume a leading role in the world Church, without

---

[1] Leo XIII brought Hergenröther into the Curia to prepare for the making available of the state archives (up to the key year 1846) for research.
[2] His work on Hippolytus and Callistus dates from this time.

having to depend on any sovereign state. The nuncio ostentatiously left the audience.[1] Döllinger was hoping for a reconciliation with the Mainz group when he was invited to attend a Congress of Scholars at Münich in 1863, but as things turned out the reverse happened. The nuncio accused Döllinger of wanting to call a sort of synod without the authority of the Church, so that the university theologians could publish a Charter of Rights and demand that German theology should take over leadership of the Church, and this charge carried the day.[2]

Neo-Scholasticism was given its most mature presentation in the dogmatic work of Mathias Joseph Scheeben, who taught at Cardinal Geissel's diocesan seminary from 1860. His system exhibited to the full the possibility on the one hand of putting greater stress on the dimension of the supernatural than was possible when it was approached from a critical or psychological standpoint, and on the other hand of placing a higher value on "ratio" than was possible in "Fideism".[3] Scheeben's concern was always the relation between "natural and supernatural". "This I call the supernatural, namely, that quality and radiance which is added to a lower being, and which grasps it in its totality, raising it up to the level of a higher nature. This requires an act 'praeter et supra omnes rationes et causas creatas'." There was a depth in Scheeben's thought which was at least partly due to his discovery in his work on the Greek Fathers that they had interpreted grace as a supernatural quality over against all creaturely existence and treated it in the context of the mysteries of the Incarnation and the Eucharist.[4]

---

[1] Döllinger's pessimistic verdict on the future of the Papal States had been fortified by the impressions he had got from his visit in 1857, and was reflected in these lectures. The negative response prompted Döllinger to publish at the end of the year a book which was an expansion of the lectures.

[2] Pius sent through Hohenlohe a telegram of blessing to the theologians' congress. Later the nuncio converted him to another point of view, and there was quite a scene when Pius tried to get Hohenlohe have this telegram withdrawn.

[3] Fideism had been developed by Bautain in Strasbourg. Bautain's method of making faith alone the source of knowledge alarmed the University. When he lost his chair he opened his own school, whither pupils who were enthusiastic about him, like the convert Ratisbonne, followed. Rome issued its condemnation in 1840. Cf. Leflon, op. cit., 481.

[4] I. C. Murray, *M. J. Scheeben's Doctrine on Supernatural Divine Faith*, Rome 1938; E. H. Palmer, *Scheeben's Doctrine of Divine Adoption*, Diss., Amsterdam, 1953. No other German-speaking theologian had such international influence. The new edition of Scheeben by J. Höfer (1941) is the first to give the original text, which had previously been revised in a conformist sense. Many have been attracted by the juxtaposition of Scheeben and Hermes. K. Barth, *Kirchliche Dogmatik I/1*, 70 (E.T., *Church Dogmatics I/1*, p. 77), comes to the conclusion that the Cologne theologian did not make the sacrament the focal point in an exclusive way. He knew also the hearing that brings grace.

5. "DÉVOTIONS PARTICULIÈRES"

The triumph of Ultramontanism was not so much its success in establishing papal infallibility as its achievement in the course of a single generation in effecting the internal transformation of Catholic piety north of the Alps. Love of external forms, imported from Rome by Ultramontanists like Faber in London, displaced piety which set little store by display, the piety of the disciples of Sailer and of the Absolvents of Ushaw and Saint-Sulpice. The Christocentric trend, new in comparison with the Enlightenment's concentration on the First Article of the Creed, was accompanied by the Jesuits' summons to "Communion fréquente". Since 1850 Guido Gezelle, the Flemish poet, had been extolling the virtue of frequent communion. In 1855 Dupanloup brought out a new edition of Fénélon's letter recommending daily communion, and had 100,000 copies printed. In Italy, Frassinetti advocated the eucharistic practice of the Early Church, and Don Bosco pleaded that communication should be allowed at an early age.[1] In 1851 the Congregation of Councils revised the decision of a Roman provincial council, forbidding communion under the age of 12. But even in 1870 the students at the German and American colleges communicated only once a week, and of the Mainz seminarists only one or two communicated two or three times a week.

Also from Italy came new forms of veneration of the sacrament. In 1851 Pius IX had commended perpetual adoration, and this was promoted in England by converts like Faber and Dalgairns, and in Canada by Mgr Bourget. (In the years 1849–60 it was taken up in twenty French dioceses, and in thirty-seven others prior to 1875.) The Jewish convert Hermann Cohen (a Carmelite), who introduced evocative eucharistic music, introduced the Roman practice of nightly veneration into Germany and into France, too, after 1848, with the help of Abbé de la Bouillerie. Thirty years later it was the common practice in twenty French dioceses.

In the "dévotions particulières" the spectacle of the suffering Christ challenged the imagination of those to whom the Bible and the liturgy alike were foreign. In the veneration of the Sacré Coeur[2] the Catholic soul of the age of bourgeois individualism discovered its share of responsibility in the sacrifice for the salvation of the world. It was the Jesuits who, by building on the visions of Margaret Mary Alacoque, spread the

---

[1] In Naples with the confessor's permission 7-year-olds were admitted without catechetical instruction.

[2] There were other groups which concentrated on other parts of Christ's body: Faber spread the cult of the Precious Blood, and Dupont, in Tours, the cult of the Holy Countenance.

mysticism of the Heart of Jesus cult. Perrone took the Sacred Heart as his subject in a series of tracts, "De verbo incarnato". In 1856 Pius IX founded the Feast of the Most Sacred Heart to be celebrated in the Church throughout the world, and the beatification of Marguérite Marie Alacoque in 1864 gave him the opportunity to emphasize that Christ had chosen the visionary to stimulate us, through her revelations, to venerate Him under the symbol of the Heart.

If Catholic France was particularly involved in this, it was doubtless due to the influence of the Legitimists. They had not forgotten that during his captivity Louis XVI had taken an oath dedicating his country to the Sacred Heart, and that the insurgents of La Vendée had worn this emblem on their breasts.

In this way the cult of the Sacred Heart ultimately acquired significance as indicating the mystical submission of political associations to the lordship of Christ. On the eve of the Vatican Council, Archbishop Dechamps of Malines dedicated Belgium to the Most Sacred Heart. After the disaster of 1870-1, there arose in political circles in France an attitude of penitence which was associated with the hope of restoring the monarchy, and on 29th June 1873 fifty members of the Assemblée Nationale made a pilgrimage to Paray-le-Monial, with banners in hand and the Sacred Heart on their breasts. When it came to the eucharistic prayer of thanksgiving, a member, called Belcastel, rose, and in throbbing tones declared the dedication of the members and all France to the most Sacred Heart of Jesus, adding, "Pardon, pardon!" The bishop of the diocese took the deputies' vows at the altar in the name of the Church. Soon 150 more members followed them. The Archbishop of Toulouse persuaded bishops of the world Church to petition the Pope, asking him to dedicate the universe to the Most Sacred Heart. The Jesuit, Ramière, who started the "Apostolate of Prayer" (1861), which pledged its members to "prayer in union with the Heart of Jesus" for the mystical subjugation of the world, and who was now also at the heart of the Toulouse undertaking, was able to deliver to the Pope, in April 1875, the signatures of 525 bishops. But all Pius IX did was to get the Congregation of Rites to circulate a formula of consecration to be recited throughout the whole Catholic world on 16th June 1875, the two hundredth anniversary of the Vision of the Heart of Jesus. During the year of consecration (1876-7), 140,760 pilgrims visited the Sacré-Coeur on Montmartre, including three cardinals and twenty-six bishops.

Side by side with the cult of the Heart of Jesus went the veneration of the Mother of God, which led to an increase in the attributes given to Mary. The start of this was the appearances of Mary, which increased in number in France in the nineteenth century: e.g. Cathérine Labouré in

Paris in 1830;[1] Abbé Desgenettes of Notre-Dame des Victoires in 1836. On 19th September 1846 two shepherds children in Savoy, Maximin Giraud and Mélanie Calvat, on the high pastures of La Salette, met a beautiful lady weeping, who told them to convey "to her whole people" her lamentation over their failure to observe Sunday, their lack of respect for God's name, and their failings in temperance. In 1851 the Savoyards sent the Holy Father an additional communication in a sealed envelope. Miracles of healing followed, and the faithful began to make pilgrimages to the place where the vision occurred. After a careful investigation, the Bishop of Grenoble, who had authority in this matter, gave in 1851 the Church's confirmation of the appearance and of the miracles.[2] Soon the fame of the Holy Mountain passed beyond the borders of France. Mgr Ullathorne's book, *The Holy Mountain of La Salette* (1854), went through six editions in England and was translated into German.

The appearance of the Virgin to Cathérine Labouré, and then, even more, the spreading far and wide of the miracle-working medal which had been revealed to her, gave numerous bishops the opportunity to propose that the epithet "Immaculata" be added in the preface for the Feast of the Assumption of Mary and that the force of litanies be increased by including appeal to this privilege of Mary. After 1840 petitions had been pouring into Rome calling for a dogmatic definition of the Immaculata Conceptio of Mary in the womb of St Anna, the first of these petitions coming from fifty-one French prelates.[3] In view of the feelings of those with Jansenist sympathies, the opposition of the Irish and English episcopate and the scholarly criticism of German university theology, Gregory XVI held back. The situation changed when Pius IX came to the throne of Peter: Marian piety was rooted in his personal experience, for it was by a prayer to Mary at Loretto that he had been cured of epilepsy—an obstacle under canon law to his being consecrated as a priest. In 1847 Perrone gave an affirmative judgment on the question of whether the Immaculate Conception could be the subject of a dogmatic definition. On 1st June 1848 the Pope set up a study commission of twenty theologians, and on

---

[1] Pius XII declared in his Encyclical on the centenary of Lourdes in 1958, "Who does not know to-day the miraculous Medal? Revealed as it was in the heart of the French capital itself to a humble daughter of St. Vincent de Paul, and bearing the image of the immaculately conceived Virgin Mary it has spread in every place its spiritual and physical miracles."

[2] In 1854 there was a change in the see of Grenoble, but the successor, Bishop Ginouilhac, confirmed the decision of his predecessor, in spite of the opposition of the priesthood and the doubts of the Archbishop of Lyons.

[3] J. v. Walter's *Die Geschichte des Christentums*, II, 846, states that, seen in terms of the history of theology, the historical struggle between Franciscans and Dominicans as to whether Mary was born without original sin (Franciscans) or had only abstained from any acts of sin (St Thomas and the Dominicans) has been decided by the magisterium of the Church in accordance with the Franciscan interpretation.

2nd February 1849 issued from Gaëta his encyclical, "Ubi primum", requesting all bishops to state if in their opinion the time was ripe to proclaim a Marian dogma such as this, and when nine-tenths of the answers were positive he ordered a bull to be prepared, laying down the dogma. Bishops in countries with Protestant majorities, who formed the greater part of the opposition, stated that the time was not ripe for a definition, while the Archbishop of Paris stated that it was incapable of formulation. The Primate of Belgium was afraid of needlessly irritating his Liberals. Three drafts[1] were necessary before the Pope was satisfied with the answers given to the question of principle as to whether a truth not affirmed in Holy Scripture could be defined, and to the question of fact as to whether proof from tradition was possible.

When the date of the proclamation of the dogma was fixed for the Feast of the Assumption of Mary, 8th December 1854, an invitation was sent out to all national episcopates to be represented at this ceremony. On 20th November, Cardinal Antonelli informed the bishops who had already arrived in Rome that the Holy Father was anxious to learn their opinion of the text of the bull, though he did not want further discussion of its principles. Criticisms were numerous, as had been expected. Prominent in their contributions in this matter were Mgr Malou of Brussels, and the Archbishops of Baltimore, München and Prague. In the consistory of cardinals on 1st December discussion was sparked off again. Under Cardinal von Rauscher's influence, a number of modifications were made. The Pope was not happy to see foreigners setting themselves up as schoolmasters to the theologians of Rome, but had to put up with it, lest it should be said that "everything depends on the Jesuits".

On 8th December, in St Peter's, Pius IX read the bull "Ineffabilis Deus" with such emotion that he had to stop three times.[2] Thus began the nineteenth-century trend of dogmatizing which was to create a deeper gulf between Rome and the Churches of the Reformation than the sixteenth century had done, and which, being rejected,[3] too, by Eastern Ortho-

---

[1] The first of the rejected drafts came from Perrone, the second from Passaglia.

[2] A letter from the Archbishop of Malines's nephew, dated 9th December 1854.

[3] F. Heyer, "Die Lutherische Kirche vor der orthodoxen Marienverehrung", in Ev. Luth, K.Z., 9 1951, 138. "The Lutheran Church decides against the doctrine of the Immaculate Conception of Mary, which separates off the mother of God from the first moment from sinful humanity, because for it the significance of the Incarnation is in the self-humiliation of God. With the acceptance of a sinless mother, God is still removed one step away from men, so that He does not need to humble Himself so deeply. For Catholic doctrine it is intolerable to think that the Holy One could have any direct contact with the unholy. Therefore it teaches that His mother was already without sin. Yet at any place where divinity and humanity meet, there must be contact between the pure and the sinful. Why should this encounter be removed from the Incarnation to the conception of the mother, why should the greatest of miracles be transferred from the womb of Mary into the womb of Anna?"

doxy,[1] still hinders ecumenical understanding today.

Nevertheless, there was rejoicing in the Catholic world over the new definition. The King of Naples issued an Order of the Day instructing the army to fire a salute.[2] The Queen of Spain sent the Holy Father a tiara worth two million reals.

In 1855 the Bishop of Le Puy asked Napoleon III to let him have 113 Russian cannon taken by the French in the Crimean War, so that they could be melted down and used to make a gigantic statue of the Immaculate Conception. But the statue made out of gun metal was far surpassed by the appearance of the Virgin in the Grotto of Massabielle at Lourdes on 11th February 1858, to the 14-year-old Bernadette Soubirous. Mary appeared here as one to whom this holy place belonged. Thither the masses streamed, to share the ecstatic experiences of the miller's daughter. The visionary child's expression, which cast such a spell on onlookers, was

---

[1] Since the time of Metrophanes Kritopoulos (d. 1639) Orthodox theolgians have rejected the Roman doctrine of the Immaculate Conception. Patriarch Anthimos VII of Constantinople rejected the Dogma of 1854 in his answer to an invitation from Leo XIII (1895) as "unknown to the Early Church". Bishop Isidore of Reval taught that Mary was subject to original sin, like all men; for according to a report by Epiphanias of Cyprus, she was baptized by John. Thus she was freed from original sin only through baptism. Had Mary been born free of original sin, as Roman teaching asserts, then "she would fall out of the posterity of Adam, and would appear as some sort of new being, higher than man, as though she were a new creation of God's, especially fashioned to be the mother of the incarnate Son of God". Bishop Isidore opposes this teaching in four ways:

1. There is a causal connection between sin and death, and death is therefore an indication of the presence of sin. But now the mother of God has died, as all men die.
2. If the mother of God appears as some sort of new being, then the connection between her and us is broken, and if Christ became flesh from her, then he took upon himself a flesh that was not of the same kind as ours. The doctrine of the immaculate conception threatens to dissolve the unity of nature which exists between us and the son of God. But it is on this unity that the whole fabric of our redemption depends.
3. The Catholic doctrine makes the Virgin an exception to the law of nature: she receives immaculacy as a property of her nature. But if immaculacy can be as it were mechanically received, the question arises why this exception cannot be universalised and applied to all Adam's posterity, and the entire human race be freed from its sin in the same mechanical way. Then doubt would be cast on the unconditional necessity for our redemption by the incarnation of the Word of God and the suffering of the Redeemer.
4. Bishop Isidore places the achievement of the mother of God in a line with the spiritual stirrings of humanity that preceded her. Already in Eve the whole of humanity was preparing for victory over evil in the power of Christ. His mother must come from the human race (*Journal Moskovskogo patriarchata*, September 1949).

[2] The protests of the opposition were insignificant. The dissatisfaction of the German university theologians was expressed in a letter from Döllinger to Michelis dated 31st January 1854.

described by a priest as follows: "Joy was reflected in her whole countenance, giving rise to a tender smile, a smile which was just beginning." The whole bearing of her body was nothing less "than a heavenward yearning". That the vision of Bernadette did not remain her own private affair, but that her experience proved capable of electrifying others—this was the new factor in the case of Lourdes. Thirty thousand people had already witnessed the appearance of 4th March. The local authorities, who had previously tried in vain to stop the movement with the help of the police, called in a detachment of infantry who turned out in parade order. On 24th February the Virgin did not let the roses bloom as Bernadette had asked her to do when the priest had demanded proof of her power, but instead signed to the child to scrape the ground to the left of the grotto. The thin stream of earthy water which sprang up and with which Bernadette smeared her face became the miraculous spring from which 120,000 litres of water now flows daily and fills the pools in which the multitude of ailing people bathe who flock there now, seeking cure.[1]

In 1862 Bishop Laurence of Tarbes pronounced the official verdict of the Church, which justified the faithful in believing in the appearance at Lourdes.[2] In 1869 the author Henry Lasserre, having himself been cured of eye trouble, compiled details of the first 200 miracle healings, and his book went to 800,000 copies.[3]

According to Bernadette's testimony, when the "Lady" appeared on 25th March 1858 she declared, in the Bigorre dialect, "I am the Immaculate Conception." Next morning, the Catholic press spread the news of this message throughout the whole of France. On the same day the Prefect of Tarbes, Baron Massy, ordered the child to be taken into custody so that doctors could examine her mental condition, and the grotto was boarded up. But the Catholic Church treasured the message to Bernadette as a

[1] Through all that was subsequently made of Lourdes it is possible to unearth the basic facts. The French Jesuit Cros embarked on this in 1877. From a careful examination of episcopal records from November 1858 and December 1860 and the testimony of witnesses he produced his three-volume work which was published remarkably late, in 1926.

[2] To clear up the question whether the appearances were of the Devil, the children of Lourdes availed themselves of the holy water test. "Sprinkle holy water," cried one of the girls and passed Bernadette the bottle. The child then uttered the formula: "If you come from God, then draw nigh!" but as there was a shining apparition of glory, Bernadette was afraid to pronounce the rest of the formula "If you come from the Devil, then depart!" It might also have been that it was the soul of a dead person that appeared in this female form. In fact, the head of a female congregation in Lourdes, Lisa Lapatie, had died four months before and the apparition at the Grotto seemed to be clad in her raiment. When Bernadette offered the lady paper and ink so that she could write her name, the lady declined to take them.

[3] Lasserre's publication unleashed a controversy between scientific and faithful doctors. Pius IX issued a brief on 4th September 1869 which was aimed at Lasserre.

confirmation of the dogmatic definition of 1854. Cros declared: "No one could have guessed that Mary would step from her throne, place her feet on the earth and say to all Christians in the person of Bernadette: This word of the Roman Pope is the oracle of divine truth. I am indeed exactly as the Pope has defined, the Immaculate Conception, and till the end of time, here, in this place where I speak, countless miracles will bear witness alike to the actuality of my appearances, to my Immaculate Conception and to the infallibility of the Pope." When Bernadette was canonized in 1933 this was reiterated as follows: "That which the Pope by virtue of his infallible teaching office defined, the Immaculate Virgin desired to confirm openly, through her own mouth, when soon after she proclaimed her identity in a famous appearance at the grotto of Massabielle."[1]

In the period 1861–6 Abbé Hamon of Saint-Sulpice published his seven-volume study, *Notre Dame de France. Histoire du culte de la Sainte Vièrge*. The idea that France was a country which belonged to Mary was revived.[2] After the defeat of 1871, "national pilgrimages" were also made to Lourdes, and in these there was a political element of legitimist aspiration. Here, for the first time, pilgrimages were methodically organized. The Assumptionists succeeded in getting special fares from the railway companies, and in 1872, for example, there were as many as 149 special pilgrims' trains.

6. THE ULTRAMONTANE SYSTEM

The political theorists of the Restoration were the first to bring to light the particular motive which was to lead to the declaration of infallibility— the nineteenth century's hunger for authority. De Lammenais's condemnation did not check the spread of his Ultramontane ideas. Between 1842 and 1849 his pupil, Abbé Rohrbacher, outlined the new Ultramontane view of Church history, and this came to supersede Fleury's Church history, which had hitherto been widely used and which was written from a Gallican standpoint. The library which Gautier had built up in his monk's cell in Paris, and which specialized in works on Gallican and Ultramontane problems, was known as "the Roman Salon in Paris". It was there that the first two French Ultramontane bishops, Mgr Gousset

[1] Pius XII included the following in the centenary encyclical: "Certainly the infallible word of the Pope, the authentic interpreter of revealed truth, required no endorsement from heaven to be valid for the faithful; but with what emotion did Christian people and their shepherds receive from the lips of Bernadette this answer which came from heaven."
[2] Pius XII in the Lourdes centenary encyclical of 1958: "Every Christian country belongs to Mary. But this truth acquires a touching significance, if one calls to mind the history of France. . . . Nevertheless, it was to be the 19th century, after the confusion of revolution, that was to be the century of the demonstration of Mary's favour."

and Mgr Parisis, had spent their time. Alfonsus of Liguori's ethical teaching, opposing the rigours of Jansenism, was prevalent in Rome and was given currency in Gousset's handbooks. Mgr Parisis, who had been told of the desire of the Holy See that the French dioceses should no longer avail themselves of the special laws which were theirs by custom, was the first to begin the practice of consulting the Roman Congregation of Cardinals on questions of worship and discipline. Nothing did more to strengthen the wave of Ultramontanism in France than the help Rome gave to the country priests, who as a result of the Concordat had been made subject to the power of the bishops. By 1837 there had been 3,500 cases of priests being transferred, and in 1839 the brothers Allijol, both country priests, had written a pamphlet in which they called for the restoration of the old securities the rural clergy had enjoyed. The bishops condemned the work; but one of the Allijols went to Rome and was given a hearing. From then on this group knew that they could always appeal to the Pope.

The Ultramontane attack was now developed by Fornari, the accredited nuncio in Paris from 1843 to 1850. In 1849 he managed to prevent the holding of a national council, which some of the French bishops tried to promote, and even put a stop to a meeting of a Provincial Council which had been summoned without papal authorization. Fornari induced Abbé Bouix to write in *L'Univers* advancing the Roman interpretation of canonical principles governing the calling of a council. As a result of his influence on Falloux, Minister of Culture, he succeeded, as new bishops were appointed, in increasing Ultramontane representation in the French episcopate. Back in Rome he did much to encourage French Ultramontanism by defending before the Roman Congregation French priests who refused to carry out decisions of their still anti-Ultramontane bishops and who had to appear to answer charges in Rome. Fornari also took steps in Rome to ensure that publications, Gallican in tone, were soon put on the Index.[1]

A group of fifteen bishops under the leadership of Mgr Sibour were preparing a counter-attack. They wanted Veuillot's dictatorial powers to be brought to an end, they sought to have the limits of papal infallibility stated, and they deplored the fact that there was so much conformity in literature and that Gallican traditions were being forgotten. It was a sign of the times that their Memorandum of 1852 had to be printed and distributed anonymously. Yet there was a recognizable faction within the

---

[1] Provincial and diocesan synods were recommended by Pius XI, and as a result, even held in France, Spain, England and the U.S.A.; but not in Germany, although *Der Katholik* (1850) canvassed for them, with references to the provincial councils of Bordeaux, Rheims and Paris.

Church in France. When Sibour banned *L'Univers* in 1853, the Pope issued his encyclical, "Inter multiplices", which effectively prevented further action.

From this point on Rome was determined to take over itself direction of the Ultramontane movement, which had prospered during the first half of the century on account of the local situation in France and Germany. A scheme was evolved to systematize Fornari's methods to bring about a general tightening of the connections between the Church throughout the world and Rome.

The Ultramontane movement was helped by modern social conditions with their increased mobility. Wiseman had himself been one of six students who had travelled from England to study at the Collegium Anglicanum in Rome when it was reopened in December 1818, and his view was that the progress of Ultramontanism was not unconnected with the growth of travel facilities.[1] "But to Rome there flock, from every region of the earth, aspirants to the ecclesiastical state, in boyhood, and well nigh in childhood; . . . and yet perhaps hardly one of them fails to come into personal contact with him, to whom from infancy he has looked up, as the most exalted personage in the world. Is it wonderful that what is unmeaningly called 'ultramontanism' should increase on every side? For what in reality is it? Not, certainly, a variation of doctrine but a more vivid and individual perception—an experience of its operation. The 'supremacy' is believed by the untravelled as much as by the travelled Catholic. Facilities of access, and many other causes, have increased the number of those who have come into contact with successive Pontiffs and this contact has seldom failed to ripen an abstract belief into an affectionate sentiment. . . ." Kurd von Schlözer, Legation Secretary at the Prussian embassy at the Vatican, wrote at Easter 1865, "Special 'trains de plaisir' or 'trains de dévotion' are arriving here from Breslau, Vienna and München",[2] and he also reported "a massive audience of 1,000 people who were arranged in nationalities". The number of bishops who came to Rome for the Marian definition in 1854 was 206, for the canonization of the Japanese martyrs in 1862, 265, and for the 1800th anniversary of the martyrdom of Peter, in 1867, 500 bishops. Cardinal Manning's comment on this was, "No pontiff from the beginning, in all the previous successions of two hundred and fifty-six popes, has ever so united the bishops with himself."[3]

Pius IX had no hesitation in summoning to his presence anyone who appeared to be too independent. His audiences could be stormy

---

[1] Wiseman, *Recollections of Rome*, London 1936, 14f.
[2] Countess Berzynska had come to Rome "to stay in a convent there for a whole week—as distinguished Catholic ladies often do—in order to perform her devotions".
[3] H. E. Manning, *The True Story of the Vatican Council*, London 1877, 41f.

affairs. When the Pope discovered how effective personal interviews could be, he sought to use them more and more, and revived the practice of periodical "ad limina" visits. To assist the centralization of the Church throughout the world, the administrative organization of the Roman Congregations was extended—a procedure which, in the same way as the organization of the "International", had been made possible by the social changes of the nineteenth century.

The Pope was more and more inclined to make appointments of bishops without regard to the suggestions of the local clergy. For him, the decisive considerations were whether the candidate had been educated in Rome and whether he would be submissive to the Curia. Better to appoint reliable men than priests of great merit who would be too independent! The length of his reign gave this Pope the chance to replace the entire body of bishops. By 1869, out of 739 Catholic bishops, there were only eighty-one left who had been appointed during the papacy of Gregory XVI. In places where concordats limited the opportunities open to the Curia to influence the choice of candidates, the Pope relied increasingly on canonical regulations or used his power of veto, in order to increase the bishops with Ultramontane sympathies. He was able to supplement this by the way he used his power to elevate individuals to the rank of cardinal. All this had a noticeable effect on provincial councils, where there was a definite weakening of opposition to control and to the amendment by the Holy See of council decisions.

In order to increase the number of priests on whom Rome could depend, Pius IX encouraged priests and seminarists to attend the universities in Rome. In 1852 he took a personal interest in the founding of the Collegium Pium for Latin America. The fact that, in 1859, a Collegium Americanum could be added to the number of national colleges existing in Rome was due to his persistent suggestion. The Irish college was reopened in 1862, the Polish Seminary founded in 1866. In 1867 the Pope appointed a new Rector of the Anglicanum without consulting the English episcopate.

7. THE ROAD TO THE COUNCIL

A day or two before the definition of the dogma of the Immaculate Conception, Mgr Talbot is said to have remarked in confidence: "You see, the most important thing is not the new dogma itself, but the way in which it is proclaimed."[1] In the critical discussion of 20th November two bishops raised the question whether it might not be better to make

---

[1] Knoodt to Döllinger on 10th July 1866.

reference in the bull to the agreement of the episcopate; they were told that if the sovereign pontiff himself pronounced the definition, and all the faithful spontaneously adhered to it, then his decision would provide a practical demonstration of the sovereign authority of the Church in questions of doctrine and of the infallibility with which Jesus Christ had endowed His representative on earth.[1]

On 6th December 1864 the Pope for the first time revealed to the cardinals the plan which he himself had been considering, namely, an ecumenical council to bring to a close the struggle against Liberalism, just as the Council of Trent had dealt with the controversy with the Protestants.[2]

Pius used the celebration of the Martyrdom of the Apostles in 1867 as the occasion for announcing this to the public.[3] It is true that Pitra was unable to suppress his anxiety. "What, calling a Council! But the French and German theologians will come, and disrupt our congregations!" The preparatory commission at first comprised only champions of Ultramontanism, but was later enlarged to include men of different opinions, e.g. Hefele, an expert in the history of the Councils. The fact that Döllinger was passed over only made him more bitter. Mgr Dechamps, Ultramontanist though he was, said with regard to Döllinger, "On ne peut pas ne pas l'écouter."

The partisan way in which the consultants were chosen made for bad blood. It appeared to be an attempt on the part of the Curia to hold the Council *before* the Council began. In the bull "Aeterni patris", dated 29th June 1868, Pius IX summoned the Council to assemble on 8th December 1869 in the Vatican Basilica. The most difficult question to be decided was whether the heads of Catholic states should participate or not. To exclude them would be to break with tradition. But the King of Italy had been excommunicated, the presidents of the South American states were Freemasons, and the Emperor of Austria tolerated an anti-clerical government. Thus an ambiguous text was chosen for the bull summoning the Council,

---

[1] Manning, op. cit., 42. (Pius IX had defined the Immaculata Conceptio alone.)

[2] Manning, op. cit., 3ff. After the cardinals had given their written comments, the Pope got a commission of cardinals to meet on 9th March 1865, who declared a "relative, not absolute" necessity for councils. "The Church is not infallible by reason of General Councils, but General Councils are infallible by reason of the Church" (ibid., 14). The setting up of an extraordinary Congregatio Directionis was recommended (ibid., 20f.). Thus began the practice of consulting the episcopate (ibid., 24).

[3] Fears had arisen that the Feast of the Apostles would be used for the proclamation of infallibility. But after difficult negotiations with Mgr Franchi and against Manning's opposition, Dupanloup succeeded in getting the word "infallibilis" removed, which had repeatedly appeared in the bishops' address to the Pope, and, in the reference of the Pope's magisterium, in limiting its scope by the formula "ad custodiendum depositum".

and Catholic heads of state were merely given the opportunity of joining in the work of the Council.

The Council claimed to be an ecumenical one and in order that justice should be done to the existence of division in the Church, the brief "Arcano divinae providentiae" provided for the invitation of all the bishops of the Eastern Rite. After a considerable period, for the first time since Benedict XIV, the relations between East and West were once more brought on to a level of fundamental principle.[1] To show the Orientals that they were not classed in the same category as the Protestants, a few days elapsed before a call was made to the Protestants to unite with Rome and to take part in the Council.[2] In the main, this papal call was provocative in tone. An Anglican bishop did start discussions with de Buck, S.J., but Pusey's attitude made any progress in the discussions impossible.

The knowledge that decisions would be taken by the Council brought the debate between the different trends of nineteenth-century Catholicism to a head. The Ultramontanists felt that the time had come to strike a great blow. On 6th February 1869 the semi-official *Civiltà Cattolica* published the following under the heading "Correspondance de France": "Everyone knows that Catholics in France are divided into two parties, one simply Catholics, the other calling themselves Liberal Catholics. True Catholics believe that the Council will be very short. They hope that it will declare the doctrines of the Syllabus, that is, that the propositions there given in negative form will be expressed in positive formulations and with the necessary expansion. They will receive with joy the declaration of the dogmatic infallibility of the supreme bishop. No one finds it surprising that Pius IX, with a sentiment of proper reserve, does not wish to take the initiative himself for a proposition which seems to relate to him alone; but it is to be hoped that this definition will be made with acclamation by the unequivocal manifestation of the Holy Spirit through the mouth of the fathers of the Ecumenical Council."

The effect of this article was fantastic. Döllinger, who had for some months been writing a work on the papal primacy, published five articles anonymously in the *Allgemeine Zeitung* of Augsburg, under the title "The

---

[1] The brief of invitation was published in the press before it was delivered to the recipients and this made an unfavourable impression. It was not tactful to have had the letters delivered by Latin missionaries.

[2] It is a matter for research to establish the circumstances of the composition of the texts of the invitations to the Orientals and the Protestants, and their reactions. The difference between reactions then and reactions to the proclamation of the Council by John XXIII is astonishing. In December 1869 the Freethinkers opened an opposition council in Naples. The future convert, Baumstark, gave a positive reaction in *Thoughts of a Protestant on the Pope's invitation to reunion in the Roman Catholic Church*. The E.O.K. in Berlin on 4th October 1868 described the Pope's action as an "unwarrantable encroachment". With this, the 15th German Evangelische Kirchentag agreed.

Pope and the Council". He accused the Jesuits and Pius IX himself of preparing for a revolution which would impose upon the Church the Pope's infallibility and primacy of jurisdiction as dogma, despite the testimony of history that the advancement of the papacy was only the consequence of a series of usurpations, beginning in the Middle Ages, "an abscess which disfigures and chokes the Church". A similar position was represented in Austria by the canonist, Schulte. An appeal to the Catholics of Baden was designed to get the support of the laity.[1]

In France a group of theological Gallicans was active at the Sorbonne, with Mgr Maret at their centre. Mgr Maret founded on research no less than Döllinger, but his influence was different from that of the creed of the German university theologians, who prided themselves on their scientific method. As a Gallican entirely disposed to co-operate with the government, Maret's technique was rather to carry confidential reports to Napoleon, but which went on occasion also to the French episcopate or the Pope. Napoleon's Minister of Culture, Rouland, and later Baroche, both of Gallican sympathies, were happy to work with Maret. Candidates from his circle were preferred in the eighteen episcopal appointments in which Baroche had a hand (e.g. Darboy's appointment as Archbishop of Paris in 1863).[2] This group had grown more bitter in 1853 when, with "Inter multiplices", Pius IX had humiliated the French episcopate before a pamphleteer like Veuillot. Liberal Catholics in France abhorred dependence of the Church upon the state as much as centralization in Rome, but they were none the less inclined to join forces with the Maret-Darboy group. A short time before the Council it was still possible for Mgr Maret to bring out his work, *Du concil général et de la paix religieuse*, on which he had been working for years with the forthcoming decisions in view. In his opinion, infallibility could not be attributed to the person of the Pope alone—it was only to be asserted when the bishops had given their approval. Rome did not conceal its displeasure. Mgr Dechamps, Archbishop of Malines, published "L'infallibilité et le concil général", and in this he defended the thesis that there could be no question of divinizing the person of the Pope or all his actions, but only of declaring an infallible authority for solemnly executed decisions on points of doctrine.

The French Liberal group, which the *Correspondent* represented, joined the debate in the issue of 10th October 1869. It was Albert de Broglie, under Dupanloup's influence, who spoke in the name of the editors. Here the hope was expressed that the Council would not contribute to the victory of a despotic monarchy in the Church, when in itself it embodied

---

[1] On 9th April, 1869, Prince Hohenlohe, Prime Minister of Bevaria, tried to persuade the governments to take concerted action.

[2] There is still no biography of Darboy.

the total authority of the Church. Instead of underlining the proposition of the Syllabus, what was needed was to make them comprehensible. Further, there could be no question of a definition of infallibility, since that would then have to apply to the actions of earlier Popes and, in some instances, such as the "Dictatus papae" of Gregory VII, or the bull, "Unam sanctam", these would be incompatible with modern precepts of public law. On 11th December 1869 Dupanloup followed Döllinger in declaring a definition of infallibility to be inopportune, and this disqualified him in the eyes of Rome for the role he might otherwise have played at the Council.

8. THE FIRST VATICAN COUNCIL

Approximately seven hundred Council Fathers, 70 per cent of the world episcopate, gathered in Rome, including many incumbents of episcopal sees which had never before been represented at a Council. At Trent, only four English-speaking bishops were present; now there were a hundred and twenty.

The Council quickly divided into two ideological groups. In the majority party of the right, the leaders were Manning and Beck, the General of the Jesuits. The minority included the Liberals and Gallicans from France, theologians from the German universities, Cardinal von Rauscher of Vienna, Archbishop von Schwarzenberg of Prague, and Simor, the Primate of Hungary. Strossmayer of Croatia considered Rome's progressive policy of centralization to be a stumbling-block to the return of the Orthodox Slavs to the Catholic Church, for which he was working so hard. The Eastern bishops rejected this policy as well, fearing that it would lead to an increase in Latinizing tendencies.

Only two out of fifty-one schemata that had been prepared were actually discussed.[1] A report that a surprise move was being planned to force through the infallibility dogma created considerable excitement. In fact, business proceeded so slowly that the discussion of infallibility was bound to be anticipated. Now both sides canvassed the fathers of the Council for support, literary activity increased and there was a good deal of agitation outside the Council. On 17th December, under the pseudonym of "Quirinus", Döllinger began to publish his "Letters from Rome" in the *Allgemeine Zeitung*, and the accuracy of the information they contained was a clear indication that the fathers of the Council were not observing the pledge of secrecy.[2] The impact on the public was all the greater, since there

[1] As early as the third public session it was possible to receive the dogmatic Constitution "De fide catholica".

[2] The Schema De ecclesia, which contained the infallibility statement and which was distributed to the Fathers on 21st January 1870, had got into the hands of the French and Austrian envoys some days before, and through them reached the press.

was no other source of accurate information.

On 18th June the Superior General of the Dominicans, Guidi, caused a sensation with his intervention in the debate. In order to overcome objections to an infallibility which was supposed to be valid for the Pope personally and "apart from the bishops", he proposed that there should be no more talk of the infallibility of the Bishop of Rome, but rather of the infallibility of his doctrinal definitions. Divine assistance extended not to the person of the Pope but to specific acts. Even if the Pope did not strictly require the consent of the bishops, he still could not proceed independently of the episcopate. The charisma of infallibility operated only to the extent that the Pope represented the traditional teachings of the Church. This meant that an examination of tradition would be essential before any definition was made, and there was no better way of ascertaining tradition than inquiring of the bishops! Pius IX created a terrible scene and told Guidi, "La tradizione son'io!"

Negotiations went on behind the scenes, so as not to drag the conflict too much into the open, and in these the Archbishop of Malines was particularly active. Guidi's initiative had thawed the ice a little between the two sides. He was responsible for the decisive fourth chapter of the dogmatic definition having the heading, "De romani pontificis infallibili magisterio". The discussion showed the infallibilists that some modification of their position was necessary. On the other hand, the controversy was so fundamental that the need to clarify this whole area of discussion became evident and this let the "Inopportunists" tone down their arguments. It became more and more important to the opposition that no formula should emerge which could give the impression that the Pope was the Church. It would have to be stated that in his definitions the Pope could not divorce himself from the faith of the Church, to which faith it was the bishops who were the authoritative witnesses. Manning, on his side, feared that infallibility might be restricted to truths of revelation. Cardinal Bilio, an assiduous mediator, persuaded Cardinal Cullen to propose a new formula, which allayed Manning's fears on the one hand by

---

With the intention of supporting the liberal Catholics, the French Foreign Minister, Daru, dispatched a note with a protest against the Schema on 20th February. With reference to Article 16 of the Concordat, he requested the transmission of the documents and the admission of a special French ambassador. A memorandum from Daru started up agitation all over Europe and found support from all the chancelleries. Antonelli was disturbed by this, but the Pope appreciated the situation in France more accurately. In fact, a telegram reached Rome on 18th April with the news that Daru had been replaced by Olivier. Döllinger's information came from the theologian Friedrich (of Cardinal Hohenlohe's circle), from his young friend, Lord Acton, and from the dispatches of the Bavarian and Prussian ambassadors which the President of the Bavarian Council of State passed on to him (C. Butler, *The Vatican Council*, 1869–70, 1962; based on Ullathorne's letters).

speaking simply of "definition of doctrine", and on the other hand ruled out the possibility of papal interference in the field of politics, which was what the governments feared. Cullen's formula, with the happy addition of the phrase "ex cathedra", prevailed. Mgr Martin of Paderborn wrote the historical preamble, which affirmed that consultation of the whole Church by the Pope was at least a beneficial custom, leaving it, however, to the Pope to choose any one of the whole range of technical possibilities as the method whereby he sought advice. When the majority showed reluctance to accept this, the minority, still trying to bring the Council round, had the satisfaction of getting the words "non autem ex consensu ecclesiae" added at the last minute to the last part of the formula which stated that papal definitions were irreformable of themselves. Anti-Gallican, anti-episcopalianist, and therefore backward-looking, the Council majority pushed through their dangerous formula, and it was at least fortunate that this was done not in connection with the actual making of any papal definitions of doctrine, but in the less important context of the possibility of their revision.[1]

On the eve of the vote fifty-seven members of the minority left the Council. Only two, who had not been informed, voted "non placet", but submitted at once. On 18th July, during a terrible storm, the constitution "Pastor aeternus" was read out, a typical product of the nineteenth century, with its craving for authority, seeking to find here a final anchorage for authority. The concept of tradition was put to one side, and understanding of the Church as the Body of Christ was impeded by the one-sided way in which the possibility was worked out that the head, the Pope, could make decisions without the whole body.[2]

The Vatican Council remained only as a torso. The heat of summer and the outbreak of the Franco-Prussian War persuaded the Pope to adjourn meetings until 11th November. But on 29th August the Italian government took advantage of the withdrawal of the French brigade from the Papal State because of the war, and declared the occupation of Rome. The Pope was given sovereignty only over the Leonine citadel.[3] Pius IX

---

[1] J. B. Torrell, *La théologie de l'épiscopat au premier concile du Vatican*, Paris 1961, demonstrates the theological work that was produced by the reaction against the Schema de Ecclesia. The infallibility of the episcopal body is not deflected by the infallibility of the Pope.

[2] Two possibilities of moderation remained open to Catholic theology. The question could be asked, when, in fact, is the *ex-cathedra* situation present, and then it could be further suggested that the Vatican Council had not succeeded in completing its task. If time had permitted further definitions, the one-sidedness of the dogma of infallibility would have been balanced out again. Thus the Orthodox theologian, Florovskij. Herein also the possibilities for the Second Vatican Council.

[3] Tüchle states that the action of the Italian government was taken on the advice of the Prussian envoy. Schlözer reports a vision of the Leonine city as the papal area.

instructed the general in command of the papal troops to capitulate as soon as the first cannon shots were fired, demonstrating that this was an act of violence. When General Cadorna, commanding the Italians, moved into Rome, Cardinal Antonelli asked him to provide police patrols in the Leonine citadel as well.[1] In view of these events, on 20th October Pius IX adjourned the Council, *sine die*.[2]

9. COLLAPSE OF THE OPPOSITION

In France the fathers of the Council who had been in opposition submitted completely and absolutely, due to pressure from the Ultramontane diocesan clergy, and to the fact that the country had been shaken by the rapid German victories. Mgr Darboy, Archbishop of Paris, wrote: "The Council is hardly mentioned now. France has so many troubles to deal with that the vergers and their Byzantine discussions fall into the background." What was now necessary was unity of moral outlook, and this was helped by the realization that even if the transactions of the Council were considered by some to be unlawful it was still the case that a sizeable proportion of the French episcopate had endorsed infallibility. Mgr Maret drew attention to the fact that Veuillot's group of integrists had not, in fact, been able to prevail at the Vatican.[3] In Austria and Germany opposition bishops agreed not to take action on their own without consulting von Rauscher and Schwarzenberg, the leaders of the opposition party at the Council, and this constituted a more serious problem. But in the middle of August a severe illness removed Cardinal von Rauscher from the scene. Geissel was afraid that if opposition continued the authority of the Church in general would be damaged, and at his initiative a conference of bishops was held at Fulda, which issued a pastoral letter confirming the validity of the Council's decisions. Roman circles welcomed this public

---

[1] Antonelli's motives are a matter of dispute; betrayal for personal gain, concern for security against anti-clerical gangs or the provocation of a solution that would in all probability be anti-papal in order that world opinion might put the worst interpretation on the Italian act of violence and cause a revolt of Catholic conscience as soon as possible?

[2] The labours of the Vatican Council commissions were by no means in vain. Canonists drew upon them in 1917 at the time of the publication of *The Codex Juris Canonici*.

[3] Mgr Maret wrote: "The aim of the extreme party was to make the Pope completely and absolutely independent of the episcopate. The lectures that were given, the pamphlets and scholarly works that were published, demonstrated this. This aim has not been achieved in the Decree. God has willed it so. The result has been secured that the infallibility of the Pope certainly does not come from the episcopate as though it was its source; but it remains nevertheless certain, that the co-operation of the episcopate, and its previous or concurrent approval is an essential condition of this infallibility."

statement with relief. But this put an end to the solidarity that had remained between Germany and Austria, and the unity in moral outlook of the bishops and the university professors was shattered. Von Scherr, the Archbishop of Munich, who had himself once said that he would not require his clergy to adhere to the new dogma, excommunicated Döllinger. Knoodt, Reinkens and Friedrich, all professors, likewise suffered excommunication. Those who felt themselves at one in conscience with the professorial group founded the Old Catholic Church. Hefele was the last of the German bishops to submit, which he did on 10th April 1871.[1] In the Austro-Hungarian Empire the old ways still persisted, and the critical situation was muddled through. The last to submit was the Croatian Bishop Strossmayer, on 26th October 1872.

In the development of piety in the nineteenth century veneration of the Pope had gone too far. A church newspaper which appeared in Nîmes in 1865 had written à propos the doctrinal definition of the Immaculate Conception: "Louis XIV said the famous words, 'L'état, c'est moi!' Pius IX has gone further. He has said, and in fact with better reason than Louis, 'L'église, c'est moi!' " He had been addressed as "Oracle" and "Vice-God of mankind". The Archbishop of Rheims, however, had spoken of an "idolatry of the papacy".

The Vatican Decree did not, however, completely endorse the opinions of Neo-Ultramontanists like Ward, Butler and Veuillot. In this connection, the Bishop of Augsburg could write to Cardinal Schwarzenberg that infallibility had been reduced to such narrow limits that it must be adjudged a victory for the minority rather than for the majority. Newman wrote at this time to Mrs Froude: "To all appearances Pius IX wanted to say a good deal more. But a greater Power prevented it."[2]

---

[1] The depth of the conflict of conscience is expressed in Hefele's letter to Döllinger dated 14th September 1870. "I thought I was serving the Catholic Church, and I served the caricature which the Jesuits have made of it." "To acknowledge as divinely revealed what is not in itself true—let anyone do it who can; for myself I cannot."

[2] E. I. Watkin, op. cit., 206f. On the occasion of Gladstone's attack on the Council in 1874, Newman, in an open letter to the Duke of Norfolk, explained that the Vatican Definition was really the result of moderation. Scheeben wrote sharply worded pamphlets against the opponents of the papal infallibility and gave a similar interpretation.

CHAPTER VIII

THE CATHOLIC CHURCH IN THE ANGLO-SAXON WORLD

Since her victory over Napoleon, England had assumed a role of world leadership. From 1830 and the beginning of industrialization, the United States was concentrating on preparing the way for the power she was later to possess. That the Catholic Church was able to establish itself within the Anglo-Saxon world, which from the days of its inception had been Protestant, was a development of the greatest importance. It was the liberalizing tendencies of the century that made this possible. The immigration of workers of foreign nationality and different language, the key role played by émigré aristocrats and clerics, conversions among the educated classes, the size of Catholic families—all these factors helped to build up the Catholic elements of the population. There was no lack of internal tension, as can easily be understood if Gallican traditions are considered alongside the abrupt Ultramontane decisions. The Catholic Church was faced with the task of welding itself together, and it succeeded, due to the fact that all elements were at home with the Roman Mass and to the formal advantages of the episcopal office, which was established in the U.S.A. between 1791 and 1808, and on English soil in 1850. This process would have resulted in a militant but quite mediocre kind of Catholicism if it had not been for one man—John Henry Newman, who opened up questions his contemporaries were unable to answer, but which have remained productive up to the present.

I. THE FRENCH EMIGRÉS

On 3rd March 1791 an English smuggler tied up at Mount's Bay and put ashore brandy and a bishop. This was Mgr de la Marche, the first of the émigré clerics, fleeing on account of the Terror from his see, St Paul de Léon in Brittany. By 1797, 5,500 Catholic priests had taken refuge in the British Isles from revolutionary France, including sixteen bishops; 5,950 Catholic laymen came, too. The assistance which Protestant England gave these Catholic refugees was not confined to fixed money payments (two English pounds a month for a priest, ten pounds for a bishop). The Oxford University Press printed 2,000 copies of the Vulgate for them, and the Marquis of Buckingham printed a similar number. As there were not enough Catholic altars in London, Bishop Douglas permitted the saying of mass in private houses. King's House at Winchester was put at the disposal of the French clergy, and there, six hundred priests lived under rule.[1] The building up of the Catholic Church in England began when the French priests got down to fulfilling their apostolic responsibilities.

The English Catholic settlements abroad, in Holland and France, which had been of an educational and monastic nature[2] were lost when the French Revolution hit them. They were important, however, in that the new situation made it possible to establish institutions to replace them in England, their motherland. The school and seminary of Douai was soon succeeded by two institutions on English soil: Old Hall, which was moved to St Edmunds in 1799, and Crookthall, which settled in Ushaw in 1808. The setting up of similar institutions, for example that at Oscott, was also made easier. The College of the English ex-Jesuits of Liège formed a new house in 1794 at Stonyhurst, in Lancashire. In 1814, when the Jesuit Order was again tolerated, this College came openly to the fore as a Jesuit institution.[3]

Two French refugee congregations found a welcome on English soil. The French Benedictine nuns of Montargis landed at Brighton, the Prince of Wales let them have Bodney Hall, and in England they have remained ever since, moving to Princethorpe in 1835. The exiled Trappists took refuge in the monastery of Lulworth which had lain deserted since 1559, but went back to La Trappe in 1817.[4]

In view of the fact that members of the orders, flooding into England, were playing such a large part in the mounting renewal of Catholic life, the Monastic Institutions Bill, which Sir Henry Mildmay introduced in 1800, constituted something of a danger. But the Anglican Bishop of Rochester, Bishop Horsby, intervened and prevented the measure getting through the House of Lords.

The Napoleonic Concordat enabled the French émigrés to move back again to France. At the same time, however, the old bishops were called upon by Pius VII to renounce their office. Out of the nineteen bishops

---

[1] E. I. Watkin, *Roman Catholicism in England from the Reformation to 1950*, London, 1957, 144f.

[2] On monastic foundations overseas, cf. Watkin, op. cit., 73ff.; P. Guilgay, *The English Catholic Refugees on the Continent, 1558–1793*; also *The English Colleges and Convents in the Catholic Low Countries*; D. V. Whelan, *Historic English Convents of To-day* (chapter on "The History of English Convents in France and Flanders").

[3] Watkin, op. cit., 151f.

[4] Watkin, 146, 166, 168. On the enrichment of monastic life in Ireland, cf. Mother F. M. T. Ball, Dublin 1961. (Because of the fact that Mgr Murray sent F. M. T. Ball to York for her education, when she returned in 1821 Mary Ward's educational institute for girls was transplanted to Ireland.)

living at that time in London, fourteen refused to obey. Of the priests, some nine hundred stayed on in England, at least for the time being.

2. THE IRISH QUESTION AND CATHOLIC EMANCIPATION

When full union between England and Ireland came about in 1800, the promise was given that the emancipation of Catholics, giving them full civil rights, would follow. In the following year Pitt wanted to meet this promise, but King George informed him that he was prevented by his coronation oath from agreeing.

In 1823, however, O'Connell started the Catholic Association. The subscription to this society was very small, one shilling a year, low enough for the poorest Irishman to join. In this way, there came into being a reservoir of Catholic nationalism in Ireland. English Catholics soon copied the Irish model. An attempt was made to undermine these associations by forcing them into illegal activities, but this was foiled by having them formally reconstituted. In 1826 the Catholic Association came out with a Declaration of Principle which Bishop Poynter had drafted and which reassured the Anglicans in that in it all claims to the property of the Established Church were abandoned. It was signed by all the English and Scottish bishops. Rallying support from the Catholic Association, O'Connell was successful in the election of 1828, and his victory stimulated something amounting to a constitutional revolt by the Catholic electorate of Ireland. Under the pressure of this development, Peel managed to get the King to agree to the emancipation of the Catholics in 1829.

Now Catholics could vote and hold office, and the last remnants of the Elizabethan laws of prohibition were swept away.[1] Napoleon's high-handed dealing with the Pope had brought into being a tacit alliance

[1] In his autobiography *From Cabin-boy* . . . Bishop Ullathorne gives a sketch of the Catholic community of Scarborough, Yorkshire, a typical picture of a community's life *before* emancipation: "Every sixth Sunday a priest would appear for the service; on intervening feast days the congregation gathered morning and evening in the chapel for prayer, under the direction of a Lector of the week." After some public prayers, the mass prayers taken from *The Garden of the Soul* "were read in a subdued tone, followed by a sermon from Archer's collection". Even after 1829 the prohibition against Catholic clerical vestments being seen outside the church was maintained. As late as the Eucharistic Congress of 1908 use was made of these limitations. After emancipation, an influential parliamentary group of Catholics grew up in the House of Commons, in 1830 with ten members, in 1831 with thirteen (B. Ward, *The Eve of Catholic Emancipation 1803–29*, II, also *The Sequel to Catholic Emancipation, 1829–50*, 2 vols—this gives most detail). As a result of emancipation, the Irish clergy were won over for England to such an extent that they refused to support the repeal movement; cf. P. S. O'Hegarty, *A History of Ireland under the Union*, London 1952, 49ff.

between England and the papacy.[1] When Pius returned from exile in 1814 he sent Consalvi to England as his diplomatic representative, to have preliminary discussions on the problems facing the Congress of Vienna. This was the first time since Cardinal Pole that a cardinal was received at the English Court,[2] but the Catholics of Ireland and England by no means all welcomed this contact with Rome. In Irish Catholicism, "Gallicanist" ways of thought continued unabated. When a settlement with Rome in 1815 gave the government the right of veto in elections of Catholic bishops, the Irish press launched a sharp attack on Consalvi. O'Connell publicly declared: "I am a sincere Catholic; but I am no Papist. The authority of the Pope in spiritual matters is limited. He cannot change our religion. Even in inessential questions of discipline, without the con-currence of the Irish bishops, the Pope can alter nothing".

In 1823, a Cambridge graduate, Kenelm Digby, whose Romanticism had led to his conversion (author of *Mores catholici* and *The Broadstone of Honour*), was the first in England to exploit the taste for medieval Gothic art in the interests of Catholic apologetic. Two years later he was joined by the young Romantic, Ambrose Philips, a wealthy country gentleman from Leicestershire who from then on used his fortune to bring about (in collaboration with Pugin, the architect) a neo-Gothic revival in church architecture (thirty-five churches between 1837 and 1845). The idea was to introduce a new age of medievalism.[3] Emulators of Gothic were later to be opposed by devotees of the Italic style. The first Italian missionaries to appear were Dr Gentili, a pupil of Rosmini, and the Passionist, Dominic Barberi, who, unperturbed by their failure to master the English language, worked away with great dedication in England.[4]

But the Gothic movement was to be countered on a second front. Since the beginning of the century the Catholic population of England had been growing through the immigration of Irish workers, attracted by the possibility of finding work in industry (potato famine, 1845–7). Into English Catholicism, which tended to be that of the landlord, the Irish

---

[1] The English General Bentinck, who had defended Sicily against Napoleon, at a meeting on 30th March 1814 placed his troops at the disposal of Pius VII, whose return to Rome was impeded by Murat's occupation of the Papal State. Cf. Leflon, op. cit., 277f.

[2] Watkin, op. cit., 161; Leflon, op. cit., 283. Consalvi, who did not meet the sovereigns in Paris, was shocked that Avignon and Venaissin remained with France, and afterwards followed the sovereigns to London. M. Sheehy, "Ireland and the Holy See", *J.E.R.*, 1962, 1–23, gives an insight into Gallican and Ultramontane trends.

[3] D. Gwynn, *Lord Shrewsbury, Pugin and the Catholic Revival*, London 1946; M. Trappes-Lomax, *Pugin, a Mediaeval Victorian*, London 1932; Watkin, op. cit., 167, 172.

[4] Watkin, op. cit., 175f.; D. Gwynn, *Father Dominic Barberi*, London 1947; R. Aubert, "Le Pontificat de Pie IX", in *Histoire de l'église* (Fliche-Martin), XXI, 1952, 68.

introduced a proletarian element. They brought their own priests with them, and their militant, unliturgical ways were ill suited to Pugin's churches. Antagonism to the Irish was later to retard the flow of conversions.[1]

3. THE OXFORD MOVEMENT

Of equal importance in strengthening English Catholicism was the influx of converts through the Oxford Movement. The movement began with a sermon which the poet, John Keble, preached on 14th July 1833, on "National Apostasy" (the Irish Act of 1833). This was really an attempt to encourage Anglicans in their conviction that they were, in fact, the true Church. Romanizing tendencies and attacks on the English reformers only came to light with the posthumous publication of Froude's works. In view of the excitement this caused in university circles, in the press and in Parliament, and because many families were refusing to send their sons to Oxford as long as it had a reputation for "romanizing", the Anglican bishops issued an official warning against the "Tractarians". This was a severe blow for Newman; for up to that time he had looked upon his bishop's concurrence as a guarantee of the soundness of his way. "I loved", he wrote later in his *Apology*, "to act in the sight of my bishop, as if it were the sight of God". In his work on "The Prophetical Office of the Church" (which Döllinger called "the masterpiece of English theology") he was still trying to find a *via media* between Protestantism and Catholicism. But in the course of his researches into Monophysitism in the autumn of 1839 the question occurred to him: "Why should the Monophysites have been heretics if Protestants and Anglicans did not deserve the same name?" The aim of Tract 90 was to keep within the Anglican Church the young generation of the Oxford Movement who, under W. G. Ward's leadership, sympathized with Rome, but it only spurred them on the more. In 1841 Newman's antagonism grew deeper when he observed that the Established Church of England was able to co-operate with the Old Prussian Union in setting up the bishopric of Jerusalem. In 1843 he resigned his Church of England appointments as University preacher at St Mary's and as Fellow of Oriel College.

On 8th October 1845, at Littlemore, his house of retreat, John Henry Newman made confession of the Catholic faith before the Italian Passionist, Dominic Barberi, and was baptized "subconditione"; on 1st November he was confirmed at Oscott by Bishop Wiseman. On that occasion, ten Anglican priests who had been converted with Newman, attended. The wave of conversions reached a second peak when the Catholic hierarchy was re-established in 1850–1. The new converts brought a high level of

[1] Watkin, op. cit., 180f.

culture to English Catholicism. Wiseman said of them: "We are their inferiors. When the Oxford theologians enter the Church, we must be ready to withdraw into the shade." In connection with the setting-up of Prior Park, Bishop Baines had already pursued the aims of Catholic education and discussed plans for a Catholic University with Wiseman, the then Rector of the Anglicanum in Rome, when the latter visited England in 1835. The Collegium Anglicanum had been closed at the time of the French occupation in 1798, but had reopened in 1815 and was now flourishing;[1] but in England itself there was no real effort to educate the public to thinking of Catholic Christians as being the cultural equals of others. Wiseman used his visit to the British Isles to give a series of lectures. When O'Connell started the *Dublin Review* in 1836 the English Catholics were able to give literary expression to their views, but it was only with the influx of converts that Wiseman's "Politics of the Catholic Presence" could reach a wider public.[2] When Newman returned from studying in Rome he offered his services as a lecturer, and from 1851 held the office of Rector in the new Catholic University of Dublin, which he hoped to make into a Catholic Oxford. The main theme of Newman's theological work was the question as to how the unconditional adherence of believers to the Church's dogma and its rational justification in the world of modern science were to be related.[3]

In view of the growth of the Catholic community, the Vicars Apostolic in England had as early as 1837 proposed to Rome that the hierarchy should be re-established. Wiseman set more store by the external trappings of a hierarchy than was warranted and when he became Pro-vicar of the London district in 1847, the English Church leader increased the pressure.[4] In 1848, after nine weeks of discussion, Mgr Ullathorne's skill as a negotiator achieved the desired end.[5] The establishment of the English hierarchy was delayed until 29th September 1850 only on account of the Pope's flight to Gaeta.

[1] Ibid., 170f.; N. Wiseman, *Recollections of Rome*, London 1936.

[2] Watkin, op. cit., 175.

[3] H. J. Walgrave, *Newman, Le développement du dogme*, Tournai, Paris 1957 (E.T. Newman the Theologian, London 1960); J. H. Newman, *Christianity and Science*; C. S. Dessain (ed.), *The Letters and Diaries of J. H. Newman*, XI, London 1961. The editor hopes to edit the 20,000 letters and all the diaries in thirty volumes, and is beginning, typically, with the Catholic period.

[4] Watkin, op. cit., 185f.

[5] Cardinal Acton in Rome had advised against the creation of the English hierarchy. He feared that increased independence would only augment the English Church's tendency to split up into parties in revolt. Acton's death in 1847 removed an obstacle to this. Cf. Ullathorne, *From Cabin-boy to Archbishop*, 1891, 247f.; Watkin, op. cit., 184. In this, Acton was thinking not only of the antagonism between the Catholic gentry and the proletarian immigrants from Ireland, but also of the tensions between the Oxford converts and the old congregations, who rejected the Italianate forms of

This action of the Roman see caused a storm of protest in Protestant England. In particular, the Prime Minister, Lord John Russell, took offence. When Wiseman was leaving on a visit to Rome, he had given him to understand, on the basis of a hint he had received from the Vatican, that he would be made a Cardinal of the Curia and would not be returning. Russell acquiesced in the Bishop of Durham's protest against the "underhand action of the Pope", and forced through Parliament an Ecclesiastical Titles Bill under which the new bishops were prohibited under penalty of a fine from using their titles within the realm.[1] Nevertheless, Wiseman, who was now Archbishop of Westminster and a Roman Cardinal, defied the attacks, returned to London and issued his "Appeal to the People". The Church, he argued, had claimed nothing to which communities existing outside the Established Church were not entitled. What the British Government had done itself in 1841 in Jerusalem was in no way different from what the Roman Church was now doing in England.

In 1851 Henry Edward Manning, Archdeacon of Chichester, was converted. Two months later, Wiseman ordained him to the priesthood and did not hesitate to make him his chief collaborator. Manning brought considerable momentum to the new Ultramontane era of English Catholicism. With the Bayswater community of secular priests, the Oblates of St Charles, he created a militant group of "romanizers".[2] When W. G. Ward was called to St Edmunds as lecturer in dogmatics—and it was a rare thing for a layman to occupy such a position—and when at the same time he took over the editorship of the Dublin Review, the most influential posts were in Ultramontane hands.[3]

For the old English bishops this was a sinister development. They therefore supported Mgr Errington, the Co-adjutor and Successor of Westminster, who did not want to see the papal influence spreading in the

---

piety which the converts were spreading. Later, it was Faber who "proceeded from the idea that the pattern of Catholic life was not to be sought in a country where the persecution of Catholicism had compelled it to disguise itself to some extent" and contended for the Italian pattern. To exert a moderating influence, Newman stopped publication of the series of lives of the saints which Faber was supervising.

[1] Repealed by Gladstone in 1871.
[2] Watkin, op. cit., 186f. Manning's conversion was one of a whole wave of conversions sparked off by the so-called Gorham judgment, in which the legal committee of the Privy Council reversed the refusal of the Anglican Bishop of Exeter to induct a cleric who denied baptismal regeneration.
[3] Watkin, op. cit., 195. Ward, in step with the dogmatic teachers of the Continent, developed a theistic metaphysic in opposition to the agnostic empiricism of J. S. Mill, with whom he was personally closely connected. It was Ward who offered the sharpest opposition to liberal Catholics in England (Lord Acton, Simpson) and drew Manning's attention to the dangerous influence of Newman.

English Church—and there was a revolt in the Cathedral chapter. The Errington disputes are certainly misunderstood if they are regarded merely as a matter of the incompatibility of his narrow pedantry with the largeness of vision of the new men. Manning wrote of Errington that his elevation to the See of Westminster would jeopardise everything that Wiseman has done since the re-establishment of the hierarchy, and would halt the progress of Catholicism for a whole century.[1] Early in 1859 Wiseman initiated the first steps in Rome against Errington, and had him removed from office in 1860.[2]

In spite of these proceedings, the Cathedral chapter was taken by surprise when Pius IX refused to accept their elected candidate, and made Manning archbishop instead. His domineering personality and the support he got from Rome forced English Catholics into a position of Ultramontane "romanizing" conformity.

For Newman, the way ahead could now not but be a tragic one. After seven years of trying to make the new University of Dublin under his charge into a Catholic Oxford, he was to see this attempt frustrated.[3] The revising of the translation of the Bible into English, which had been entrusted to Newman at the Episcopal Synod of 1855, came to a halt for financial reasons, though behind them lay suspicions of his theological position.[4]

When the liberal Catholic journal *The Rambler*—started by intellectuals among the converts in 1848 and concerned with modern questions—was about to be disowned by the Catholic episcopate, Newman offered his services as mediator and the April and July numbers of 1859 appeared under his editorship. Bishop Ullathorne, however, called for the concentration of all Catholic literary resources in the *Dublin Review*, and Newman obeyed. Nevertheless, suspicions still remained and attached to his essay, "On Consulting the Faithful in Matters of Doctrine", which appeared in July. Bishop Browne of Newport lodged a complaint against Newman with the Congregation of the Index, and this finally foreclosed the possibility of his being elevated to episcopal rank.[5]

---

[1] Letter to Mgr Talbot, in Purcell, *Life of Manning*, II, 171.

[2] Watkin, op. cit., 194f.

[3] In 1864 Manning shattered Newman's plan to settle in Oxford and be spiritual adviser to the Catholic students there. Catholics were not allowed to study at the universities until 1893 (Watkin, op. cit., 204f.).

[4] The suspension of the translation of the Bible was viewed in various ways. Laros: "As the greatest living master of English prose, Newman would have performed the task brilliantly." Cf. Watkin, op. cit., 193: "One can be glad the project failed. The scrupulousness which Dr. Martin brought to the Reims-Douay translation would have been intolerable for Newman's literary genius. Anyway, he would not have been the actual translator."

[5] Watkin, op. cit., 200. This expresses present-day Catholic opinion: "Unfortunately the bishops were blind to the need for such a periodical. An opportunity was missed."

Acton, who had carried on the editorship of *The Rambler*, replaced this journal in 1862 with *The Home and Foreign Review*. The address made at Döllinger's Congress of Scholars in Münich which criticized authoritative judgments of the Church inhibiting scholarly research, was given an enthusiastic welcome in this journal as representing its own point of view, whereupon Pius IX intervened with a brief which emphasized the merits of scholasticism over against liberal Catholic scholars. Newman's comment on the brief was that here doctrinal decisions were being set up as norms of research. Acton published the brief with Newman's interpretation and suspended the publication of the *Review*, since its continuation would have led unavoidably to conflict with Rome. At this point links between English cultural life and the Catholic Church were for the time being severed.[1]

Newman was hurt by a passing reference that was made to him in *Macmillan's Magazine* in 1864: "Truth for its own sake has never been a virtue with the Roman clergy. Father Newman informs us that it need not be." As a result, Newman wrote an account of the progress of his development in a series of articles from Thursday to Thursday. Thus emerged in barely five weeks under the title "Apologia pro vita sua", the biography which was to serve as a model for the converts of modern times.[2]

4. THE HIERARCHY AND CATHOLIC IMMIGRATION IN THE U.S.A.

Of the thirteen old colonies of the U.S.A., only one was Catholic: Maryland, the first colony to put into practice the principle of religious toleration. It was founded by the first Lord Baltimore, a nobleman who shortly before had gone over to Catholicism. In his toleration he was not inspired by considerations of a philosophical nature (e.g. as to the nature of the state), as Roger Williams was; rather, his was the practical aim of gaining non-Catholics as well as Catholics for the colony he had founded, and in which he had invested his entire fortune. From 1634 on the settlers who streamed into the country were almost all Protestants. But the government was under Catholic control, and two Jesuit fathers arrived with the first ship of immigrants. When their success in converting Indians and settlers became known in England and when dispute arose with Lord

---

[1] On the English reception of Döllinger's appeal, cf. Watkin, op. cit., 201; these proceedings, too, belong to the prehistory of the Syllabus.

[2] Watkin, op. cit., 202f. Biographical note: From 1859 Newman was taken up with simple educational tasks in the Oratory at Edgbaston, and was made a cardinal in 1879 by Leo XIII. He died in 1890. How right Newman was in thinking that his influence would not be felt until the coming century is clear from the foundation of the German Cardinal Newman Curatorium in Nürnberg and the first international Newman conference in July 1956 in Luxemburg, which brought together thirty of his interpreters from eight different countries.

Baltimore over direct purchases of land among the Indians, they were replaced by secular priests. An aggrieved band of Puritans forced Lord Baltimore in 1649 to instal a Protestant Governor.[1] Despite the fact that Maryland was declared a Crown Colony in 1692, with the result that the Anglican Church then became the state church, the Catholic Church in America owed its beginnings to Lord Baltimore.

After the Declaration of Independence, Talbot, the Vicar Apostolic resident in London, refused to accept responsibility for jurisdiction over the U.S.A. Out of regard for the general feeling against bishops in the States, the American clergy, who had gained popularity through the positive role they had played in the Revolution, were unwilling to commit themselves on the question of bishops. Diplomatic reasons also made the Pope hesitate. In 1784 he began by giving John Caroll the title only of "Apostolic Prefect". But in 1785 Caroll's authority was not weighty enough to enable him to get his way in a dispute with the Trustees of the New York community. (The Trustees insisted on withholding the emoluments of a duly qualified priest, Father Whelan of the Capuchins, so that they could give them to another priest, Father Nugent, whose preaching had made him more popular.) It now began to dawn on Rome that only the office of bishop could preserve unity in American Catholicism. The clergy of the U.S.A. were given the right to elect bishops, and in London on 15th August 1790 Caroll was consecrated the first member of the American hierarchy.

At the beginning of 1791 the Superior of Saint-Sulpice, Mgr Emery, who was worried about the future of his seminary in revolutionary France, got a group of his Sulpicians to go to the U.S.A. to set up a daughter house there. Mgr Caroll therefore commissioned them to start the diocesan seminary in Baltimore. The same year saw the establishment in Georgetown of the first Catholic university.[2]

Dmitri, Prince Gallitzin, although baptized in the Orthodox Church, had been led to conversion by his mother, the same Princess Gallitzin who was prominent in Romantic circles in Münster. In the course of an educational journey to the U.S.A. in 1792 he decided that he should serve as a

---

[1] M. B. Andrews, *The Founding of Maryland*, 1933; C. E. Olmstead, *History of Religion in the United States*, 1960; J. T. Ellis, *American Catholicism*, Chicago, 1957.

[2] A. M. Melville, *John Caroll of Baltimore*, 1955; P. Guilday, *The Life and Times of J. Caroll, 1735–1815*, 2 vols, 1922; M. A. Ray, *American Opinion of Roman Catholicism in the 18th Century*, 1936; C. J. Nuesse, *The Social Thought of American Catholics, 1634–1829*, 1945; Olmstead, op. cit., 234f. The sharp reaction which the XYZ affair of 1798 produced against France affected the French Sulpicians of the St Mary Seminary at Baltimore. Hence the opposition of the College at Georgetown against St Mary (Melville, op. cit., 146f.). When Mgr Emery wanted to recall the American Sulpicians, Caroll had to fight for their remaining. The issue was settled by Pius VII, whom Emery met at Napoleon's coronation in Paris.

priest. He therefore entered St Mary's Seminary in Baltimore, and as the first priest to complete his ordination entirely on the soil of the new Continent he became the father of the American clergy.[1]

In a manner similar to the Protestant "awakening", the Roman Church discovered the settlements in the West, Kentucky, and the forgotten French stations of Kaskaskia and Vincennes. Two French priests, Badin and Flaget, tackled head-on the task that here confronted them. In 1792 their service became that of "circuit riders".[2] After 1808, Flaget, who was by then Bishop of Bardstown, carried through the organization of the new territory.[3]

The unexpected growth of the Catholic Church in the U.S.A. was determined by three factors: the political gains which accrued when territories which had been founded as Catholic were added to the Union of American States; the immigrants; and the systematic support of Catholics in Europe.

After the War of Independence, there were only 35,000 Catholics in the States; but in 1803 Louisiana was purchased from Napoleon, and with it came a block of conservative French Catholics.[4] The Texas Revolution of 1836 and the Mexican-American War of 1848 brought Texas, New Mexico and California into American possession.[5] The new territories were

---

[1] D. Sargent, *Mitri, or the Story of Prince Demetrius*, 1945; *Gallitzin's Lettres: A Collection of the Polemical Works*, Loretto, Pa., 1940; S. Bolshakov, *Russian Non-conformists*; Olmstead, op. cit., 255; H. Lemcke, *Life and Work of Prince D. Gallitzin*, London, New York, Toronto 1940, 2, 1941.

[2] I. H. Schauinger, *Cathedrals in the Wilderness*, 1952; Olmstead, op. cit., 245f.

[3] 1808—date of the enlargement of the American hierarchy by Pius VII by the creation of a metropolitan with four additional episcopal sees.

[4] H. I. Priestly, *The Coming of the White Man*, 1929; G. M. Wrong, *The Rise and Fall of New France*, 2 vols, 1928; J. H. Kennedy, *Jesuit and Savage in New France*, 1950; Olmstead, op. cit., 33ff. The French missionary effort was an answer to the Iroquois threat to the five Jesuit chapels among the Hurons, west of Montreal. This could only be met by the conversion of the Iroquois (*Martyrdom of Fr. I. Jogues*). In 1660, Fr R. Menard led the Jesuit missionaries in the tracks of the explorers Nicolet and Esprit into the unknown interior. Within ten years their stations on the Upper Lakes were centres of Christian culture. In 1670 Marquette founded St Ignace at the mouth of Lake Michigan. Fascinated by descriptions of the "Great River", Marquette followed the Wisconsin as far as the Mississippi. In a second expedition in 1674 he founded Kaskaskia. Following on this discovery, de la Salle pushed on to the Gulf of Mexico, accompanied by the Recollect Fr Hennepin. The gigantic geo-political network from the St Lawrence river to the Gulf of Mexico would have been more effective if opposition had not prevailed between de la Salle and the Canadian authorities, and also between Recollects and Jesuits. Connections between Illinois and Canada were difficult because of the hostility of the "Fox" who lived in between. The Treaty of Paris of 1763, which ended the French-Indian war, interrupted French missionary work.

[5] H. E. Bolton, *The Spanish Borderlands, a Chronicle of Old Florida and the South-West*, 1921; also *The Rise of Christendom*, 1936; C. E. Casteneda, *The Catholic Heritage of Texas*, 6 vols, 1936–50; M. Espinosa, *Crusaders of the Rio Grande*, 1942; Z. Engel-

detached from the Mexican See of Durango and put under the charge of two French priests, Latour and Vaillant. In the main communities in the country, in Santa Fé, Albuquerque and Thaos, these two quickly came up against the opposition of the local clergy who were a turbulent set, living in concubinage, and refusing to accept the new American jurisdiction. The strength of the ties that still existed with Mexican piety was to be seen in the veneration of the Madonna of Guadeloupe (the only appearance of Mary in the New World), and in the esteem given to the bell of St Joseph of Santa Fé. Latour, who had attended the Seminary of Montferrand himself, got four young priests from there to assist him, installed a Spanish priest, Talabrit, in Thaos, so as to put the Spanish-speaking Mexican priests in the shade, and got five nuns from Loretto in Santa Fé to start a Catholic school. The dispute became even worse with Padre Martinez, whom priests with Mexican sympathies supported. These latter formed a splinter group which was declared to be schismatic. Father Vaillant preached for three weeks in Thaos against the schism and read out in churches the notice of excommunication of the rebel priests.[1]

President Jackson's policy of 1830 paved the way for industrialization and the immigration of an industrial labour force. As a result, Italians and Poles streamed into the country, as did the Irish after the Irish famine of 1846, giving rise to an urban Catholicism in the big cities among the lowest levels of society.[2] 1848, the year of revolution, brought Catholics from Germany, who settled in farming communities in the Middle West.[3]

---

hardt, *The Missions and Missionaries of California*, 5 vols, 1908–15; J. P. Dolan, "A Note on the Spanish Missionaries of California", *N.Z.M.W.*, 1962, 127–35; Olmstead, op. cit., 25f. The Franciscan mission in New Mexico, started in 1581, was responsible for twenty-five missions in 1630. The exploitation of Indian labour led to the revolt of 1680 under the medicine-man, Pope. With the re-conquest in 1692, the Indians soon found themselves within the Church again. The pioneer in Texas from 1670 was the Franciscan J. Larios. The arrival of the Frenchman, Juchereau, in 1714 speeded up the founding of mission settlements. (San Antonio, in 1718, known as Alamo.) In California, Junipero Serra founded San Diego in 1769, the first settlement in a chain of Franciscan missions, intended as a barrier against the Russian advance, and up to 1823 the most influential institutions existing under Spanish control. When Spanish rule in Mexico came to an end in 1821, there was uncertainty about the loyalty of California to the new Mexican government, so the Mexican politicians seized the mission territories between 1834 and 1840 and expelled the Franciscans.

[1] Historical novel by W. Cather, *Death comes to the Archbishop*.
[2] M. R. Mattingly, *The Catholic Church on the Kentucky Frontier, 1785–1812*, 1936; G. Shaugnessy, *Has the Immigrant Kept the Faith?* 1925.
[3] C. Barry, *The Catholic Church and German Americans*, Milwaukee, 1953. Of German immigrants after the Civil War, 35 per cent were Catholics, numbering 700,000 between 1865 and 1900, the largest Catholic group entering the U.S.A. P. Wehlinger, the first to undertake missionary work among the German immigrants, maintained on the language question that the language preserved the faith. Bishop Neumann in Philadelphia was convinced that linguistic assimilation was bound to be

By 1840 the number of Catholics had grown to 650,000; by 1850, to 1¾ million, and by 1860 it had doubled again.[1] This rapid development created difficult problems, with the various nationalities of Catholics wrestling for leadership in the Church. In the first generation of priests the French émigrés had predominated. Until 1825 it was they who provided the bishops. The fact that their mastery of the English language was far from perfect gave substance to the idea that Catholicism was a foreign confession. The Irish element, who already spoke English when they arrived, and excelled both in militancy of spirit and in organizing ability, ended up by taking over leadership in the Church.[2] Of one Irishman, Mgr England, a contemporary said that he was the first to make the Catholic religion respectable in the eyes of the American public. Mgr England managed to tone down the rivalry between the various nationalities.[3] With Neumann, Provincial of the Redemptorists, who came from Bohemia, and Friedrich Reese from Hanover, who had been active in Cincinnati since 1824, the Germans, too, ultimately entered the American episcopate.[4]

---

a slow process. When School sisters were sent in 1847, Ludwig I stressed that they must remain German. In 1840 Fr Benedikt Bayer from Baltimore complained to the Ludwig Society that charitable donations were not being used for German projects. In the "central union" an association of German Catholics was formed. Cahensly, who had noticed the circumstances of the emigrants in Le Havre, formed links between Germany and the "central union" and in 1865 and 1868 brought the problem of German Catholics in America before the German Catholic Assemblies.

[1] Of the fifty American cities with over a million inhabitants thirty-five have a Catholic majority. Since the civilization is predominantly urban, none of the great newspapers can take an anti-Catholic line.

[2] On the rivalry between French and Irish groups in the Boston congregation, founded in 1788, and the overcoming of this by Fr Matignon, see Olmstead, op. cit., 235f.; Melville, op. cit., 189ff. On the influx to the U.S.A. of French emigrant clergy, which was increased by fugitives from San Domingo, cf. Melville, op. cit., 157f. The German-Irish conflict began with the dispute between the founder of the American Benedictines, Boniface Wimmer, and the Irish Bishop M. O'Connor of Pittsburg, in whose diocese Wimmer wanted to build his (independent) abbey. The Irishman, who was keen on total abstinence, refused to allow the monastery brewery, built by the Benedictine from Bavaria, to continue. Ludwig of Bavaria had to use his connections in Rome to enable the monks' brewery to carry on (Barry, op. cit., 16f.). In 1788 a separate German national church had already been founded in Philadelphia, with the intention of choosing Fr Heilbronn as its own priest. When the separation was renewed under the Austrian priest Götz, Bishop Caroll argued that the *ius patronatus* could not be allowed to the congregation, and even if this were the case, the congregation would only have a right of presentation. After the excommunication of the priest, the schism was healed. Cf. Melville, op. cit., 203f. Later attempts, renewed by Cahensly, to create at least special German-speaking congregations, failed because of the objections of the Irish bishops.

[3] Th. Maynard, *The Story of American Catholicism*, New York 1942, 276; J. McSorley, *Father Hecker and his Friends*, St Louis 1952, 5f.; P. Guilday, *The Life and Times of John England, 1786–1842*, 2 vols. 1927; H. J. Nolan, *The Most Rev. F. P. Kenrick, Third Bishop of Philadelphia, 1830–51*, 1948.

[4] Barry, op. cit., 16ff.

The crippling shortage of priests could only be overcome with the help of Catholics in Europe. On 3rd May 1822 Bishop du Boury of New Orleans, who came from France, and was paying a visit to Lyons, managed to get a society founded with the aim of providing financial support for American Catholicism (Society for the Propagation of the Faith). This idea soon caught on among other European nations. Friedrich Reese, in Vienna in 1827, gained the sympathy of the Archbishop. He published a short history of the Bishopric of Cincinnati in the Annals of the Society in 1828, and this aroused the interest of the Austrian episcopate. An audience with the Emperor, Franz I, was arranged and this led to the setting up of the Leopold Society which was run under the auspices of Cardinal Archduke Rudolf of Olmütz and administered by Viennese Dominicans, and which gave most effective aid, particularly between 1831 and 1860. In 1838, when the King was visiting Münich, Reese succeeded in getting a similar institution, the Ludwig Society, started there.[1]

To ease the shortage of priests, in 1857, at Mgr. Spalding's instigation, an American College was founded at the Free University of Louvain by the Belgian, Pierre Kindekens, who up to that time had been Vicar General of Detroit. In the next fifty years this college trained eight hundred priests for America. In 1859 a similar American College came into being in Rome. By these means the number of priests was trebled inside twenty years, increasing from 1,320 priests in 1852 to 3,780 in 1870.[2]

Anxiety on the part of the old American Protestants over the wave of Catholic immigrants from Ireland was responsible for the rise to the "Know-nothing" movement. Alarm was first raised by a report which came from Missouri in 1829 from a correspondent of the *Home Missionary*. According to this report, the aim of the European aid societies in Lyons, Vienna and Münich was the conversion of the American West, and its effect was that feeling became more intense. Samuel Morse, the inventor of the telegraph, was convinced that the Leopold Society was an agency for the undermining of American democracy by means of Catholic infiltration (*Foreign Conspiracy against the Liberties of the United States*, 1835). The Catholic despots of Europe were said to be alarmed at the vigorous development of democratic principles in the U.S.A., and to have decided to protect themselves from the dangers that threatened by using Catholic immigration to corrupt the American character.

In 1834 the "revelations" of a former Ursuline nun who had been dismissed from her Order had such an effect that the masses, whipped up by Lyman Beecher's anti-Catholic preaching, burned the Order's convent

---

[1] B. Blied, *Austrian Aid to American Catholics, 1830–60*, 1944.
[2] J. v. D. Heyden, *The American College*, Louvain 1909; J. R. Foley, "St. Charles College", in *The Catholic World*, 168, 1948, 61ff.

at Charleston to the ground. (There were, it should be said, plenty of Protestant voices which spoke out against Catholic-baiting). With the rise of the Native American Party in 1837, anti-Catholicism acquired national significance. In 1849 the patriotic "Order of the Star Spangled Banner" was formed in New York, and its function was to see that key positions in society were kept exclusively for native-born Protestant citizens.

Demonstrations took place against the first Plenary Council of Baltimore and against the visit of Mgr Bedini, the first papal envoy to America, in 1852. In 1854-5, the "Know-nothing Movement" controlled the legislatures of several States. It influenced the legislature of Massachussetts in 1854 in its drafting of the Monasteries Inspection Law. "Bloody Monday" at Louisville (5th August 1855) demonstrated its fanatical character anew.[1]

From the start America's Catholic laity was more liberally minded, and participated more fully in community organizations. The Trustees, whom the American legislators held responsible for the legal representation of the Catholic communities, portrayed an element in the structure of American Catholicism that was basically Protestant.

Since the New York Trustees' stand over against priest and bishop in 1785, there was a clear danger that a limit might be set to authority of priests and bishops.[2] At Baltimore's instigation, Pius VII condemned "Trusteeism" with his brief "Non sine magno". John Hughes, the first Archbishop of New York (1842-66), an Irishman, solved the problem by introducing a law giving the ecclesiastical authority freedom to organize the community in accordance with Catholic Canon Law. Gradually, the New York law was copied in other states.

Numerous church buildings in the Catholic states of the South were destroyed in the Civil War. Moreover, the War had a direct influence on the history of Catholics in the U.S.A. by bringing about the economic ruin of the Catholic landed aristocracy in the Southern States, thereby eliminating the one cultured section among Catholics. Patrons could now no longer provide funds to support priests in the coloured communities.

---

[1] Olmstead, op. cit., 326; R. A. Billingston, *The Protestant Crusade*, New York, 1938; McSorley, op. cit., 10f. Connected with the demonstration against Bedini was the hostility of the Italian emigrants against the politics of Pius IX, which they considered anti-liberal and opposed to the national unification of Italy.

[2] In the South, Trusteeism was connected with the opposition to the assignment of French priests. On the same grounds, the instructions of Archbishop Maréchal of Baltimore—a Frenchman—were ignored. Only with the creation of two dioceses (Charleston and Richmond) and the nomination of two Irishmen as bishops in 1820 did the strength of the opposition decline. In 1831 Bishop Kenrick's answer to Trusteeism in Philadelphia was to interdict St Mary's Church. In New York, in 1839, when Bishop Hughes was unable to rescind the removal of one of the Sunday school teachers whom he had appointed, he waited for the next election of the Board of Trustees, the composition of which was more favourable to him (Olmstead, op. cit., 324).

Half neglected, these communities were open to evangelization by the Protestant denominations. The bitterness which arose at that time between former white masters and black slaves caused a racial separation in worship which is only now being overcome.[1]

5. PROBLEMS OF CATHOLIC UNITY

The question of how American Catholicism was to be united had to be faced. As early as the second decade of the nineteenth century the suggestion had been made by the Irishman, Dr Gallagher, that an apostolic delegation and a national Catholic university should be set up in Washington, D.C. In 1853 the future Cardinal Bedini toured the States at the Pope's bidding to sound opinion on whether a papal delegate could be accredited, but this provoked such a storm in Protestant circles that he wisely disowned the existence of such an idea altogether.[2] Instead, it seemed obvious to try to bring about unity among Catholics in the U.S.A. by calling Plenary Councils. The Archbishops of Baltimore presided over the councils with the powers of papal delegates. The first Plenary Council took place in Baltimore from 8th to 20th May 1852, under the new Archbishop, Francis Patrick Kenrick, and was a unique event for Catholics in the New World. Canonical regulations which had been drawn up at the Provincial Council of Baltimore in 1849 were extended to all bishoprics, the power of national groupings to segregate themselves was curbed, and the extent to which the laity might participate in Church administration was cut down to the limits allowed by canon law. At the second Plenary Council, in October 1866, the education question came to the fore. Contrary, as it seemed, to the guarantee of religious freedom in the American Constitution, the Minister of Education, Horace Mann, had tried to introduce religious instruction of a non-confessional nature into the public schools. To the Catholics, this appeared in practice to be very like "laicizing" schools altogether and the Catholic Church felt obliged to take the

[1] R. J. Murphy, "The Catholic Church in the U.S. during the Civil War Period", in *Record of the American Catholic Historical Society*, 39, 1928, 271ff. Bishop Lynch of Charleston sought in vain to get the Pope to recognize the Confederate Government. Cf. L. F. Stock, "Catholic Participation in the Diplomacy of the Southern Confederacy", in *Catholic Historical Review*, 14, 1930; B. J. Blied, *Catholics and the Civil War*, 1945; W. E. Wight, "Bishop Verot and the Civil War", in *Cath. Hist. Review*, 1961/2, 153–63.

[2] McSorley, op. cit., 12. At the Third Plenary Council the bishops still declined to have an Apostolic Delegate for fear of public opinion. The nomination of a delegate would be taken to be incompatible with the constitutional separation of Church and state. Only when Archbishop Satolli had been well received as papal representative at the World Exhibition in Chicago in 1892 was he appointed as delegate in the following year, though without diplomatic status.

initiative itself in the matter of education. The episcopate took up Arch-bishop Hughes's slogan: "The school before the Church!"[1] Now, amid great financial sacrifice, parochial schools began to multiply. The Provin-cial Council of Cincinnati in 1858 had led the way, and the Plenary Council of 1866 standardized collections to be made for schools.[2] The Plenary Council also put forward the clear outlines of a plan to start a Catholic university which would serve to integrate theological education throughout the Continent. Archbishop Spalding, who had been educated himself at Louvain, saw the Free University there as the model for the projected university in Washington. Its chief aim was to be able to offer those who were to be priests a better opportunity for specialist study than was possible in the seminaries. It was only at the Third Plenary Council in 1884 that firm decisions were taken on the plans.[3]

6. THE APOSTOLATE OF THE ORDERS IN THE U.S.A.

The number of Catholic immigrants flooding into the country was so large that no adaption of the existing framework of pastoral care could possibly cater for them. In this situation, the activity of the Catholic Orders and their missions, not unlike the Protestant "revivals" in structure, was indispensable. When the Jesuit Order was reinstituted in 1814 there were twenty Fathers in the United States, working in Maryland and Pennsylvania. But by 1815 they had founded the Maryland Mission with its Pioneer College. In 1821 they were joined by a group of young Belgian Jesuits, whom Bishop du Boury set to work under van Quickenborne in a mission in Missouri, concerned with the Indians and catering for the hosts of Catholic immigrants arriving in New Orleans from Ireland and Germany. Popular missionary work was begun by the Austrian, Father Wehlinger, and he alone conducted more than eight hundred missions. In 1831 a group of French Jesuits set to work in Kentucky; in 1843 Holy Cross College was founded in Worcester, Massachusetts; and in 1848 Swiss Jesuits who had been exiled following the passing of the Jesuit Law in Switzerland appeared on the scene. In 1867 the Mission to Mexico and

---

[1] Bishop Hughes of New York was narrow-minded in his anti-Protestant polemic, and his attack on the Public School Society in 1840 aroused the New York legislature to form a City Board of Education and to initiate a one-sided system of subsidy for the public schools. Olmstead, op. cit., 325.

[2] Ibid., 290. The Presbyterian Synod of New Jersey led the way in 1845 with the slogan of the Church School. On 24th October 1875 the Propaganda endorsed the American hierarchy's call to Catholic families not to send their children to the public schools. The Germans took the lead in setting up parish schools, since the Irish had no experience of work in schools at home.

[3] Preparatory work for the third and last Plenary Council (1884) was done in Rome.

Colorado was founded by Neopolitan fathers who had been driven out by Garibaldi. In 1860 the Order opened its college in Boston.[1]

The diocese of Cincinnati had, through Reese, formed connections with Vienna and in 1832 asked Redemptorists of the Hofbauer circle for help. Their resources were absorbed in the task of setting up parishes for German immigrants. It was out of the Redemptorists' only mission in New York that there came into being the first American Order, and one that was to be typical of the New World—that of the Paulist Fathers.

Hecker, who had been converted in 1844 as a young man and along with other American converts was trained as a novice at St Trond in Belgium, began the first missionary work among Catholics as member of a "Band of Mission" in St Joseph's Church, New York, in 1851. In St Patrick's Church in Norfolk, in 1856, he was astonished to discover how effective such a mission could be among non-Catholics. The Redemptorists' settlement was still German-speaking and what their missionary team lacked was a vision of an English-speaking Catholic America. When Father Hecker went to Rome to get the General of the Order to set up an English-speaking house, this was condemned as disobedience and led to his discharge. Then, in 1858, with the support of the American episcopate and of Barnabo, the Prefect of Propaganda, and Bedini, its Secretary, he founded the diocesan congregation of the Paulists.[2] The new congregation set out to win America, now under the sway of the Unitarian movement, for the Catholic Church. Of Father Hecker it was said that with him every Catholic argument was given the stamp of America. He wanted to see those who were fighting in this field armed with the weapons of their foes. In his evening lectures in a rented hall, Hecker could hold a Protestant audience of 2,500 enthralled for a whole week. He would announce a subject of mixed theological and secular interest. First he would show how near Catholicism was to the natural, reasonable man, nearer than Protestantism. Then he would pick up misunderstandings of Catholic doctrine and patiently explain them, and finally produce positive arguments for the Catholic answer. He always went the whole way, step by step from scepticism to Catholicism.[3]

In a report to Propaganda in 1833 Bishop England had already drawn attention to the growing power of the press in America. Hecker took up this theme: "The providence of God makes the press of our day an artificial medium of human intercourse more universal than the living voice itself." From Assisi, he wrote: "The special battlefield of attack and

[1] M. Horney, *The Jesuits in History*, New York 1941, 399f.; Olmstead, op. cit., 427f.
[2] McSorley, op. cit., 15ff.
[3] Ibid., 154f., 157; Hecker's Report to Cardinal Barnabo, 1862. In 1822 Bishop England had founded the first Catholic weekly, the *United States Catholic Miscellany*. Cf. Olmstead, op. cit., 324.

defence of truth for half a century to come is the printing press." So in 1865, the same year in which the *Atlantic Monthly* started, he founded *The Catholic World*, to mould the American mind, and five years later *The Young Catholic*, which eventually became the most successful of Catholic children's papers. His efforts led to the starting up of the "Catholic Publication Society".[1] In face of common misunderstanding of the place of formality and ceremonial in the Catholic Church, he affirmed American freedom, combining it with a strong doctrine of the Holy Spirit.

In his publishing activities Hecker collaborated with Orestes Brownsen, who, since his conversion in 1844, had edited the *Brownsen Quarterly*, but contributed no fewer than seventy articles to Hecker's journal. He was the most brilliant and controversial American Catholic of the nineteenth century, an unusual mixture of self-conscious dogmatism and Christian humility. Hecker felt that Brownsen was good at defeating his opponents, but did not succeed in actually winning them over. Brownsen is an interesting case, too, in that the vitality he brought to American Catholicism came from one who, originally Episcopalian, was converted through the Oxford Movement.[2]

The idea of sending nuns to the U.S.A. was put forward by Father Thorpe in Rome as early as January 1788. He had Ursulines in mind, while Father Thayer of Boston was thinking of Carmelites. In the event it was the Carmelites whose safety was threatened by revolutionary unrest in the Belgian Hoogstraet, who moved to Port Tobacco in 1790. Bishop Caroll tried to get Propaganda to extend the Carmelite rule so that a girls' school might be attached to the convent, but failed. When Louisiana was purchased in 1803 an Ursuline convent, which had been founded in 1727, came under the jurisdiction of Baltimore.

The first American Order of nuns was founded in 1808 and was the work of Elizabeth Bayley Seton, a widow and a convert, under the spiritual direction of Bishop Caroll. (Sisters of Mary and Joseph; in 1809 Emmitsburg school for girls was opened, the first independent parochial school, the staff being drawn from members of the Order; in 1840 St Joseph's Orphanage was started in Philadelphia, the first Catholic institution.) The settlement of Benedictine nuns from St Walburg (Eichstätt) in St Mary, Pennsylvania, in 1852 was the starting of the famous congregation of Saint Scholastica.[3]

---

[1] McSorley, op. cit., 162ff.

[2] Th. Maynard, op. cit., 423; A. M. Schlesinger, *Orestes A. Brownsen*, 1939; H. F. Brownsen (his son), *Life of Brownsen,* 2 vols, Detroit, 1898–1900. A number of members of the Episcopal Church were converted as a result of the Oxford Movement and joined the Paulists: William Baker, Augustine Heved, Tillotson.

[3] A. M. Melville, *Elizabeth Bayley Seton, 1774–1821*, 1951; also John Caroll, op. cit., 170ff.; Olmstead, op. cit., 427.

7. CATHOLIC CANADA

The Treaty of Paris, 1763, handed over French Catholic Canada to England with its established Anglican Church and the Penal Laws. Article IV did indeed provide for the right of French Catholics "to worship according to the rites of the Roman Church", but with the ambiguous qualification "in so far as the laws of Great Britain permit". The Test Act consequently excluded Catholics from holding public office. In the following six years sixty of the 196 priests left the country. Governor Murray had begun by applying the Treaty provisions as fairly as possible, but he received orders from London that he was to allow "no kind of ecclesiastical jurisdiction which derived from Rome" and must promote the establishment of the Anglican Church.[1]

It is an astonishing fact that despite this French Catholic Canada did not lose its unity. In 1763 there were 65,000 French Catholics living in the Province of Quebec. By 1871, as a result of the large size of the normal family, this number had grown to 930,000. The policy followed by the Church leaders was, with the faithfulness of subjects of the "ancien régime", to adopt an attitude of loyalty vis-à-vis England so as to be in a better position to demand equal rights and to withstand the official Anglicanism of the state. After ten years, English policy swung round, and in 1774 George III signed the Act of Quebec, releasing Catholics from the Test Act oath and confirming French judicial procedures and freedom of worship. Only in this way was Catholic Canada prevented from joining the movement for independence which was now breaking out in America. When the American army appeared before Quebec, French Canadians helped the English to drive back the rebels. Nevertheless, American independence did not work to the advantage of Catholic Canada: 50,000 English loyalists emigrated across the St Lawrence river, and when the English failed in their attempt to assimilate the French, the country was divided in 1791 for administrative purposes into a French Lower Canada and a more English Upper Canada.[2]

The position as regards churches and schools remained particularly difficult because of the lack of priests. To meet this situation, Mother d'Youville (who was beatified on 6th May 1959), started her "Sisters of Charity of Quebec" (of whom there are now 7,500). Two facts led to an improvement: apparently fifty priests, escaping from revolutionary France, were allowed in by the British authorities, and proved to be

---

[1] Daniel-Rops, op. cit., 701ff. (E.T., 355ff.). There is no detailed general history of the Catholic Church in Canada in the nineteenth century. A. Tessier deals at length with ecclesiastical developments in *Histoire du Canada de 1753 à 1958*.

[2] Daniel-Rops, op. cit., 703ff. (E.T., 354ff.).

models of culture and apostolic zeal; and for twenty-three years (1806–29) the episcopal See of Quebec was administered by an outstanding bishop, Octave Plessis.

At that time a twofold attack was being made on the Catholics: a new schools organization was introduced by the creation of "Royal Institutions", which alone were entitled to receive public support, and which were accordingly intended to replace the Catholic system of schools and colleges. At the same time new grants of land enabled landlords of Anglican origin to settle. On the resolute instructions of Mgr Plessis, the French Canadians conducted a boycott of schools, and in seven years they succeeded in setting up 1,500 "parish workshops" for the support of Catholic education.[1]

In the war of 1812 the French Canadians' loyalty stood the test once more, and as a token of gratitude Mgr Plessis, who up to that time had been referred to in official documents merely as "Superior", was given recognition of his hierarchical rank. A leadership crisis arose when Papineau started a radical nationalist movement which for a time displaced the episcopate from the leadership of the popular group as being too ready to be assimilated with the English. At the same time this movement provoked the government into taking punitive action and, despite 40,000 Catholic signatures of protest, passing the Act of Union which, with the reuniting of Upper and Lower Canada, introduced a system of parliamentary representation which was far from favourable to the Catholics. Nevertheless, a young Catholic member, Hippolyte Lafontaine, managed to represent Catholic interests most effectively. Lord Elgin accordingly proposed the settlement which was guaranteed by Queen Victoria in 1851.[2]

The situation of the churches improved when Ignace Bourget, Bishop of Montreal, mobilized the help of clergy from France to counteract the Protestant French-Canadian Missionary Society. Two encouraging factors had suggested that this would be a practical step: in 1837 four teaching friars from France had succeeded in getting permission to work in Montreal by arguing that they were not, in fact, priests, and they had continued to give a boost to education. In 1840 the former bishop of Nancy, Mgr Forbin-Janson, who had to leave his diocese as a result of the upheaval in Paris in 1830, had come on a missionary journey to Canada and was an outstanding success. Whole villages had accepted the faith as a result of his preaching. With these facts in mind, Mgr Bourget tried to increase his contacts with his former homeland, and set off on a journey to France, in

[1] Ibid., 705f. (E.T., 357). In 1854 the first Catholic university in Canada was opened in Quebec. In 1867 Dominion status was granted, which left each province to administer its own school system.
[2] Ibid., 737f. (E.T., 358f.).

the course of which he persuaded numerous French Orders to undertake new work in Catholic Canada.

With this additional strength, the Canadian clergy succeeded in checking the flow of emigrants from among the Catholic population into the United States and led the next generation to open up new territories in Canada itself, the groups of settlers being accompanied by priests.[1]

In the middle of the century Catholic organization forged ahead westwards and northwards along the Pacific coast. French-Canadian half-castes, with the support of their clergy, offered armed resistance when the Hudson's Bay Company took over the prairies of central Canada. Mgr Taché, who was responsible for the organization of the Church in the West, was, however, able to arrive at an understanding and get another Catholic immigration accommodated.

It has often been noted that colonials tend to be conservative in holding on to their status and do not co-operate in developments in their mother countries. In Canada's case, however, the influence of anti-revolutionary émigré priests made itself felt on two occasions—with the influx of priests after 1791 and again after 1830 with Forbin-Janson and his Restoration outlook—and this was a contributory factor in the Catholics' holding on to the ecclesiastical forms of the "ancien régime". The whole of French-Canadian society was enclosed in a net of clerical vigilance. Even if originally this provided society with security against the English-speaking Protestants, it also had the effect of preventing any infiltration of French free thinking. "Ce n'est pas l'Eglise qui est dans l'Etat, c'est l'Etat qui est dans l'Eglise."[2] Traditional Gallicanism was replaced, in fact, by an Ultramontane outlook. The Syllabus and Pius IX's policy of infallibility were received with unqualified approval in Canada, and when the Papal Zouaves were formed, no fewer than five hundred young Canadians enlisted.[3]

[1] Ibid., 708ff. (E.T., 361ff.).

[2] Pastoral letter of the episcopate of Quebec, 22nd September 1875.

[3] Daniel-Rops, op. cit., 713f. (E.T., 362); C. Lindsay, Rome in Canada, Ultramontane Struggle for Supremacy over the Civil Authority, Toronto 1877.

CHAPTER IX

UNION WITH THE EASTERN CHURCHES

The attempts made at Lyons and Florence to end the schism between East and West through the heads of the Churches meeting as a Council of the whole Church were doomed to failure. After Trent, there was a new era of effort towards union, and this has now to be examined. Characteristic was the application in this area of the methods of mission, just because these had proved so successful among the heathen peoples of the colonial territories and among Protestant subjects of Catholic princes.

Missionaries from the Orders worked feverishly at their task, and, under the jurisdiction of Propaganda, exploited every opportunity, however, partial or local, or merely political. Minor successes were achieved, offers of better schooling being made by way of enticement. But the unforeseen reaction was the building up of resentment, which still exists among those Eastern Christians in whose areas incursions were made and who have seen Rome as the disturber of the peace of the Church.

The Papacy must be given the credit for never having given up its understanding of the Church in terms of which the unity of the Body of Christ is to be actualized on earth. The Catholic Church could have found common ground with the Orthodox if the Gallican and Josephinist idea of territorial churches had been more generally seen as being quite compatible with the autocephalous principle of the Orthodox Churches and if the function of the Papacy had been reduced, as it was in Febrionianism, to a mere "centrum unitatis". It was not by chance that the Orthodox took up the Febrionian formula. The development of Ultramontanism, however, was bound to repel the Orthodox, especially as there was on the part of the East, where social development, had not gone so far, additional alarm at the extent to which the machinery of the Curia with its specialist congregations was in fact able to bolster the primacy of the Pope.

The price the Roman Church had to pay for the gains it made through the unions of this period was the danger of a disturbance in Catholic uniformity. Whatever promise for the future was contained in Leo XIII's attitude of respect for the separate tradition of the East, Chevetogne and Istina were even more significant and it was the great tragedy of the period under review that such an approach was lacking. To a man like Prosper Guéranger, associated as he was with Mme Svečin, the question of union was dear to his heart, and he was quite confident about the theory of union he supplied. He thought it was possible to detect a "policy of the Roman Popes to unite the Churches within one and the same liturgy". "Any union of the two Churches must, if it is to last, be accompanied by a change in the Oriental liturgy." We can recognize today that the efforts towards union between the Council of Trent and the Vatican Council, in spite of impressive individual successes, were bound to be fruitless because of the insistence upon latinization of the liturgy and canon law. This most highly organized of attempts at union has broken down once more.

1. JURIJ KRIŽANIC'S MISSION TO MOSCOW

In its zeal to end the schism with the East and to spread Counter-Reformation piety, Rome turned to the Orthodox of Moscow. The policy which the Polish king, Stefan Bathory, laid down and which was put into practice in 1579, was to seize Moscow from Warsaw and at the same time bring about an affiliation with Rome. This policy miscarried when "the false Dimitri" was murdered in the streets of Moscow in 1606. At first, Rome was unable to devise any new policy. Then that unique figure, Jurij Križanic, devised such an unusual approach that it is something of an enigma to know whether to think of him as the most important missionary Propaganda ever had or as an early founder of Pan-Slavism.

In his home in Croatia, Križanic had first-hand experience of the unhappy split in the Hapsburg and Ottoman ruler. It appeared to him that the greatest obstacle to the coming together of the Slavonic peoples lay in their division into Orthodox and Catholic confessions. The most important of the Slavs, the Russians, would have to be allied to Rome, not by force of arms but by force of conviction. He saw that if union was eventually to be achieved, the first step would have to be to bring the Orthodox Wallachians of Croatia into the Catholic Church.

As a student, Križanic developed a real animosity against the Germans. The Jesuit colleges at Agram, Graz and Vienna, sharing this outlook, therefore turned out to be more congenial to him than the Moravian colleges of Bohemia which the Czech Jesuit, Balvin, had criticized for promoting non-nationalist ideas of a united Germany. Križanic developed an anti-Greek outlook at the Greek College of St Athanasius in Rome, where he went to study because he felt that his plan for a mission to Moscow would require a thorough knowledge of Greek theology. It had been the Greeks who had constantly stirred up Russian hatred of Rome. The Emperors, whether Roman or Greek, had never shown sufficient understanding of the Slavs.

In 1641 Križanic worked out his mission plan. No one could go to the

Russians who was not engaged on mission solely for the glory of God; consideration must be shown for the old Slavonic liturgy; there were to be no illegal entries into Russia, but all involved would have to achieve sufficient literary distinction to earn an invitation from the Tsar. He, Križanic, would commend himself to the Tsar by writing a history of the Slavonic people. He would offer his services as translator and also as tutor to the royal family. He would study mathematics, so that he could impress upon the Russians the urgency of correcting their calendar. Only after four to five years spent in gaining their trust would he divulge his actual plan in Moscow. The projected union would then be based not on theology but on power politics. In the struggle against the Turks, Moscow certainly needed the support of western Europe, if only because of the technical military skills of the West. Such support could only be expected if there was a union of the Churches. Ingoli, the Secretary of Propaganda, was deeply impressed by this plan, and therefore had Križanic ordained as a priest of Propaganda in 1642, with special permission to use the liturgy of the Eastern Church.

Three times he tried to make a start with his assignment in Moscow, but each attempt proved to be in vain. In 1644 he was sent to Bishop Parczewski of Smolensk, only to discover that the Pole looked upon the See of Smolensk as no more than an outpost. In 1647 Križanic did reach Moscow with a Polish legation which he had joined as an interpreter, but he realized that merely appearing with the Poles would be enough to discredit his commission. In 1651 he entered the service of the Imperial Internuncio at the High Port, but it emerged that there was no possibility of entering Russia from Constantinople. When, however, he was on leave studying at the Library of Gran, he discovered a route from Hungary to the Ukraine and from there to Moscow. So, in September 1659, Križanic entered the Tsarist capital and, assuming the name Jurij Bilic, got a post in the embassy. The situation was not unfavourable: following the uniting of the Kingdom of Moscow with the Ukraine in 1654, interest in languages and science had been growing in Moscow and scholars from Kiev Academy had been called to Moscow, thus forming a bridge with Latin scholasticism. In the Ukrainian monks' monastery Križanic could hope to find a group who would favour the idea of union.

One day, however, when Križanic let slip a reference to his real mission, some Russians grew suspicious of this missionary from Propaganda in the embassy, and in 1661 Križanic was banished to Tobolsk in Siberia. He did not regain his freedom until fifteen years later, in 1676, on the death of Czar Alexei. The Tsarist government was eventually forced to recognize that even now Križanic had no intention of switching his allegiance to Russia and Orthodoxy, and he was threatened with banishment even more severe. It was only because the Danish ambassador intervened on his behalf that Križanic was allowed to make his departure for the West.

2. UNION IN POLAND

If attempts to promote union in Moscow came to nothing, efforts in the Ukrainian and White Russian Voivodeships of the Polish-Lithuanian aristocratic republic did meet with success. At the end of the sixteenth century the Orthodox nobles in these districts were trying to get an alliance with the Catholic Poles, because they hoped to acquire the same aristocratic privileges as had been granted in Poland. The Jesuit schools exerted their influence in support of this policy. In 1588 the ecumenical Patriarch, Jeremias II, in the course of a visitation, brought new life to Orthodoxy which was at a low ebb, and the Castellan of Brest, in order to check this movement, took up the question of the union of the Churches. The nuncio in Warsaw declared that the Union concluded at Florence was still valid, and when a synod of Orthodox bishops met in Brest in October 1596, and resolved upon Union, the King did not hesitate to give official state recognition to it.

The Latin bishops, however, insisted on their own interpretation of territorial jurisdiction, and refused to allow the Uniate bishops independent rights of administration in their territories, demanding that the tithes which the Uniates paid over to their episcopate be also paid to them, and finally blocking the Uniate bishops' admission to the Polish Senate. Thus the union was soon in grave difficulty. On the other side, Theophanes, Patriarch of Jerusalem, consecrated new Orthodox non-Uniate bishops for all bishoprics in Uniate territories and the Polish king, John Casimir, began to see that the union offered no prospects of a constructive policy. He therefore sacrificed it, in the Treaty of Hadiacz which he made with the Cossack enemies of union and their Russian allies, who, in the course of the campaign, had already captured the cities of Smolensk, Polock and Vilna, and expelled their Uniate bishops.

It looked as though the Uniate Church in the Polish-Lithuanian dominion had come to an end. But in 1668 John Casimir, prior to his abdication, withdrew all the privileges he had given to the new Orthodox and reaffirmed the Union. At this point Joseph Szumlánski stormed the Svjatyj Juryj, the cathedral hill at Lemberg, like a robber knight, and had himself installed there as the Orthodox bishop. His aim was to hold the senior Orthodox office of Metropolitan of Kiev, but he was let down by Moscow, and, in 1677, secretly went over to the Union. So, for the second time, the Uniate Church was established. Szumlánski did not comply with Roman wishes that he should forthwith act to enforce the law of the

Church. Psychologically, he shared the feelings of the people, who for the time being were still Orthodox in outlook, and he let them keep the Eastern rite, to which they were accustomed. But he did get the support of King John Sobieski, who saw in the Union a chance to separate the Eastern Christians in his kingdom from Constantinople and the Turks on the one hand, and from Moscow and the Russians on the other.

In 1680 the King and Szumlánski invited both Orthodox and Uniates to Lublin to discuss union. This step was opposed as much by Rome, which objected to non-Catholics being treated on equal terms with Catholics, as by the Orthodox Bishop of Luck, Gedeon Četvertinskij, and indeed came to nothing. But in 1681 the Bishops of Lemberg and Przemyšl and the Igumen of Univ publicly accepted the Union, and this met with such a response that Četvertinskij had to withdraw to Russia. (In 1685 he was translated from Moscow and became Orthodox Metropolitan of Kiev). The only thing now holding up progress was Szumlánski's break with the King, John Sobieski, when the latter, with the "perpetuation" of the Treaty of Andrussov in 1686, in supplementary clauses dealing with religion, gave Gedeon Četvertinskij jurisdiction over the whole of Poland-Lithuania. Szumlánski would rather have been directly responsible for a fixed period to the Patriarch of Moscow.

It was only in 1699, under King Augustus the Strong, that the Theatines, who ran a seminary in Lemberg for the Armenians, persuaded Szumlánski to come round again and publicly accept the Union. As Rome was hesitant about accepting this bishop who was always changing sides, Szumlánski got authority from the Diocesan Synod of Lemberg in 1700 to carry through the Union. Never had the Union been so complete as now. (In 1702 the Bishop of Luck also joined, and in 1708 the Lembergers in Bratstvo came in as well.)

The Uniate Church of Poland-Lithuania suffered more and more from a lack of balance in its structure. The reason for this was that the monasteries belonged to an independent, super-diocesan association of "Basilians", for whom the Metropolitan, Joseph Rutski had made provision between 1617 and 1621. Eastern monastic life in this area thus quickly achieved a stage of development which it had taken Western monasticism centuries to arrive at. But in a different way from the West, Basilian monasticism was bound to become a real threat to episcopal power.

Initially, the Metropolitan had always had himself elected Superior of Basilian monasteries. But during a vacancy in the Metropolitan See the Basilians, following the letter of the rule of their Order, held an election and elected an ordinary monk as their Superior. As a result, as far as the Order was concerned, the reins were taken completely out of the Metropolitan's hands, and the dangerous possibility of separate administration was realized.

The Basilians were also the driving force behind changes in the liturgy. Modelling itself on the Jesuits, the Order converted itself into an Order of priests. The young members of the Order, who were sent to Rome to study, formed an association with Grotta Ferrata which gave them the model for their liturgy.

Daily celebration by all the monks who were priests necessitated the removal of the iconostasis of the Eastern Church and the erection of side altars within the Church. The latinizing of the liturgy in this way constituted a real threat to the unity of the Uniate Churches, since the Basilians came from the old Uniate districts of White Russia and Polessia, and as a body, considered themselves quite separate from the new Ukrainian Uniates, who did not want to change the rite of the Eastern Church. Rome supported the independence of the Order, as this was in line with Western thought, and the Order's power grew to such an extent that in the "Nexus" settled at Novogrodek in 1686 the bishops' dependence on the Order was only thinly veiled.

There were so many unresolved questions that Metropolitan Leo Kiszka, with Rome's approval, called a Synod for the year 1720. As there was an outbreak of plague in Lemberg, the Synod actually met in Zamość.

With Grimaldi, the Nuncio, presiding, and, strangely, with no representation from the Polish State, the Synod hastily drew up nineteen articles which have been normative for the Ukrainian-White Russian Uniate Church ever since. Roman dogma and official Roman thinking were now reflected in the introduction of the "Filioque" and of commemoration of the Pope in the liturgy. The practice of the Old Uniates of Lithuania with regard to celebration of the sacraments was merely set out in the form of notes to the Trebnik. Indeed, the conservative nature of its wording, which the printing press of the Stauropegium at Lemberg tried to perpetuate in the liturgical books it printed, necessitated the setting up of a commission to revise it between 1730 and 1732. Zamość made reforms in all the offices in the Church, from that of Metropolitan to nuns in Orders. The monasteries even in the new Uniate bishoprics of the South were to be united in one congregation. (This took place in 1739, under Metropolitan Afanasij Szeptyckij.) Under the heading of "Simony" the results of twenty years' discussion between Rome and the Uniates on the question of Church taxes were set out, to be posted up in chancellories. On the question of the visitation of country parishes, Zamość drew up a form of questionnaire to be completed. Throughout, references to the law of the Eastern Church were omitted, so great was the zeal to carry through the Tridentine reforms in matters of union as elsewhere.

The bulls in which Clement VII and Paul V had confirmed the use of the Eastern Rite by the Uniates were not even mentioned at Zamość. It is true that when Rome ratified the decrees of the Synod of 1724, the Secretary of the Congregation of Rites, Prosper Lambertini, (subsequently Benedict XIV) had a provision inserted contradicting the actual proceedings, to the effect that earlier papal concessions were not to be thereby annulled, and on this the "Purism" which developed in the nineteenth century in Uniate circles in Galicia, influenced by Pan-Slavism, was able to found. The proviso, however, could not conceal the fact that after the Westernizing that had taken place at Zamość, Rome's practice in matters of union was not to be trusted by the Eastern Churches. The half-latinized Ruthenian rite certainly assisted political separation from both Moscow and Constantinople, and this was to the advantage of the Ukrainian people and the Warsaw government, but it none the less made it impossible for this union to serve as a bridge between Rome and Orthodoxy.

Rome inisted on completely transforming Uniate monasticism after the pattern of a Latin congregation, and, at a General Congregation of all the Basilian monasteries at Dubno in May 1743, the northern province and the southern province were brought together under one authority by the election of a common Proto-archimandrite. At this point, in the Order of Basilians, the Eastern practice, in which the monks took the place of the episcopate, coincided with the Western feature of comprehensive organizational unity, with the result that all power in the Church was concentrated in the hands of the Proto-archimandrite.

In their struggle for power with the secular clergy, the Basilians declared that any rectory in which the duties were being discharged by a monk was to be considered a house belonging to the Order; indeed, in this way they even laid claim to bishops' palaces.

The predominance of the Order continued undisturbed until 1750, when the Metropolitan tackled the problem of giving dioceses their own seminaries for secular priests, a policy that had been decided upon at Zamość. Rome assisted this arrangement in 1756 by extending the provision made for the Gallican bishops in 1670 in the constitution "Superna magni patris" so as to apply to the relation between the Basilians and the Uniate bishops, and in terms of this provision regular priests were subordinated to the local bishop. Thereafter the monks were subject to the bishops in matters of pastoral care and preaching anywhere other than in the Order's churches.

In 1743 Benedict XIV ratified the rule of the Basilian Order which had been drawn up at Dubno, and thus took a step which was to have momentous consequences in the history of the Uniate Church. The great canonist on the papal throne insisted that the final version should include a reference to the apostolic Constitution which he had just issued for the Uniate Melkites in Syria. From then on it was possible to argue in terms of canon law that papal constitutions which were issued for one rite might be applied unilaterally in individual cases to other Uniate rites as well. The Latin bishops of Poland soon exploited this possibility, when they appealed to a decree of the Pope concerning the Italian Greeks, "Etsi pastoralis", which gave the Latin rite priority over the Greek. This decision they wanted to use to advantage in their relations with the Uniate episcopate.

Overall cohesion was completely restored to developments in Uniate church law for the different Uniate rites in the following manner: the Latin bishops and the Polish king wanted to make it possible for the laity to switch over from the Uniate to the Latin rite (with the abrogation of Urban VIII's decree of 7th February 1624). Taking the advice of the nuncio, Archinto, who was well disposed to the Union (and who had been Secretary of State since 1756), the Pope finally put a stop to this tendency with his constitution "Allatae sunt". Changing over from one of the Uniate rites to the Latin rite was now generally forbidden without special apostolic permission.

3. PODCARPATHIA AND TRANSYLVANIA

To Hungarian Catholics, the kind of union that had taken place in Poland–Lithuania appeared to be a practical possibility for the Orthodox Slavs of Podcarpathia as well. The Primate of Hungary showed no lack of initiative in this question, but he was opposed by the local ruler, Georg Rakoczy, who was a Calvinist and who was anxious to ensure that the Bishop of Munkacs should be of the Orthodox confession. In January 1652 Bishop Parfenij Rostošynskij (1649–68) succeeded in getting almost all the clergy of Podcarpathia and many of the laity as well to sign a letter to Pope Innocent X stating their readiness to submit to Rome. If negotiations within the Roman congregations had not dragged on until 1655, probably not so many priests would have gone back again to the side of the rival Orthodox bishop, who had Rakoczy's support. But now the Emperor, Leopold I, who was so strenuously pursuing union with the Protestant princes of North Germany, and promoting the "politica nova" in Hungary, now liberated from Turkish rule, made his influence felt in Podcarpathia and also in the Roumanian settlement of Transylvania. In 1660, both the Emperor and the Primate of Hungary confirmed Rostošynskij as occupant of the See of Munkacs. After the death of Georg Rakoczy, his widow, Sophia Bathory, joined the Roman Church and commissioned the Jesuits to conduct a thorough-going mission throughout the whole territory. The Jesuit University of Tyrnau then became the centre of Union activities. When Rostošynskij died in 1668 Podcarpathia again became the scene of strife between rival candidates for the office of bishop, until, in 1689 a former student of the Greek College in Rome, Johannes de Camillis, was sent as Vicar Apostolic to Munkacs. As one who had been a fellow student with Cyprian Žochovskij, who was at this time Uniat Metropolitan of Kiev, de Camillis got on well with the Ruthenian Union. By 1693 he had already won over some four hundred parishes for the Uniate Church.

Like the Orthodox of Podcarpathia, the Orthodox Roumanians of Transylvania, at the end of the seventeenth century, fell under the influence of Calvinist Hungarian landowners. In this situation, the Roumanians turned to Rome. On 5th September 1700 the Orthodox Bishop Athanasius, together with the Protopopes and priests, meeting at Alba Julia, declared that they had united with the Roman Church. At the time when Moldavia and the Wallachians were discarding the unserviceable mantle of the Slavonic liturgy, the Roumanian Orthodox of Transylvania were ridding themselves of Calvinist and Magyar influences by means of union with Rome. After 1683, Emperor Leopold I gave encouragement to this development by promising civil equality to Roumanians who became Uniates.

Here again, Rome acted with such circumspection that it was possible for a group to be organized to protect Orthodox traditions and the Roumanians of Transylvania were split into "Uniti" and "New Uniti". The Uniate Roumanians, who now for the most part did their studying in Rome, there discovered Roumanian "latinity", the affiliation of their people to the family of Romanic peoples, and this was to become an important factor in the development of Roumanian national consciousness during the wave of nationalism in the nineteenth century.

4. UNION IN THE NEAR EAST

Notions of union were also current in the Near East. In 1625 Urban VIII formed the idea of utilising political relations between Paris and the High Port, which were a source of irritation to Christian Europe, to foster effort towards union between the Chalcedonian and Non-Chalcedonian Churches of the Ottoman Empire. With the agreement of Louis XIII, he got the French Carmelites, Capuchins and Jesuits to send out members of their Orders, particularly to Syria. The King commended the missionaries to his ambassador in Constantinople, M. de Césy, and French consulates became centres of union activity. It is true that it was the Franciscans who were responsible for preventing a French consulate being established in the Holy City—the first settlement there was founded by Rey in 1713. Aleppo, at the crossroads of caravan routes, leading to Iraq and Persia, became the centre of the new missionary activity; from there it was possible to develop useful contacts with the Maronites of the Lebanon, who were united with Rome.[1]

The Patriarch of Alexandria, Samuel Kapasoules, was being hard pressed by his rival, the Metropolitan of Sinai, who could rely on the support of the Turks and Phanariots and on the advice of the Franciscan Custos of Jerusalem, submitted to Rome in 1712.[2] In the case of the Capuchins, their provincials directed the union movement in the Near East from France, the Provincial of Paris being responsible for Constantinople and Smyrna, the Provincial of Tours for Aleppo, Mesopotamia and Egypt, and the Provincial of Rennes for Damascus and Lebanon.

In view of the fact that the Eastern Christians received these monks who had recently been appearing in their midst, without suspecting them in any way, the method of achieving union which commended itself was that of secret conversion taking place in the confessional. In their eagerness to promote union, the monks drew a distinction between the uneducated and the educated. The former were thought of as "material schismatics", basically of goodwill and who could, therefore, be allowed to remain in the confession of their fathers; the latter, consciously adhering to false doctrines, were required to recant.[3] It was only when the Roman Church refused to allow its monks to celebrate according to the Eastern Rite that the rifts, hitherto concealed from the ordinary Christians, became open.

France's protectorate over the Christians of the Near East (granted in the Capitulations between François I and Suleiman the Magnificent in 1535, and renewed eleven times, being finally revoked by the Sultan on 1st October 1914, at the outbreak of the World War), also formed the background to the resumption in the nineteenth century of Roman efforts towards union in these parts of Christendom which had been divided by the dogmatic controversies of the Early Church. Their extensive network of consulates meant that the French were in a position almost

[1] In Aleppo, too, the Armenian monk, Peter Mechitar, was won over to the Roman Church. In 1701 he founded his Uniate Armenian Order in Constantinople, but because of strong opposition soon moved to the Morea peninsula, which was still under Venetian control, and finally, in 1717, founded his settlement on the island of San Lazzaro, near Venice. The Order, which was ratified by Clement XI in 1711 on lines based on the Benedictine rule, has sought ever since to bring national and Christian renewal to the Armenian people through ties with Rome. The Mechitarists worked on the restoration of the Armenian language and literature, translated the Armenian Fathers into Latin, likewise the Latins into Armenian, and educated Uniate Armenian priests.

[2] Picot, in Paris in the middle of the nineteenth century, was the first to draw attention to Kapasouleas's union. In 1911 Chrysostomos Papadopuolos still declared Latin claims to be false. In 1928 Georg Hoffman, S.J., published the Vatican documents in *Orientalia Christiana* (cp. 1934).

[3] The Carmelites had to follow a stricter method of union. This appears from a report of Fr Anselmus in 1657, contained in the important source work, A. Rabbath, *Documents inédits pour servir a l'histoire du christianisme en Orient*, Paris 1907.

everywhere to take effective action. For Turkey, it was preferable that the protectorate should be exercised by their allies of the Crimean War rather than by the Tsarist Empire.[1]

The Turkish "Millet System", to which the divided churches of the Near East were subject, was relaxed after 1830 by a number of Firmans making it possible for individuals to change from one confession to another.[2] This situation was exploited by the missionaries of the Catholic Orders, who entered into rivalry both with the missionaries of the American Board and with the Orthodox Tsarist Empire by setting up parallel Catholic Uniate congregations in all the communities which stemmed from the divisions of the Early Church.

It was a pupil of Félicité de Lammenais, Eugène Boré, who became the architect and organizer of Catholic missionary strategy. In 1837, when he was Professor of Armenian Studies at the Collège de France, a research project for the Ministry of Education took him to the East. Leleu, the Apostolic Prefect of the Lazarists' mission at Constantinople, got him interested in that Order, and when, in the course of his studies, Boré travelled to the Lake of Urnia, to Teheran, Isfahan and Mosul, he paved the way for the Lazarists. Boré was no longer able to resist his own vocation to the priesthood and in 1849, he entered the Mission Seminary of the Lazarists in Constantinople and eventually worked as the Order's Provincial Visitor in the Ottoman Empire. (In 1874 he became Superior General.) What the Catholic Church put into practice in the nineteenth century in the Near East was basically none other than the strategy for the return of the schismatics of Asia which Boré, with his expert knowledge, had suggested to the Lazarists in 1839. No nation appeared to be better suited to carry out the plan than France, which could add new lustre to her "gloire" by exercising her traditional protectorate in this new way. When the ambassador of Orthodox Russia prevailed upon the Shah of

---

[1] During the Revolution the Pope was glad to see Naples and Austria maintaining their rights of protection. But in the peace treaty of 1802 with Turkey, the First Consul let the capitulations come into force again. A circular from Propaganda dated 29th May 1888 advised missionaries to consider France alone as the protecting power.

[2] Until Catholics were emancipated in 1830, Catholic converts from the communities of Gregorian Armenians, the Nestorians, Jacobites, Greek Orthodox and the Copts were dependent on the non-Catholic patriarchs of their "nations". As a result of connivance between the Orthodox patriarchs and the Turkish pashas, persecution of converts took place. The opposition of the Orthodox Patriarchs Sylvester and Daniel was particularly evident in Aleppo and in Damascus. Even in 1817 the Orthodox got the authorities to issue a firman under which converts were compelled to return under threat of confiscation of their goods, and Catholic priests were expelled from the country. On 16th April 1818 eleven Catholic Uniate priests were executed on the orders of the Governor. This started an emigration movement. The Orthodox Bishop Gerasimos of Aleppo brought his methods of co-operating with the Turkish pasha with him to Damascus.

Persia to expel the Catholic missionaries, Boré was able to get the French ambassador to take counter-measures. Copying the American Board's practice of issuing tracts, Boré began in 1853 to flood the ancient churches of the Near East with his pamphlets. He did not shrink from indulging in Oriental-style polemics in his attacks on the Americans, and declared that their strongest argument was their money.

Rome made its presence felt in the Near East in 1847, when it sent a missionary in Mosul, Joseph Valerga, to take up residence as Latin Patriarch in Jerusalem. Up till then, the Latin tradition had only been represented by a titular bishop resident in Rome. The extent to which this was an act of rivalry becomes evident when it is remembered that between 1842 and 1847 the Kings of England and Prussia had set up their joint bishopric of Jerusalem, the Orthodox Patriarch, who had hitherto resided at the Phanar, had returned to the Holy City, and Orthodox Russia had established a Religious Mission in Jerusalem. France chose the installation of the Latin Patriarch in 1847 as the time to require the Greeks to hand over the sanctuaries, which they claimed the Greeks had usurped. The new French ambassador in Constantinople, the Marquis de la Valette, was a man devoted to the Holy See, in whose appointment Montalembert had taken a hand, and he laid stress on the demands of the Latins. A firman dated 9th February 1852 did not go very far towards satisfying Latin desires, and the Holy See remained disappointed that after her victory in the Crimean War, France did not exact complete satisfaction.[1]

The integration of the Eastern Uniate groups within Roman Catholicism made for difficulties which came to the surface at three points: their acceptance, through Germanos Adam, of Josephinist doctrine; their opposition to the Armenian Catholic Patriarch, Hassun of Constantinople; and the revolt of the Uniate Nestorians on the Malabar question.[2]

The Melkite Uniate Bishop of Aleppo, Mgr Germanos Adam (from 1777), had been a student at the College of Propaganda in Rome and at that time had come to know the Josephinist bishop of Pistoia, Scipione Ricci. Adam's writings indeed displayed underlying Josephinist ideas,

---

[1] Cardinal Antonelli thanked Montalembert for his help, as a service to the whole of Christendom. On the vexed question of the Holy Places, the French envoy wrote in 1890, after discussions with Cardinal Barnabo: "L'un de ses griefs principaux est à Jérusalem."

[2] With the codification of Oriental Canon Law, which was omitted from the C.I.C. of 1917 and was brought into force by the Motu Proprio, "Cleri sanctitati" on 2nd June 1957, the inflammatory problems of those days were carried forward into the present. On 10th February 1958 the Melkite hierarchy protested against the subordination of the Uniate patriarchs of the East to cardinals and nuncios, the curtailment of the patriarchs' privileges and the granting to converts of a choice of rites. "Our Orthodox brothers must be able to recognize in our law the pattern of authentic oriental law."

such as the Orientals' sense of their independence over against Rome. Adam adopted the Conciliar theories of Constance and Basel, the Gallican Articles of 1682 and Febronius's propositions. Even in his first work in 1799 (a pamphlet written in reply to a work entitled "Opinion of the Missionaries consulted by His Holiness, Patriarch Mar Ignatios Michael"), Adam intervened in a controversial situation: his Patriarch, Agapios II Matar, had to resist the suggestion of founding a new order in Kalat Sem'an, which Bishop Ignatios Sarruf of Beirut and the Latin missionaries were promoting and which seemed highly dubious in view of the fact that there were already two rival communities of Melkite monks, the "Schuwairites" and the "Salvatorians".

At the Synod of Qarqafé in 1806, Adam's Josephinist ideas prevailed. Surprisingly, the decisions of this Synod were accepted in 1809 by the Maronite Patriarch, Joseph Tyan, or rather, by Gandolfi, his Apostolic Visitor.[1] As the provisions of Qarqafé with their Josephinist interpretation of the primacy of the Pope came near to the Orthodox outlook, when they became known in Orthodox circles in Aleppo they forged new links between the Uniate and Orthodox Eastern Christians.

Possibly the solemn condemnation of Germanos Adam on 6th March 1812[2] would have halted the influence of Josephinism in the East had not Patriarch Agapios in 1810, after Adam's death, appointed as Bishop of Aleppo one of Adam's pupils, Maximos Mazlum who had at one time been Secretary of the Synod of Qarqafé. The Roman party in the Melkite Church appealed to the Holy See, which responded by temporarily suspending Mazlum. However, the Melkite Church did not want the talents of such a man to lie idle, and so their Episcopal Synod of May 1811 made him director of the new seminary at Ain Traz, which was intended eventually to supply the Melkite Church with secular priests.[3]

Patriarch Anathasios V, the second successor and brother of Patriarch Agapios, sent a submission to the Holy See defending Mazlum and subscribed by all the bishops. Moreover, he defied Rome by making Mazlum his procurator in the Curia. Now it came to a contest in Rome

[1] C. Charon, *Histoire des Patriarcats melkites*, II, 1, Rome 1910, stresses that in his will Mgr Adam submitted his writings to the judgment of Rome. Possibly Gandolfi subscribed simply because he was not familiar with the Arabic tongue.

[2] On 3rd June 1816 Rome issued a decree forbidding the reading of Adam's books.

[3] Previously the care of the congregations had fallen to the monks, who had shown themselves able to withstand the persecutions (Salvatorians and Schuwairites, the latter splitting in 1826–9 into an urban group (the Aleppines) and a rural group (the Baladites)). Since the monks rejected all reforms, the formation of a (celibate) secular clergy was now an urgent task. In 1845, for the same reason, the Jesuits founded their Oriental seminary at Ghazir in the mountains of Kesruan. It transferred to Beirut in 1875 and was given university status by Leo XIII in 1881. Mgr Mazlum had already made plans for a foundation in St Anna in Jerusalem, but this was only brought into being by Patriarch Gregor II Yussef and Mrg Lavigerie in 1881.

itself between the Orientals with their tactical agility and the Romans with their church diplomacy which now had greater scope as a result of Napoleon's defeat at Waterloo.

Mazlum quickly came to recognize that his position would have to be regularized under canon law as the Romans understood it, and he resigned from the episcopal see of Aleppo. Fearing that his return to the Near East would provoke new disturbances, Propaganda insisted that he remain resident in Rome, but concealed the true state of affairs by elevating Mazlum to the office of Titular Metropolitan of Myra.[1]

It was only in 1831, at the beginning of the pontificate of Gregory XVI, that Mazlum's requests to return to Syria succeeded. He volunteered to bring about the Jesuits' return to the Middle East and to have them put in charge of the seminary for secular priests at Ain Traz. But as soon as they had landed at Beirut, Mazlum left the Jesuit Fathers to fend for themselves. Although prior to his departure from Rome he had declared that he had renounced any episcopal function, in 1833 he was directing his energies towards having himself elected patriarch. This situation also provided opportunities for curial diplomacy. On 16th September 1833 Propaganda refused to confirm his election until he rejected the Synod of Qarqafé and the teachings of Germanos Adam. Now even Mazlum was prepared to concur in his teacher's rejection.

Mazlum was really one of the greatest patriarchs in the history of the Melkite Church. In his administrative measures, he continued to demonstrate a spirit of independence from Rome.[2] He took advantage of the Egyptian occupation of Syria to make his solemn entrance into Damascus in 1834. In 1836 he appeared in Egypt and organised the Melkites there. For five years he was at work in the Ottoman capital with a view to getting the Sultan to emancipate the Uniate Christians. Yet traces of Pistoia and Qarqafé were still to be discerned in a constitution drawn up by his Council of 1849.

A second focus of conflict developed in Constantinople. In 1830, the High Port emancipated Uniate Catholics who had originally been Orthodox from the civil jurisdiction of the non-Catholic patriarchs of their "nations". It was specified that all these Catholics were to be

---

[1] In order to stop the persecution of Uniate Melkites in Syria, Mazlum persuaded Propaganda to get Austria to approach the High Port and entered into negotiations himself in Vienna, making direct contact with influential persons close to the Sultan. When he travelled to Trieste and Marseilles he promised on each occasion to return to Rome, and when this promise was not punctually fulfilled Rome stopped his monthly salary. In March 1821 Mazlum managed to have a Melkite Uniate congregation formed in Marseilles for Christians who had come there from Egypt following Napoleon's expedition.

[2] In 1835 M. called a council without Roman approval. The Holy See only gave it belated sanction in 1841.

represented by *one* man, the so-called "Patrik", at the Sultan's court. Pius VIII took this opportunity of emancipating the Armenian Uniate Catholics who had, up till then, been subject to the Apostolic Delegate in Constantinople, with regard to their spiritual jurisdiction as well, and created the office of Armenian Patriarch of Constantinople. In 1845–6, both the office of Patrik and the patriarchate were held by a protégé of the Propaganda, Mgr Hassun, and when it came to filling the vacant see of the Armenian Catholicate of Cilicia, this office, too, was given to the same man, so congenial was he to Rome.

This accumulation of offices was confirmed by Pius IX in 1867, in his bull "Reversurus", but at the same time the Pope rescinded certain ancient Armenian privileges, in particular the participation of the laity and lower clergy in nominations and even elections of bishops.[1] There was a further extension of Western canon law to Oriental affairs in that from that time on, the elected patriarch was not, prior to Rome's confirmation, to be enthroned or to make use of the five acts of hierarchical jurisdiction. In addition, he was obliged to make "ad limina" visits to Rome, and without Roman confirmation no Church property was to be disposed of. These decisions were stated to be "perpetuis futuris temporibus inviolabiliter observanda".[2]

For long enough an "Oriental" group had been in existence among the Armenian Uniates. The laity of the Gregorian Armenians had certain rights which were highly treasured, and the existence of these rights impressed the nationalist wing of the Uniates as the kind of rights they desired. Opposition from this quarter forced Mgr Hassun to relinquish his "civil" function as "Patrik". When Pius IX founded six new Armenian dioceses and designated their bishops without any prior consultation with the clergy or the laity, on the day of their ordination, rebellion broke out among the people. Hassun consecrated the newly designated bishops at night behind closed doors, and formal recognition was only obtained from the Sultan because of French diplomatic pressure. At this point,

[1] According to Aubert, the laity's participation in elections was stopped because they tended to take more account of their material interests than of the spiritual welfare of the Church. This assertion has not been sustantiated.

[2] The bull "Reversurus" partly contradicted decisions taken by Propaganda in 1827, which, following the old Oriental usage, allowed patriarchs to exercise their right of jurisdiction immediately after their election. Pius IX, in opposition to Propaganda, inclined to the view that the Eastern patriarchs should conform to the practice obtaining with regard to the "little" patriarchs of the Latin Church. This being so, it was logical to refuse the Eastern patriarchs their rights. In Aubert's view, the Pope's measures were in order, since the patriarchs' rights were only privileges "*iure humano*". But in these proceedings an enactment which Benedict XIV had sanctioned "*in forma specifica*" at the Maronite Synod of 1736 was annulled. R. Aubert poses the question for research in the archives as to whether the tactical error encountered here was due to Pius IX or to the two prelates who advised him.

the opposition was provoked to extremes by the bull "Reversurus".

On his first visitation of the Cilician dioceses, Hassun discovered so much smouldering discontent that he summoned a Council to meet in Constantinople in July 1869. At this Hassun was accused of sacrificing to the Pope rights which had for centuries belonged to the Cilician Catholicate, and his deposition was called for. The patriarch was forced to suspend the Council. But during Hassun's absence at the Vatican Council, revolt against Romanizing tendencies broke out anew; the patriarch's church was taken by storm, the bull "Reversurus" publicly burned, and the patriarchal see declared vacant. The Superior of the Antonine monks, Gazandian, assumed leadership of the rebel movement and four opposition bishops left the Vatican Council. Unperturbed by excommunication, the rebels elected Bahbiarian as a rival patriarch in February 1871, had him recognized by the Turkish government and appropriated the property of the Church.[1]

The wave of agitation over the bull "Reversurus" spread from the Armenian Church to the other Uniate groups of the Near East as soon as they realized that it was the Pope's intention to extend the new legislation to all the Eastern patriarchates.

The third conflict broke out in the Chaldean Church (which owed its origin to the missionary work of Catholic Orders among the Nestorians in the seventeenth and eighteenth centuries). This Church had the chance to develop freely after the Armenian "Patrik" gave them civil emancipation in 1844. When Joseph Audo was elected patriarch in 1847, there was, apart from a small seminary which the Lazarists had started in 1845, no school and no printing press. Audo showed considerable initiative and brought twenty Nestorian villages into the Union.[2]

The struggle began in 1856 when two priests of these Uniate Nestorians joined Audo from Malabar. They were under the jurisdiction of the Latin Apostolic Vicar in India, but were keen to have a bishop of their own "nation", as they had had in the sixteenth century when their bishop had been consecrated by the Chaldean Patriarch of Mesopotamia. Mgr Audo took up their cause and was quite prepared to consecrate Malabar bishops, but when he informed Propaganda he was curtly told that he had no right to meddle in Indian affairs. However, Audo, foreseeing the danger that the Malabar delegation might turn to the non-Uniate Nestorians of Mesopotamia, consecrated a priest, Thomas Rokos, on 23rd September 1860, as titular bishop without jurisdiction, and sent him as his Vicar to

---

[1] The struggle between Hassunites and anti-Hassunites raged long in Turkey. Mgr Hassun only returned to Constantinople for a brief period, but in 1880 he was made a cardinal of the Curia.

[2] 1867—70,000 Chaldeans.

India. Audo was thereupon summoned to Rome, and after being given a very brusque reception by Pius IX was compelled publicly to disown his action. Humiliated and full of bitterness against the Dominicans of Mosul, whom he blamed for the trouble he had had in Rome, Audo went back to the East.

At this point, agitation against the bull "Reversurus" which was spreading from the Armenian Church to the other Churches of the Near East reached the Chaldeans as well. The constitution "Cum ecclesiastica disciplina" of 1869 extended the provisions of the bull to the Chaldean Church. Audo, however, refused to consecrate episcopal candidates who had been nominated by the Pope in terms of the bull. A second dramatic audience with the Pope, in which the Apostolic Delegate, Valergo, pressed Pius IX into a position of complete inflexibility, only resulted in Audio's entering into relations with the Armenian opposition party. He was the last member of the hierarchy to acquiesce in the Vatican Council, in which he thought he could detect an intention to do away with the ancient rights of the Oriental patriarchs. From then on, there was a group within the Chaldean episcopate who were hostile to Rome. On two further occasions (1874 and 1875) Audo had a bishop elected without observing the provisions of "Reversurus". Rome was not able to show any indulgence towards this 87-year-old man, and in 1876 threatened Audo with excommunication if he did not submit within forty days. At that time the whole of the East was looking towards the Patriarch of Babylon, and it is impossible to say what might have happened if Audo had not decided on total submission.[1]

5. CONVERSIONS IN BULGARIA

Conversion movements among the Armenians and Arabs of the Ottoman empire attracted the attention of the Orthodox Bulgarian people who were set on national emancipation and separation from the Greeks in matters of religion. The kind of Church action which seemed best suited to their political aims was that which was directed to the creation of an autocephalous, national Church. But in 1859, union with Rome was also being canvassed in the press. Among a group of the Bulgarian intelligentsia in Constantinople, who were inflamed by the Polish Committee in Paris, a number of individual conversions took place as a result of contacts with the Apostolic Delegate. They hoped to be able to further the cause of Bulgarian emancipation by joining the papal Church, provided the Pope agreed

---

[1] Bishop Mellus, having been sent to India by Mgr Audo, went on with the organization of his Indian congregation, although in 1872 Rome had again rejected his claim to jurisdiction over Malabar, and despite excommunication by the Latin bishop. He only left Malabar in 1882, withdrawing his claims in 1889.

to retain the old Slavonic liturgy. In 1860 Mgr Hassun, the Armenian Patriarch of Constantinople, was asked to transmit an address to the Pope, and on 21st January 1861 Pius IX granted the Bulgarians the privileges they asked for. In Thrace and Macedonia there was a swift extension of this movement. So as to strengthen their position, the Bulgarians claimed a Uniate bishop. The Pope accepted the old Igumen, Joseph Sokolski, and consecrated him himself, on 14th April 1861, as Archbishop and Apostolic Vicar of Uniate Bulgaria. This gesture led to the conversion within a few days of 60,000 Bulgarians. However, the old Archbishop lacked experience. Orthodox Russia, whose ambassador had already intervened when the movement was beginning to gain ground in Constantinople, managed to induce Mgr Sokolski to "resettle" in Russia. The small Uniate remnant left in Bulgaria after this scandal was put under the care of the Assumptionists. At this time, the Orthodox Bulgarian Exarchate was founded and this removed the political motivation of this particular conversion movement.[1]

6. RUSSIA'S RELIGIOUS POLICY

Government policy in Russia was aimed at incorporating the non-Orthodox churches into the political system as state churches. This applied as much to the Catholic Church in Poland as to the Uniate Church in White Russia and the Ukraine. To this end, Church government was integrated in a "College" in St Petersburg, of which the "Uniate College" became a separate branch again in 1805.[2]

The Polish uprising in November 1830 was the signal for Metternich to exert his influence in conclave to secure the election of a Pope who would oppose popular national movements and who would give his support to the Restoration. In February 1831 Gregory XVI, in the brief "Impensa Charitas", was already calling on the Polish clergy to obey their Tsarist superiors. The encyclical "Cum primum", dated 9th June 1832, and addressed to the Polish bishops, in words binding upon their consciences, pressed upon them their duty to co-operate with the Tsarist authorities. The encyclical suffered from the defect that it was served by the Viennese nuncio directly on the Polish bishops without having received the Tsarist exequatur, but it was in fact circulated by the Tsarist authorities and added as an appendix to the Polish catechism.

There seemed to be a sudden change of climate when, in his allocution

---

[1] Scholars are not agreed on whether the Russians displaced Sokolski, exploiting his great age and virtually holding him prisoner, or whether his return to Orthodoxy was a matter of conviction.

[2] Rome received reports on the College from the legate, Bernetti.

of 22nd July 1842, the Pope charged the Tsarist government with persecution. This allocution was made at the instigation of the Austro-Slavs and was supported by a volume of evidence listing ninety cases. The Tsar replied by reproaching the Pope for supporting revolutionary movements in Europe. Nevertheless, this affair did not really halt the trend towards closer collaboration between the Tsar and the Pope; rather, Concordat negotiations being conducted by Lambruschini and Butenev were now simply pursued the more urgently. The Concordat was concluded on 3rd August 1847,[1] and was intended as an alliance between Tsardom and Papacy as restoration powers. But the Polish uprising in 1863 forced the Tsarist government to take steps affecting the Catholic Church on its own and without regard to the Concordat.

With the Ukase of 26th December 1865 Alexander II reorganized the Polish hierarchy. Pius IX issued a public complaint in October 1866, but the Tsar replied by unilaterally revoking the Concordat, breaking off diplomatic relations with the Vatican and also transferring the spiritual supervision, which had hitherto been distinguished from the "ecclesiastical administration" of the Catholic Church, to the College at St Petersburg.[2]

It suited the Russian government's policy well enough that the episcopal leaders whom the Tsarina, Catherine, had brought into office in the partitioned Polish areas, both the Catholic Archbishop of Mogilev, Stanislaus Siestrzecewicz-Bohusz, and the Uniate Archbishop, Heraklius Lisovskyj, were Gallican and Josephinist in outlook, and therefore proved co-operative in the matter of state churches.[3] It was their attitude to state

---

[1] It was conceded to the Pope that information concerning episcopal candidates should come from Rome, but should not, however, be based on what Polish émigrés said. This was aimed at Gutkowski, the former Bishop of Podlasia, who was now in Lemberg. Metternich's information service regularly furnished the Curia with material for complaint, which enabled Rome to embarrass the Tsar's negotiator. Provision was made for mutual consultation on the nomination of bishops, and from the Tsar's side a seventh bishopric (Cherson) was promised. The question of civil procurators in the consistories gave rise to the greatest difficulties. Rome's greatest success in the era of the Concordat was the appointment of Ignatius Holwinski as coadjutor of Mogilev with the right to appoint his successor.

[2] A concession by the Russian government in 1875 made possible a more satisfactory solution. The Pope could state in a circular to the Russian and Polish bishops that the government had declared its agreement that the College would no longer be concerned with spiritual matters. Therefore the Pope allowed Catholic bishops to take part in sessions of the College. Here, for the first time, the College was given ecclesiastical sanction.

[3] Both hierarchies acknowledged the judgement of the Sorbonne which Peter the Great had sought in 1717 and which had made Jansenist ideas of a national church influential in Russia. In 1782 Catherine made Mogilev an archbishopric. The Warsaw nuncio, Archetti, who came as legate to St Petersburg in 1783, brought the requested pallium for S. The literary purchases which Archetti made on that occasion form the basis of the collection in the Papal Oriental Institute. The filling of the Uniate archiepiscopal see of the territories annexed to the Tsarist Empire through the partition of

religion which led the Uniates to abandon their association with Rome. Their central seminary, which had been founded in Vilna in 1803, was filled with Josephinist teachers. One of this seminary's students, Joseph Siemaszko, who at the age of twenty-four had been active as an assessor in the Uniate department of the Catholic College in St Petersburg, produced in October 1827, at the time of the issue of new ordinances for the Basilian Order, two reports for the authorities, outlining a plan for the return of the Uniates to the Orthodox State Church.[1] In accordance with this plan, in 1833 rights of patronage were removed from the landowners and the appointment of priests was made the business of Russian officials at the St Petersburg College. Landlords were also forbidden to refer the religious grievances of their peasants. In this way, the Uniate populace lost its supports. In the Uniate College, a secret committee for the "preservation of the purity of the Rite" was formed, with the object of eliminating romanizing elements and by a process of assimilating the Uniate rite with the Russian Orthodox rite making it easier for individual communities to go over into union with the Orthodox State Church.[2] In 1835, part of the central administration of the Uniate College—the department for schools —was annexed to the Religious Commission for Schools of the Orthodox Ruling Synod, and in 1837 the whole Uniate College ceased to be the responsibility of the Ministry of Internal Affairs and was placed under the Ruling Synod. Finally, in February 1839, Siemaszko and Bishops Losinski and Zubko, all former students of the Central Seminary at Vilna, with twenty-one other priests, acting in the name of the entire Uniate Church of the Tsarist empire, formally went over to the Orthodox State Church. (This involved $2\frac{1}{2}$ million members.) All the Uniate priests were compelled to sign a declaration of conversion.[3]

The bishopric of Cholm—simply because in 1809 it had been incorporated in the Grand Duchy of Warsaw and therefore after 1815 also belonged to the kingdom of Poland which was under the jurisdiction of the Tsar—

Poland (Polock) was also settled by Archetti. The liturgical reforms which Lisovskyj prepared as a move to counter Austrian advances were, however, rejected by Propaganda in 1787. From then on the Tsarist Empire found that its Uniates acted as a bulwark against anti-Russian influence.

[1] In Nicholas I's ukase of 9th October 1827 the decree of Alexander I forbidding change from the Uniate to the Latin rite was sharpened, the acceptance of Latins into the Order was forbidden and a purist liturgy was recommended. In 1832 the Basilians were dissolved as an Order and the individual monasteries were placed under the control of the bishops.

[2] Realized in Zlužebnik in 1831.

[3] Gregory XVI refused to get involved with the Polish revolutionaries at the Palais Lambert in Paris, because he did not want to forfeit diplomatic possibilities of arriving at an understanding with the Tsar, and did not commit himself publicly on the Disunion until very late, namely with his White Paper of 1842.

was not quite so quick to participate in disunion. When the Metropolis of Halisch was created in 1807 with its centre at Lemberg, Cholm came under its jurisdiction. In 1830 this bishopric was again detached from Halisch and placed by Pius VIII directly under the Holy See, and this did much to deprive the Uniate diocese of its supports. Bishop Szumborski did indeed take steps in 1831 to prevent a takeover by the purist Služebnik, but in 1839 a reform of the rite according to Eastern ideas was put in hand to counteract the suggestion that a number of men should be sent to the Orthodox Religious Academy at Kiev. After Szumborksi's death in 1851 the government had a free hand in pressing on with disunion. Ukrainian nationalist, anti-Polish priests who came over from Austrian Galicia, in particular Marcel Popiel, began to oust the Cholm clergy from the more important offices in the Church.

The Uniate seminary in the bishopric became the centre of resistance, and it was put under the jurisdiction of the anti-Roman Commission for Worship and Education in Warsaw in 1861. When it became clear that the episcopal administrator of Cholm, John Kalinski, was secretly on the side of the Polish rebels in 1863, the government resorted to coersive measures. In June 1864 it deprived the administrator of control over his clergy and made his entire administration dependent on the concurrence of the Warsaw authorities. In the same year, four of the five Basilian monasteries in the bishopric were closed.

To replace Polish, Russian was introduced as the official language. On 3rd October 1866 the administrator was arrested and exiled to Wjatka. In 1875, Bishop Popiel got village after village to support petitions professing loyalty to the Russian State and at the same time asking to be received into the Orthodox Church. A deputation was dispatched to convey these petitions to St Petersburg, and thereafter union with the Orthodox Church was finalized. Thus in the Cholm district as well the Uniate form of the Church was wiped out.

Only in Galicia, which was administered by Austria, was the Uniate confession able to survive, having acquired a new significance as a result of "Austro-Slavism".[1] Certainly, from the middle of the nineteenth century a movement had also developed there which was deeply conscious of the special ties between the Galician-Ukrainian Uniate Church and Orthodoxy and which repudiated the Latin customs and ideas which had been forced upon them. This "purism" originated in the Greek-Catholic Central Seminary set up in Vienna in 1851, where the Galician students

[1] In 1875 the ablest of the young leaders of the church of the union, Bishop Rytto, whom the Tsarist authorities wanted in the Uniate see of Polock, went to Pržemyšl in the part of Poland occupied by Austria. He soon gained the favour of Joseph II. The seminary of the Theatines in Lemberg was soon converted into an Austrian general seminary.

could prepare themselves for their spiritual office in an atmosphere free of the Polish and Latin influences to which they would have been exposed if they had been educated at home. This movement was later strengthened by an increase in pro-Russian feeling among the Galicians at the time of the settlement between the Hapsburg monarchy and Polish Galicia to surrender them to the Poles once again. In the years following 1860 the Galicians were prepared to abandon the idea of their own Ukrainian nationality and the existence of the Uniate Church was now seen as an obstacle to speedy integration with the Russian people. The total loss of the missionary gains of Brest seemed to have come about. The only indication of an interruption in this development was Pius IX's encyclical of 13th May 1874, which gave a warning against accommodation with the Eastern schismatics and condemned the purists.[1]

7. ARISTOCRATIC CONVERTS AND ROMAN SYMPATHIES IN RUSSIA

Meanwhile, in the heart of Russian Orthodoxy itself, a new movement had got under way. This expressed a quite fresh interest in Rome and opened up new perspectives of contacts between Russian Orthodoxy in its entirety and Rome. It arose through the activity of French Catholic émigrés at the time of the Revolution, who were accepted into St Petersburg society. In this mileiu, Jesuit Fathers collaborated with the Sardinian and Neopolitan ambassadors resident in St Petersburg, de Maistre and Serracapriola.[2] A French father called Rozaven[3] was responsible for several conversions among the nobility, for instance, the conversion of

[1] There were many revolts against the Encyclical. The Russophile attitude was only overcome through the influence of East Ukrainian emigrants who sought to develop Galicia as a base for the national liberation of the whole of the Ukraine. In this, however, the Uniate priests of Galicia lost their role of leadership, being ousted by liberal and socialist politicians. About the turn of the century a new Church movement came into being, the so-called Uniatism, which wanted the Uniate Church to act as a prop to nationalism and to keep the union separate both from the Roman Catholic Poles and the Russian Orthodox.

[2] Jesuit influence in the Tsardom was not new. Antonio Possevino, S.J., had managed to enter into discussions with Ivan the Terrible. In 1685 the Society of Jesus had set up a school in Nemeckaja Sloboda, the European quarter of Moscow, but it was closed five years later because it was attracting too many of the aristocracy. When the Order was dissolved in 1773 the Tsarina Catherine II made it possible for the Jesuits to remain in the Empire. The number of Jesuit fathers rose to 200. Paul I granted the Order a special rule, making it independent of the Catholic hierarchy, restored its property and opened a school for it (the Polock Academy, with the right to supervise schools in the district). Eventually Paul I produced the brief "Catholica fidei", which restored the Society in Russia.

[3] Rozaven's letters to Russian nobles were published posthumously in 1862, an untimely publication according to de Buck.

Sophia Svečin, the daughter of a Tsarist Secretary of State (8th November 1815).[1]

The Tsarist government reacted abruptly to this Roman invasion of St Petersburg society: by a decree of 20th December 1815 the Jesuits were expelled from the two capitals. Five years later the fathers were banished from Russian soil, their property being made over to the Roman hierarchy, and their gymnasium in St Petersburg and their academy in Polock being abandoned.[2]

Nevertheless, sympathy with the Roman Church survived as one of the elements in Russian philosophy of religion. Čaadaev gave a dominant place to the idea of unity through a spiritual monarchia. From eternity God is one—the world *becomes* one in history. It is from this point of view that Čaadaev considers the course of history from Creation to the Last Judgment. History up to the time of Christ shows that the world cannot achieve unity of itself. In sending Christ to lead men out of their isolation into organic unity, God makes possible a continuous growth towards the goal of history: *ut omnes unum sint*. This development is brought about through the Church instituted by Christ, and the characteristic of the Church is in its turn the unity it already possesses to be imparted to the world. Čaadaev adopted the ideas of the Restoration philosophy of de Maistre and de Bonald when he expounded the unity of the Church as being represented by the *"monarchia St Petri"*. In the *"Treuga Dei"* the Middle Ages of the West had already developed political unity out of ecclesiastical unity. "L'histoire du Moyen-Age—l'histoire d'un seul peuple, du peuple chrétien." This unity Byzantium had destroyed. Christianity had come to Russia already in a "form disfigured by human passion". There was hung over Russian history the fateful *"extra ecclesiam nulla salus"*. The question of the meaning of Russian history which was posed with such emphasis by Čaadaev at the start of the Russian movement in philosophy of religion was answered by the affirmation: that in Russia there could be no spiritual continuity.[3]

---

[1] Sophia Svečin, betrothed at 17 to General Svečin, was unfortunate in her marriage and sought the consolation of faith.

[2] The Order's official restoration brought a loss of confidence in it in Russia. The Jesuits, however, also suffered defeat at the hands of their rivals, the Bible Society. One hundred and four fathers left Russia for Austria, residing mainly in Tarnopol, near the frontier.

[3] Reactions of the Russian world to Čaadaev's "Philosophical Letters": the journal *Teleskop*, which published a Russian translation in 1836, was banned, the Censor was removed from office and Čaadaev was placed under the supervision of the Moscow police doctor as a mental defective. Pushkin entered into controversy over the "Philosophical Letters" and wrote to the author: "You see Christian unity in Catholicism, that is, in the Pope. But does it not rather lie in the idea of Christ, which is also present in Protestantism?"

Čaadaev and his aunt, now "Madame Svetchine", in Paris, greatly impressed Prince Gagarin, who later became an attaché at the Russian Embassy in Paris, and on 19th April 1842 the young Russian diplomat, hoping to unite all Russia with Rome, but, in fact, sacrificing his own career, went over to Rome.[1] From 1856 Gagarin's publications followed one after another in quick succession. Translated into Russian, German and English, they reverberated throughout Europe. The starting-point of Gagarin's thought was that the Roman Church must of necessity be seen as the *centrum unitatis*. What was required was not a general melting down of differences into Latin forms, but rather a reconciliation of the East with the West. The trouble which continually beset the Russian Church, namely the clergy's state of dependence over against the civil power, could only be cured by establishing connections with the papacy.[2]

These ideas of Gagarin's began to influence the decisions of Leo XIII, thus heralding a new period of activity towards union.

[1] Schelling had already suggested to Gagarin in Munich in 1833 that he considered Čaadaev "one of the worthiest men he had ever met". Gagarin's curiosity having been roused by Schelling, he made Čaadaev's acquaintance in Moscow in 1835.

[2] Gagarin's ideas led to the Encyclical of Leo XIII which was favourable to the union and to Vladimir Solovev, who, after 1889, abandoned Panslavic criticisms of Rome, who was critical of Juri Samarin's polemical book on the Jesuits, and who found in the idea of a spiritual head independent of the state the affirmation of the papacy. In 1896 Solovev received the sacrament from a priest called Nikolai Tolstoi, a convert in Rome. Yet it remains unclear whether this is to be regarded as a conversion to the Roman Church or whether spiritualizing elements in his thinking about the Church made it possible for him to take communion at the Roman altar.

SELECT BIBLIOGRAPHY

of Works in English touching on
the Catholic Church in Germany, 1648–1870

———

The New Catholic Encyclopaedia. New York, 1967.
A Catholic Dictionary of Theology, Vols. 1 & 2 published Edinburgh 1962, 1966.
The New Cambridge Modern History, Vols. V–X. Cambridge 1957–1965.

Atkinson, C. T.:	A History of Germany, 1715–1815. London 1908.
Becker, C.:	The Heavenly City of the 18th Century Philosophers, New Haven 1932.
Bright, J. F.:	Maria Theresa. London 1897. Joseph II. London 1897.
Bury, J. B.:	History of the Papacy in the 19th Century (1864–1878). London 1930.
Bruford, W. H.:	Germany in the Eighteenth Century. Cambridge 1935.
Butler, E. M.:	The Saint-Simonian Religion in Germany. Cambridge 1926.
Cassirer, E.:	The Philosophy of the Enlightenment (E.T.). Princeton 1951.
Cecil, A.:	Metternich, 1773–1859. London 1933.
Cottrell, C. H.:	Religious Movements in Germany in the 19th Century. London 1899.
Eckhardt, C. C.:	The Papacy and World Affairs in the Secularisation of Politics (E.T.). Chicago 1937.
Gooch, G. P.:	Germany and the French Revolution. London 1929.
Goodwin, M. C.:	The Papal Conflict with Josephinism, New York 1938.
Hales, E. E. Y.:	The Catholic Church in the Modern World. London 1958.
	Pio Nono: A Study in European Politics and Religion in the Nineteenth Century. London 1954.
Hazard, P.:	European Thought in the Eighteenth Century (E.T.). London 1954.
	The European Mind (E.T.). London 1953.

Hughes, P.:   A Short History of the Catholic Church. London
                     1967.

Leman, A.:   The Church in Modern Times, 1447-1789 (E.T.).
                     London 1929.

MacCaffery, J.:   A History of the Catholic Church in the Nineteenth
                     Century, 1789-1908. Dublin 1910.

Meissner, E.:   Confusion of Faces. London 1946.

Moffatt, M. M.:   Maria Theresa. London 1911.

Moore, E. C.:   An Outline of Christian Thought since Kant. London
                     1909.

Nielsen, F.:   History of the Papacy in the 19th Century. New
                     York 1906.

von Pastor, L.:   The History of the Popes from the Close of the
                     Middle Ages (E.T.). London 1891-1940.

Pinnow, H.:   History of Germany (E.T.). London 1933.

Pinson, K. S.:   Pietism as a Factor in the Rise of German Nationalism.
                     New York 1934.

Poulet, C.:   History of the Catholic Church (E.T.). London 1934.

Pullen, L.:   Religion since the Reformation. Oxford 1924.

Smith, Preserved.:   A History of Modern Culture: The Enlightenment,
                     1687-1776. New York 1934.

Troeltsch, E.:   The Social Teaching of the Christian Churches (E.T.).
                     London 1931.

Walzel, O.:   German Romanticism. New York 1932.

Willoughby, L. A.:   The Romantic Movement in Germany. Oxford 1930.

Works awaiting publication:

Holborn, H.:   A History of Modern Germany, Vol. 2.

Rogier, L. J. and du
Bertier de
Sauvigny, G.:   A New History of the Catholic Church, Vol. IV.
                     A Catholic Dictionary of Theology, Vols. II and
                     following.

INDEX